The Roman Villa at Lullingstone, Kent

The Europa Panel.

Monograph Series
of the
Kent Archaeological Society
(General Editor: A. P. Detsicas, M.A., F.S.A.)

No. I

The Roman Villa at Lullingstone, Kent

Volume I: The Site

By

Lieut.-Col. G. W. Meates, F.S.A.

Published by
The Kent Archaeological Society
1979

Published with the aid of a grant from the Department of the Environment

ISBN 0 85033 341 5

PRINTED IN ENGLAND BY
THE WHITEFRIARS PRESS LTD, LONDON & TONBRIDGE
AND DISTRIBUTED BY
PHILLIMORE & CO. LTD, SHOPWYKE HALL,
CHICHESTER, SUSSEX

CONTENTS

LIST OF FIGURES

LIST OF PLATES

ACKNOWLEDGEMENTS

During the long course of excavation, covering thirteen successive seasons from 1949 to 1961, the most encouraging interest and help was freely given by public bodies, and by private persons, and is gratefully acknowledged.

The site of the villa was originally in the ownership of the late Sir Oliver Hart Dyke, Bart., the Kent County Council, and the Kemp Town Brewery Company of Brighton, all of whom gave permission for the work to be done. Subsequently, the Kent County Council acquired the whole site, and when the Ministry of Public Building and Works took it over, with a view, not only of financially assisting the excavation but also of erecting a protective building over the villa, the Kent County Council agreed to the administration of the site by the Ministry, provided that it was protected for the general public and for posterity. The County Council had previously diverted the road and the valley sewer at considerable expense to allow complete excavation, and subsequently the Ministry designed and erected the present magnificent protective building and museum, together with an extensive car-park and landscaped surroundings. Prior to this, to allow the excavation eastwards of the Deep Room, the late Mr John H. Evans, F.S.A., most kindly provided a concrete revetment at that point.

Financial grants were made by the Society of Antiquaries, the Haverfield Bequest Administrators, and the Kent Archaeological Society, and three interim reports were published in *Archaeologia Cantiana* (Vols. LXIII, LXV and LXVI). The Society of Antiquaries also conducted an investigation, directed by the late Professor R. G. Goodchild, F.S.A., and the author, of the area between the villa and the river, prior to the construction of the new road.

The work was initiated and directed for the first few seasons by Mr E. Greenfield and the late Mr E. C. Birchenough, M.A., with the author, who expresses his gratitude to his colleagues during the earlier part of the excavations. From the outset, the greatest encouragement was received from the late Miss M. V. Taylor, C.B.E., M.A., F.S.A., and Professor J. M. C. Toynbee, M.A., D.Phil., F.B.A., F.S.A.; the late Mr C. D. P. Nicholson, F.S.A., gave most generously of his time to the assembling of the painted wall-plaster, from which the Christian character of the villa was established, work which was made possible in a room very kindly provided by the Director at the Institute of Archaeology. The painted plaster has since been deposited in the British Museum, where, with the marble portrait busts, assembled sections are displayed, while further work on it is proceeding. Mr D. A. Broodbank, A.R.I.B.A., and Mr C. B. Mears, A.R.I.B.A., prepared many of the plans, and the late Mr R. J. Rook, who remained throughout a very valuable and helpful colleague, prepared scale drawings of the wall-plaster, with a fine series of accurate reconstructions and models of the villa in whole and in part.

Since assuming control of the excavation, the Ministry of Public Building and Works, in the persons of its inspectors and scientists, has been throughout most helpful, and to further the work of research on the wall-plaster, pottery, etc., it took a lease of a range of rooms at Lullingstone Castle.

The late Professor F. E. Zeuner, D.Sc., F.Z.S., F.G.S., F.S.A., very kindly visited the site on several occasions and gave his opinion as regards the course of the river in Roman times, in which he said that it had not appreciably changed at this point in its course, but that it had bounded, as it does today, the Roman garden area on the east.

During the long period of excavation, some hundreds of persons, including groups of students from universities and many schools, gave their services to the work, including site administration, lecturing to the public and, in some cases, long and scholarly investigation into different areas and problems of the site. Without their ready assistance, the results we see today could not have been achieved.

The author wishes to express his indebtedness and gratitude to the Kent Archaeological Society, for accepting this report for publication, and especially to Mr A. P. Detsicas, M.A., F.S.A., for his most valued help in its editorial preparation for publication.

POSTSCRIPT

The appendices, covering the finds in their various categories, and from the study of which this account of the villa has received its interpretation, will be provided in a second volume to be published in due course. This volume will also include a comprehensive report, with illustrations, describing the painted wall-plaster and a full report on the marble busts and their significance.

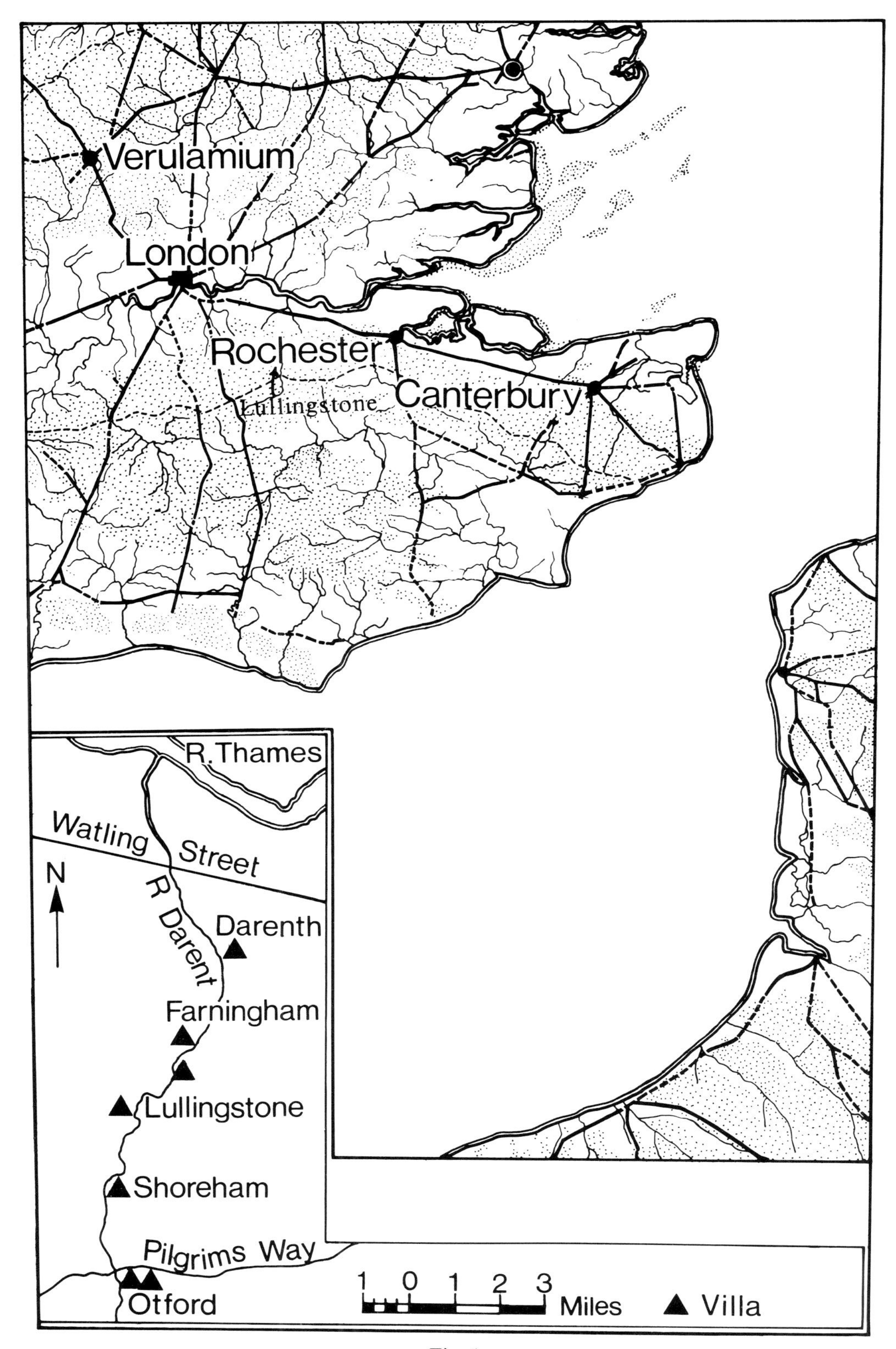
Verulamium
London
Rochester
Lullingstone
Canterbury
R.Thames
Watling Street
N
R Darent
Darenth
Farningham
Lullingstone
Shoreham
Pilgrims Way
Otford
1 0 1 2 3 Miles
Villa

Fig. 1

INTRODUCTION AND SUMMARY

A Roman site in the neighbourhood of Lullingstone had been suspected since the years immediately preceding the second World War, when an archaeological survey of the Darent Valley was initiated and partially carried out by Mr E. Greenfield and the late Mr E. C. Birchenough. During the course of their investigations they had observed in the immediate neighbourhood of the north gate of Lullingstone Park some evidence of Roman occupation. Their work was interrupted by the war, and in 1947 the author joined with them in a renewal of their archaeological survey.

Literary references of some antiquity already existed, and these were examined. In his work *Custumale Roffense,* published in 1788,[1] John Thorpe, M.A., F.S.A., refers to the probability of a Roman building having existed in the vicinity of the north gate of the park, and that Roman coins and objects had from time to time been recovered nearby. He also records that when the park fence was renewed in about 1750, a Roman tessellated pavement was discovered a short distance from the gate. He was, however, mainly concerned with the ruined church of Lullingstane which was visible in his day near this point, and not only does he publish a woodcut depicting this church, but he also states that from its small size it appeared to him to have been of Saxon architecture and built of flint and Roman bricks, of which the west end was mainly composed.

There was here a noticeable concentration which pointed to Roman occupation, and a closer investigation was made. Among the tangle of undergrowth with which the area was covered lay one or two fallen trees. Among the roots of one of these trees was found Roman pottery and fragments of tile, and this endorsed the opinion of the investigators that here might lie hidden the remains of a Roman building. It remained to determine its character and extent.

The north gate of Lullingstone Park was situated 668 m. north of Lullingstone Castle, and set back 55 m. from the west bank of the river Darent (TQ 529651), and part of the Roman villa was later found to underlie it (Site Plan, Fig. 2).

The river flows from south to north, cutting through the chalk massif of the North Downs, and eventually falls into the Thames north of the Roman Watling Street. In addition to the Lullingstone Roman villa, other comparable buildings of Roman date have been noted, and in some cases excavated, along the course of the Darent, which therefore communicated with each other by water in addition to a valley road. The chalk of the North Downs bears a deposit of clay-with-flint, and where the chalk dives steeply beneath the valley, the clay-with-flint has washed down leaving the slopes on either side steep, but of even gradient, thus concealing any natural or man-made terraces. The river meanders through this clay-with-flint and has left a deposit of alluvium over the valley bottom. The buildings that were discovered during the prolonged excavations at Lullingstone were found,

[1] *Custumale Roffense* (1788), 126–8, and Plate XXIV, Fig. 3.

therefore, to have been constructed mainly of local selected flints and blocks of the hard chalk. An abundant use was made of tiles and bricks which had probably been manufactured in the locality, possibly where the valley opens out at its south end upon wide deposits of Gault clay. Imported stone was found to be exceedingly rare, and the heavy wooden frameworks of most of the buildings clearly suggest that where much of the higher ground has long been used for agricultural purposes, in Roman times its was extensively woodland in character. As with so many Roman villas, the situation selected was a desirable one—a clear stream running through pasturage, a steep slope protecting the house, a clear south-easterly view, sufficient open land for cultivation, and extensive woodland.

Excavation began in 1949, at the north gate of the park and a trench was dug at the root of one of the fallen trees and Roman building débris and pottery fragments were immediately discovered. A second test was made on the west side of the gate, and at approximately 1·20 m. down a floor of fine Roman concrete was encountered. A third test made 14·65 m. south of this, near the west edge of the road, revealed what proved later to be the red brick tessellated surround of the main mosaic floor. A grid system was then devised to cover the presumed extent of the mosaic floor and any extensions of the building north and south of it. On beginning the excavation, the boundary fence of the park ran from the gate alongside a cart-track diagonally up the steep slope in a south-westerly direction, and the grid system was first taken up to this boundary fence. It was later found that the park fence did in fact run diagonally across the underlying Roman building, and to complete the excavation of the building the fence was removed, the cart-track diverted, and a complete rectangular grid system was evolved. The major part of the residence, containing as its central feature the mosaic floors, came to light within the grid system during the year 1949.

It was thought at this early stage that the Romano-British house was small and was not likely to contain any features of particular interest; but as excavation proceeded unusual features were in fact revealed. In addition to the mosaics, which incorporated figure subjects and a Latin inscription, a room began to be excavated immediately north-east of the mosaic floor and west of the road, and after prolonged work it became clear that this room was seated deep in the earth. The walls were of unusual height, and at the south end of the house, where the baths were later recognized, the walls also rose to an unusual height. It was becoming clear that the problem would prove to be three-dimensional, and the probability of other buildings in the immediate neighbourhood had to be taken into account for future excavation.

The complete excavation at Lullingstone lasted from 1949 to 1961, a period of thirteen years. The first seven years' excavation was undertaken by members of the Darent Valley Archaeological Group, under the direction of Mr E. Greenfield, Mr E. C. Birchenough, and the author for the first four years, and by the author alone for the next three years. In May 1956, the then Ministry of Works assumed responsibility for the excavation, which continued under the direction of the author until its conclusion in 1961.

Three Interim Reports were published during the early years of excavation; also, by the good offices of the then Ministry of Works and the Kent County Council, the latter began the diversion of the valley sewer and road, which hitherto had traversed the site from north to south on its east side, work that was designed to allow the complete excavation of the Deep Room into which had fallen the presumed Christian house-church immediately above it, the great importance of this house-church, as evidenced from the designs painted upon the wall-plaster from its walls, having been generally recognized. No other example from Roman Britain of such a house-church had hitherto been known, and complete excavation was considered essential to make an important addition to the understanding of early Christianity in Britain.

The flooding of the site in July 1956 was at first thought to be a complete disaster as the flood-water rose to the wall-tops which in the Deep Room stood to a height of 2·45 m. It happened, however, that the water flowing over the top of the south wall dislodged a number of flints and disclosed the rounded top of an arch constructed of chalk voussoirs, and in this way was discovered the blocked niche which was found to contain painted at the back a representation of three water nymphs. Had it not been for the flooding this painting would not have come to light.

By the year 1958 when excavation of the Temple-Mausoleum was approaching completion, the general lay-out at Lullingstone was beginning to be recognized. It became clear that the site had been planned to make use of the hill slope behind it; and this had, in fact, been terraced to receive the Temple-Mausoleum and the Circular Shrine, so that both these buildings rose prominently some 6 m. above and to the west of the residence, which in its turn had been founded upon a levelled area including a roughly semi-circular excavation to receive the second-century kitchens immediately west of it. This level stood between 0·915 m. and 1·22 m. above the garden area which stretched evenly to the bank of the river, flanked on the north by the granary and on the south by the presumed stack-yard or cart-standing. Lullingstone can therefore be classed as a terraced villa similar to that at Witcombe, near Cheltenham, though upon a more gentle slope than the latter. The steep path discovered in 1961 that leads westwards and upwards between the Temple-Mausoleum and the Circular Shrine proceeds to possibly a still higher terrace. This terrace has not been excavated and may contain upon it the foundations of further Romano-British buildings. These terraces were found to have been completely concealed by the downward creep of clay-with-flint hill-wash since Roman times. It will, however, be noticed that the first terrace had been made use of in, probably, the late Saxon period when the Lullingstane Church was erected, and the remnants of this church, consisting today of the truncated west wall and parts of the north and south walls, proved to have been founded upon the underlying walls of the Romano-British Temple-Mausoleum. This Temple–Mausoleum not only had a central cult-room whose interior walls were decorated with painted human figures, but also a tomb-chamber beneath it in which had originally been buried two individuals in decorated lead coffins with accompanying grave-goods, the burials dating to *c.* A.D. 300. It will at once be noticed that not only do we have at Lullingstone a late Saxon church positioned above what had been a building devoted to pagan worship, but also in the Romano-British residence itself we have a Christian house-church positioned above what had been a room devoted to the cult of the water spirits, and later to that of the marble portrait busts. The more one contemplates the complex of buildings at Lullingstone the more important becomes the religious aspect during the centuries of occupation. Throughout almost its entire history, religion, both pagan and Christian, has played a prominent part, as the following schedule of datings shows.

In *c.* A.D. 80–90 the house was constructed in flint and mortar. An earlier establishment is known to have existed by the abundant early pottery which has come to light and by the two *speculum* coins (Allen Class II); but its site is still unknown, though the increasing density of pottery fragments towards the north suggests that it stood in that region. In *c.* A.D. 100 the circular shrine was built. This had a tessellated floor with a small rectangular space reserved opposite the entrance, possibly for accommodation of a cult image; but the dedication, if any, is unknown. The Deep Room, which hitherto had been devoted merely to storage, was reorganized *c.* A.D. 180 as a *nymphaeum*, and not only was the niche constructed in the south wall to accommodate the painting of the three water nymphs with a flat space in the niche before the painting for a votive lamp, a vase, or other cult object, but a well, 0·83 m square and lined with chalk blocks, was sunk opposite the niche in the floor of the room into the flood-plain gravel to the underlying water-table. The walls of this *nymphaeum* were decorated with large panels outlined in red, green and yellow, upon a deep dado displaying squares and lozenges filled in with "marbling" technique in the same colours; and yellow date-palms rose vertically in the corners of the room, from which hung clusters of red dates. This decoration was repeated immediately to the north of the *nymphaeum* where a four-sided ambulatory surrounded a rectangular room which contained near its centre the seating in its floor for a circular water receptacle 0·76 m. in diameter. This is strongly reminiscent of the Romano-Celtic pagan temple plan, as with the Temple-Mausoleum on the terrace, and here again we probably see a building dedicated to a pagan cult, associated closely with the cult of the water spirits. From early in the third century up to the last decade or so the house was deserted, but at this latter time newcomers re-established it, placing the two marble portrait busts, which were already in a damaged state, on the steps leading into the Deep Room, and *c.* A.D. 300 they built the Temple-Mausoleum.

Christianity did not come to Lullingstone until late in the fourth century, when the house-church with its associated ante-chamber and vestibule was erected, the church itself, as already mentioned, immediately above the Deep Room, which now was no longer a *nymphaeum* but contained the portrait busts with two votive pots before them in the floor. It is clear that libations had periodically been made in front of the portrait busts, and this pagan practice continued throughout the remaining history of the house while Christianity reigned above. Indeed, when the house-church was erected, two further votive pots were added in the Deep Room for continued pagan ritual purposes. We have here an example of pagan and Christian worship running parallel.

A study of the distribution over the site of the coinage of Gratian (367–383), Valentinian II (375–392), and the House of Theodosius (379–423) suggests a likely dating sequence for the establishment of Christianity and the length of its continuance. The twenty-four recognizable coins concerned fall into two groups, divided the one from the other by the mosaic rooms which were devoid of coinage of this late period. The group to the south, which included the baths, filled in about this time, showed six coins of Gratian and four of the House of Theodosius. The group to the north showed no Gratian coins and eleven of the House of Theodosius, all concentrated about the Christian house-church and its associated rooms. The three coins of Valentinian II, two to the south and one to the north, are unlikely to be significant in this connection. Gratian having died in A.D. 383 and Theodosius I having begun to reign in A.D. 379, but his sons Honorius and Arcadius not until the 390s, the filling-in of the baths is likely to have taken place towards the end of Gratian's reign, about A.D. 380, and the foundation of the Christian house-church very shortly after this, about A.D. 385. The state of wear of some of the coins of the House of Theodosius suggests that the Christian establishment continued in being until perhaps the second decade of the fifth century.

When the family embraced Christianity, the Temple-Mausoleum, being a pagan establishment, fell out of use; but by late Saxon times its foundations were probably visible, as were certainly the higher parts of the walls of the baths below. A folk memory may have persisted not only of the pagan significance of the Temple-Mausoleum, but also of the Christian significance of the house itself; and this may well have conditioned the building of the Saxon church upon the foundations of the Temple-Mausoleum in a Christian continuity. It is orientated neither on a west-east axis nor upon the point of sunrise on St. John the Baptist's day, to whom it was dedicated. It may, therefore, prove to be an example of the precept of Pope Gregory to St. Augustine to utilize the places of former pagan worship.[2] To sum up, within a very small area we have, over a long period of time, buildings devoted both to pagan and Christian worship, making this site of a unique religious importance.

When excavations began, it was found that here the land was split up between different owners, the boundaries meeting at this point. The owners were Sir Oliver Hart Dyke, Bart., the Kent County Council, the Ecclesiastical Commissioners, and the Kemp Town Brewery of Brighton. These owners proved most co-operative, all allowing excavation to be conducted on their respective land; and when the Ancient Monuments Department of the then Ministry of Works assumed responsibility in 1956 negotiations resulted in the happy solution by which the Kent County Council acquired the interests of the other land owners and handed over the area of excavations to the then Ministry of Works, while retaining the ownership themselves, provided that the Ministry would both conduct all necessary archaeological investigations and would preserve for the future the ancient buildings so discovered. This allowed the excavations at Lullingstone to remain throughout a research project, and as the site was never in any danger of destruction sufficient time could be allocated to the excavation of each building as it was encountered. The evidence could, therefore, be slowly obtained and its significance systematically determined, and this proved of the greatest advantage in the elucidation and interpretation of a most complex site.

The thirteen years of excavation have provided a detailed history of the site.

It is clear that there was an occupation here, probably going back before the Roman invasion of A.D. 43. The evidence for this lies in the abundance of pottery of bead-rim native fabric, pseudo-Belgic ware, and Gallo-Belgic material, in which three categories a large number of vessels is represented. Large fragments were recovered from the footing-trenches of the earliest flint and mortar building, which was constructed *c.* A.D. 80–90. The two *speculum* coins of Allen Class II already mentioned support the pottery and are reinforced by a small British coin; and when it is understood that on several other sites in the Darent Valley such pottery has come to light in quantity, together with four other *speculum* coins, it is probable that the valley was quite intensively occupied and cultivated at the time of the Roman invasion. At Lullingstone the end of a ditch which was found to underlie the north-west corner of the granary contained much pottery of this character, and this ditch may be part of a boundary surrounding the original farmstead of which, however, there is so far no

[2] Bede, *A History of the English Church and People,* i, Chapter 30.

trace. Such a building at such a period would almost certainly have been constructed of wood, wattle and daub, with a roof of thatch, and therefore it would only be observed when its charcoal and rubbish spread and post-hole complex came to light, and this has so far not occurred. The owner of such a building would have been a native farmer possessing very slight knowledge of Gallic civilization and even less experience of its products.

In this connection three sites have been recently discovered (1964–66) in Lullingstone Park in the neighbourhood of the villa, together with a similar site at Hulbury (TQ 524660), known for some years. All these sites have produced an abundance of pottery which may be allocated to the period *c.* 50 B.C. to *c.* A.D. 50, with examples of Iron Age A derivation. These sites comprise (1) a ditched enclosure (TQ 524641), (2) a large refuse-pit (TQ 523646), (3) a farmstead (TQ 524649), and (4) the Hulbury site (a pit). All appear to have become disused about the middle of the first century A.D., and it was shortly after this time that the flint and mortar house was built. The distances between the sites, from south to north, are 576 m., 421 m., and 457 m., and their distances from the Lullingstone villa are 1153 m., 851 m., 604 m., and 668 m., respectively. They probably provide the late-Iron Age prologue to the Lullingstone villa itself.

In accordance with the Roman policy of Agricola, when progressive steps were taken towards the romanization both of town and country, such native farmers would have been induced progressively to accept romanization for themselves and their families, and to them would have been applied the new agrarian policy of the Roman government. This would have involved the inclusion of the original group of small farmsteads within a very much larger villa area, with re-organized and more efficient farming methods under a single farmer, still probably a native Briton working within the new Roman rural framework, and with official Roman help and advice. A suitable residence for this man and his family would be constructed, of durable materials and on the Romano-Gaulish plan. In several instances in Roman Britain such rebuilding under Roman influence has been found to overlie the older and more primitive establishment; but at Lullingstone this is not so. Here, the new building was constructed upon virgin ground; and on excavation it was quickly noted that the flint and mortar walls were, in their straightness and smooth rendering, the work of architects and masons who were almost certainly other than native British. The most important feature of this early house was the Deep Room at its north end, a feature which persisted throughout the whole history of the house, but devoted from time to time to different purposes. In dimensions 7 m. from west to east, and 4 m. in width, it occupies a similar position to the cellar in the Park Street villa near St. Albans, and in its first period it fulfilled that function, probably for the storage of grain. At this time, the approach to this Deep Room was threefold, consisting of a wooden stairway from the interior of the house, a walking-ramp from the exterior on the north, and a horizontal loading-platform of wood leading into it from the south through an aperture in the wall some 1·20 m. above the floor. The early house exhibits nothing of a luxurious nature and was, as would be expected, a continuation in durable materials of an original wooden house nearby, though planned in a far more civilized manner.

From this time into the early years of the second century occupation probably continued without event; but a new building was constructed as this century opened. This was the circular shrine, the siting of which, immediately to the north-west of the house and upon a higher level, suggests that at this time the value of a terraced slope was first appreciated. Also, this is the earliest manifestation of pagan cult worship on the site. There is no evidence that occupation ceased during the second century, though Trajanic and Hadrianic material is sparse in quantity compared with its abundance in the subsequent Antonine period; and it is to this latter period that the next development of the house belongs. Perhaps as late as A.D. 180 can be placed the great expansion and reorganization of the residence. From this time to perhaps the first decade of the third century the house was of a purely residential character, farming having ceased.

The alterations were fundamental. A large and comprehensive bath-house was added on the south, and on the north a total reconstruction took place. The Deep Room was transformed into a *nymphaeum*, the wooden stairs and loading-platform were removed, wall-blocks being inserted in their places, and on the north side the walking-ramp was replaced by a square landing from which tiled stairs proceeded downwards into the *nymphaeum*, upwards towards the north and towards the east, and westwards up into the interior of the house. The stairways directed north and east led to an ambulatory that proceeded round a rectangular room; and as has been said, the painted decorations upon the walls of the *nymphaeum* and on those of the ambulatory, where some were constructed of clay, showed a similar palm-and-panel design, thus drawing together the *nymphaeum* and the rectangular room with its ambulatory into a single complex of pagan religion. It would seem that here we have a pair of pagan cult-rooms organized to the specification of a new owner. The character of the wall decorations, showing as they do date-palms, and the presumed existence at this time within the house of the two marble portrait busts, which were sculpted from Greek Pentelic marble by artists in the eastern Mediterranean tradition, suggest that this new owner may have had a Mediterranean connection; he was certainly not a native Briton. Typologically, these two busts may be allocated as to one bust to the reign of Hadrian (A.D. 117–138), and as to the other to at least a generation later, and they are likely to have formed part of the portrait gallery of a Roman of consequence. The social standing and wealth of this individual are also evidenced by a study of the samian ware, which falls mostly in the last two decades of the century, by the metallic-glazed imported Rhenish ware, of which some 60 vessels are represented, by the numerous fragments of Castor "Hunt-Cup" ware, and by the coinage which includes issues from Hadrian through to Faustina II. One of the most important finds in this connection was a carnelian oval *intaglio*, nearly 2·5 cm. in length, depicting a winged Victory writing on a shield before a military trophy, from a gold finger-ring, which was found with a small group of these coins; and such a gold finger-ring would almost certainly have belonged to a Roman of equestrian or higher rank. This concentration of evidence of building, of decoration, of material wealth, and of Roman dignity, is strongly suggestive of a individual who had acquired the Lullingstone villa for personal residence, and who may well have been a person of consequence in the government of the Roman province, using his Lullingstone house as a small country retreat.

A careful observation of the late second-century building disclosed in many places the partial destruction of walls, and the fall over the adjacent areas of wall-plaster by direct weathering. This was particularly notable at the northern end of the building and to a lesser degree in the baths; and the large rectangular building containing the second-century kitchens, which occupied an excavated area immediately outside the house to the west, was radically altered, a small tannery taking its place. It is clear that the house was no longer occupied in the early years of the third century, except perhaps as the site of a short-lived tanning industry; and the relinquishment of his residence by the Roman owner may well have been a sudden decision. If the pair of marble portrait busts had adorned his house, they were abandoned within it on his departure, which therefore suggests a precipitate retreat. If there is substance in the suggestion that this man had been employed, perhaps as a senior civil servant, then his fortune would have been affected by the political disturbances that distracted the province of Britain after the assassination of Commodus in A.D. 192; and especially in A.D. 197, when the governor, Clodius Albinus, stripped the province of its military forces to contest the empire with Septimius Severus with disastrous result; and again during the short period A.D. 197–202, when the new governor, Virius Lupus, was sent into Britain by Severus for its reorganization. Throughout this whole period the political circumstances in Britain would have created a most difficult position for any senior official who had served under Clodius Albinus. It is difficult to assess at which of the three times listed above was the house finally deserted. From a consideration of the abundant late-Antonine pottery which has been recovered from these levels, a date before the end of the century may be premature; occupation could have continued into the first years of the reign of Severus. Much of the East Gaulish samian, together with the metallic-glazed Rhenish wares, and especially the great quantity of late-Antonine pie-dishes, the production of which is now thought to have persisted into the third century—all this mass of pottery tends to reinforce this slightly later dating for the end of the occupation.

The tannery did not last long, but was soon dismantled and began to be concealed from view by a rapid downward creep of the clay-and-flint hill-wash from the high ground behind the house; to such an extent that by the end of the third century the area immediately west of the house, hitherto level, presented a steep and even slope upwards. Towards the end of the third century the house was re-occupied, repaired, and at the northern end remodelled. During this lengthy period of desertion the tiled steps that led downwards at the northern extremity of the house had become concealed from view by the fall of the cement and plaster wall-facing, as on excavation the tiles were found to be virtually intact; but where the steps debouched into the Deep Room, and where they had never been so covered, the tiles had been removed. The baths were repaired by raising the floor of the cold room and remodelling the cold plunge bath; and at the northern end of the house where the stairs led down, these were covered by a rectangular room with under-floor heating, the walls of the room being completed by a wall-block at the point where the stairs turned down into the Deep Room, these latter steps becoming, as it were, shelves upon which to place the marble portrait busts, which had presumably been recovered from the semi-ruined building. The room with its surrounding ambulatory to the north of the Deep Room was finally reduced almost to ground level and a new north wall of the whole building was constructed 4 m. southward of the original north wall, making the building shorter from north to south. At the same time, the niche in the south wall of the Deep Room containing the now weathered remains of the water nymphs painting was blocked; and to appease the spirits of the persons whose features were depicted in the marble busts two pottery vessels were inserted in the concrete floor in front of them. The nearer of these was a Rhenish "motto-beaker" bearing the word SVAVIS (Sweetness), a vessel which can be confidently dated in the first half of the third century. It was found to contain a portion of rib-bone of a sheep to which a small snail firmly adhered. The second of these two vessels was inserted in line with the former and the busts, but near the south wall, and was a cooking-pot of late-second to early-third century type.

The largest construction at this time was the granary. This building, 24·40 m. long by 10·68 m. wide, and substantially built of flint and mortar with a roof of thatch, was sited exactly at right-angles to the long axis of the residence, but separated from it by 20·74 m., and occupying the northern side of the garden area, its east end being only a few yards from the river-bank. On the evidence of this large building the new owner of the villa can be described as a Romano-British individual whose main occupation was farming on a large scale, to which the great capacity of the granary bears eloquent witness. It is likely that the reconstruction of the house preceded by some years the building of the granary, as coins of the early third century were recovered from the former while coins of Allectus were recovered from the latter.

At the end of the century, the terrace upon which still stood the circular shrine, now probably in a ruinous condition, was extended to receive the Temple-Mausoleum, and there is no reason to doubt that the same family may well have continued in occupation of the house, perhaps indeed until its final destruction in the early decades of the fifth century, though there is slight evidence that secular residence may have ceased before the end. By the middle of the fourth century the apsidal dining room had been extended beyond the west wall of the house, and both it and the large central reception room were provided with the mosaic floors which survive today. The baths were further repaired and a third floor was laid over the cold room, the level of the cold plunge bath being further raised, and a small additional plunge bath added to it on its south side. The coinage becomes abundant, as does also the typical fourth-century pottery; and as the dining and reception rooms were not provided with under-floor heating, it is likely that the residence, which now had assumed the aspect of a luxurious farmhouse, was used by its owner only in summer and during the time of harvest, while for the rest of the year its agricultural activities were probably conducted by a resident bailiff, the owner concentrating on his urban interests. However, by *c.* A.D. 380–385, the owner and his family embraced Christianity, and their house at Lullingstone was deemed of sufficient importance for them to establish within it their house-church. About this time the baths were disused, being deprived of their heavy tiled floors with their brick supports for other purposes, and filled-in. This left open the area south of the central mosaic rooms, leaving these, with the house-church and its associated Christian rooms, standing, a compact but truncated building. This was finally burned down early in the fifth century. As suggested above, this building for some years before its destruction may have continued as a centre for Christian worship for the surrounding neighbourhood, secular residence having ceased.

The following Table of Events sums up the history of the Lullingstone Roman Villa:

Date A.D.	*Event*	*Type of owner*
To *c.* 80	Pre-villa occupation.	A native farmer becoming romanized.
c. 80–90	Building of the first flint and mortar house. The Deep Room constructed as a grain store.	Ditto.
c. Early second century	Siting of the circular tample.	A fully romanized native farmer.
c. 180	Expansion of the house by addition of the baths, the kitchens and the north cult rooms. The Deep Room becomes a place of worship of the water nymphs. The marble portrait busts now present.	A Roman, possibly of Mediterranean origin. No evidence of farming.
c. 200	Abandonment of the house.	
c. Early third century	Establishment of the tannery.	Probably a local individual.
c. 220–280	The house derelict.	
c. 280	Re-occupation by a different family. The baths rebuilt, the northern steps blocked, and the room rebuilt as a heated apartment. The marble portrait busts deposited in the Deep Room. Building of the granary.	A Romano-British individual farming on a large scale, whose descendants continue to own the villa until late in the fourth century or to its final destruction.
c. 300	Building of the Temple-Mausoleum.	Ditto.
c. 330–360	Construction of the apsidal dining room and the reception room with their mosaic floors.	The owner is now using the house as an intermittent residence, though farming continues.
c. 380	The baths dismantled.	Ditto.
c. 380–385	Foundation of the Christian house-church and its associated rooms. Pagan rites continue in the Deep Room.	The family now embrace Christianity.
c. 390	The granary, its north wall recently buttressed, is used as a cart-standing, being shortly afterwards pulled down. The Christian rooms continue in use with the house-church.	Farming ceases, and secular residence may have come to an end, leaving a centre of Christian worship only.
c. Early fifth century	The final fire.	

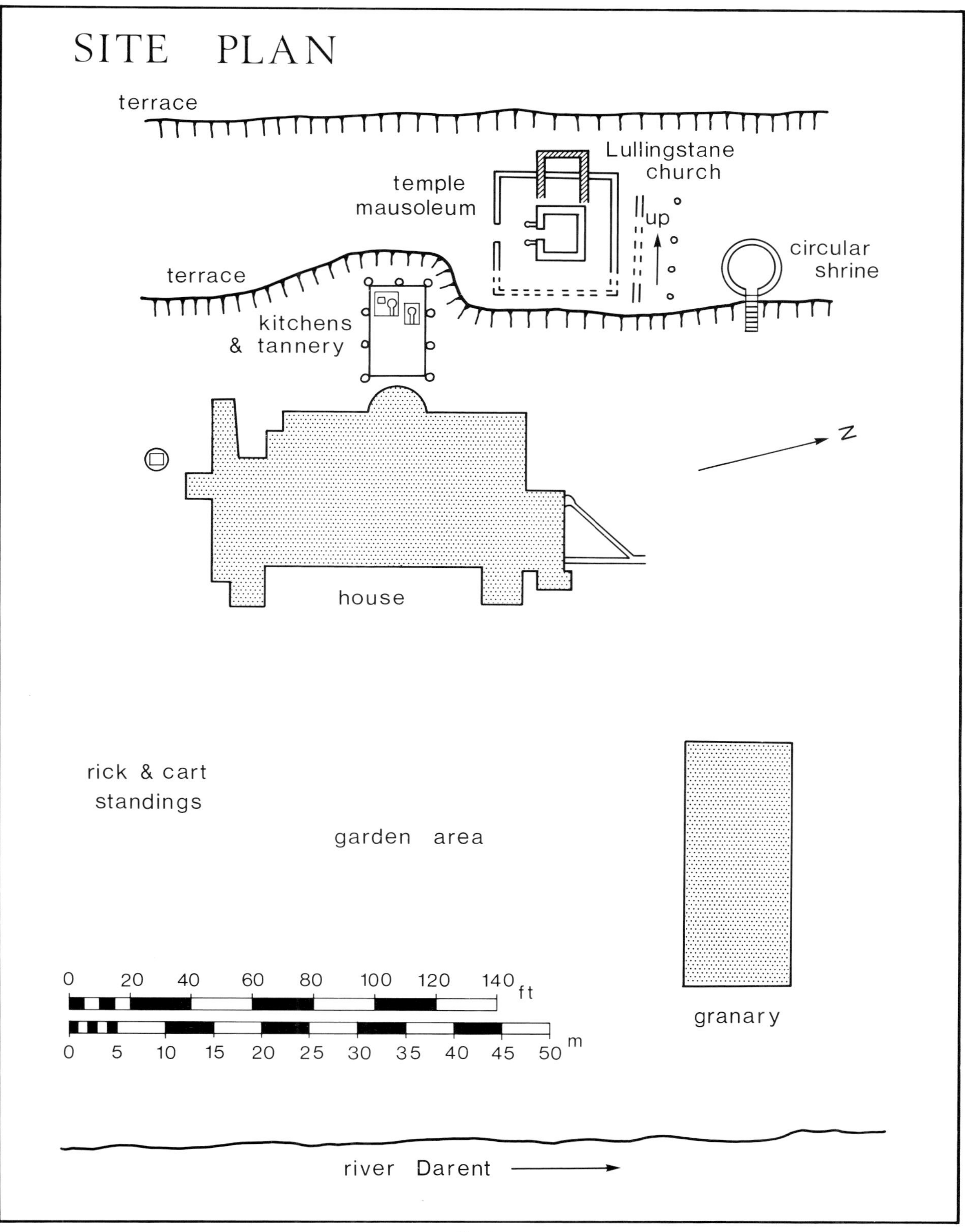
SITE PLAN
terrace
Lullingstane
church
temple
mausoleum
up
circular
shrine
terrace
kitchens
& tannery
N
house
rick & cart
standings
garden area
granary
0 20 40 60 80 100 120 140 ft
0 5 10 15 20 25 30 35 40 45 50 m
river Darent

Fig. 2.

PART I

THE NORTHERN GROUP

Room (6)—The Deep Room
Room (10)
Room (10A)
Room (11)
Room (14)
Rooms (3) and (8), Corridors (2)—The Northern Complex

The Deep Room (6) in the first Century (Fig. 3a)

The Deep Room formed part of the original building, constructed *c.* A.D. 80–90. The site selected sloped downwards from the west at a gradient of approximately 1 in 6, and for the reception of this room the clay-with-flint coverage was cut into, so that at its west end the surface of the slope was approximately 2 m. above the floor of the room, and its east end approximately 0·70 m. above the floor. The room was thus sunk into the ground to the level of the flood-plain gravel, but stopping short of the underlying water-table by at least 0·60 m. A firm wall of flint and mortar was built up at its west end, and a similar wall, most of it free-standing, at its east end; north and south walls completed the apartment. This depth of the room was not designed to admit water into it, unless the water-table has radically altered since Roman times. It would seem to have been a continuance of the Iron Age custom of storage below ground-level, as seen especially at the Iron Age farmstead site in Lullingstone Park less than 805 m. west of the new building. That the room was designed as a cellar or storage-room is made clearer by a study of its three approaches (Fig. 3b).

(1) A walking-ramp, between 0·76 m. and 0·91 m. wide, from the direction of the north exterior, leading down at an approximate gradient of 1 in 3·6, in the north-west corner. This slope had a rammed flint and gravel surface, and continued horizontally towards the north exterior as a covered way, five post-holes for the supporting uprights still remaining along the west wall of this passage, 1·52 m. apart and nearly 0·30 m. square. Some fragments of first-century native-type pottery were recovered from them, though no trace of the wood remained, the uprights having been removed when a new flint and mortar wall was built along the front of the wall that had contained them at the reconstruction *c.* A.D. 180. The passage referred to above was joined by a further, walled, steep slope, 1·45 m. wide, mounting at right-angles to the west for 1·98 m., where it led into a north–south corridor about 1·45 m. wide. This slope was roughly gravelled. Whether the passage northwards from the Deep Room debouched on the north exterior remains uncertain.

(2) A stairway of wood leading down from the interior of the house in the south-west corner of the Deep Room, directly opposite the walking-ramp (Pls. Ia and b, IIa). This

stairway was fitted between two beautifully straight and rendered walls forming a staircase-well 1·37 m. across. The ground had here been cut back and down in a steep and irregular slope of a gradient of approximately 1 in 1·3, and lightly rendered with puddled chalk. The wooden stairway did not rest upon this, but was securely fixed at the top (south) to a heavy plate of wood set on edge and embedded in thick mortar; at the bottom (north) it rested upon a second heavy plate of wood, lying horizontally in a seating of immensely thick mortar, positioned nearly 0·60 m. above the floor of the Deep Room. The rising string-course of the stairway was visible intermittently in the west wall of the staircase-well, as was the grain of the wood upon each mortar seating. This wooden stairway was removed *c.* A.D. 180, a substantial wall-block being inserted where it had once debouched into the Deep Room; and the empty staircase-well was filled up with a packing of clay, flints and lumps of mortar, with some loose red-brick *tesserae* scattered among the filling.

Both the walking-ramp and the wooden stairway were separated from the rest of the Deep Room by a strong wall running north–south, with perhaps a doorway in it for admission into the Deep Room. But at an early time, possibly associated with the reorganization of the Deep Room *c.* A.D. 180, this wall had been removed, except for 1·20 m. of its foundation at its south end, over which was laid the concrete floor at this later reorganization.

(3) A horizontal wooden platform was inserted parallel with the wooden stairway and 1·83 m. further east of it, the north end of the platform debouching through a narrow opening in the south wall of the Deep Room (Pl. IIb). The north–south corridor (13A), 2·45 m. wide and containing this platform, seems partially to have been divided by a centre wall 0·45 m., the stub of which only survives. Two narrow parallel corridors were thus formed, surviving at the northern end, each of equal width (1 m.), and the central wall probably extended southwards beyond a point 6 m. from the south bounding wall of the corridor, and it may have stopped at that point, merging into the floor level. Thus, two narrow corridors existed at the northern end, abutting directly upon the south wall of the Deep Room. Of the western of these nothing is further known, as it had been completely altered in Period IA (between first construction and *c.* A.D. 180). The eastern of the two, however, contained the wooden platform. At a distance of 3·35 m. south of the outer face of the wall of the Deep Room, the horizontal treading-level turned downwards towards the Deep Room, forming a slope, surfaced with chalk, at an approximate gradient of 1 in 4. Cut in the east wall was a horizontal slot for a beam, 0·70 m. above the slope next the wall of the Deep Room, and running back for 1·53 m. southwards, where it met the rising slope. Three vertical slots to contain squared-off wooden supports for this horizontal beam were also cut into the wall at regular intervals. The corresponding west wall enclosing this slope had been totally destroyed by the Period IA alterations, but it must have had similar horizontal and vertical slots opposite those remaining in the east wall. It can be concluded from this that a horizontal wooden platform originally led northwards above the slope, ending at an aperture in the wall of the Deep Room, the platform debouching upon the latter 1·22 m. above the flood-plain gravel which in Period I formed the floor. The platform therefore probably served as a loading and unloading stage, perhaps for sacks of grain or other material; indeed, it is the presence of this horizontal wooden stage that strongly suggests that the Deep Room was in Period I a large storage-room whose floor lay below the surrounding Roman treading-level—checked by excavation immediately outside the east wall of the Deep

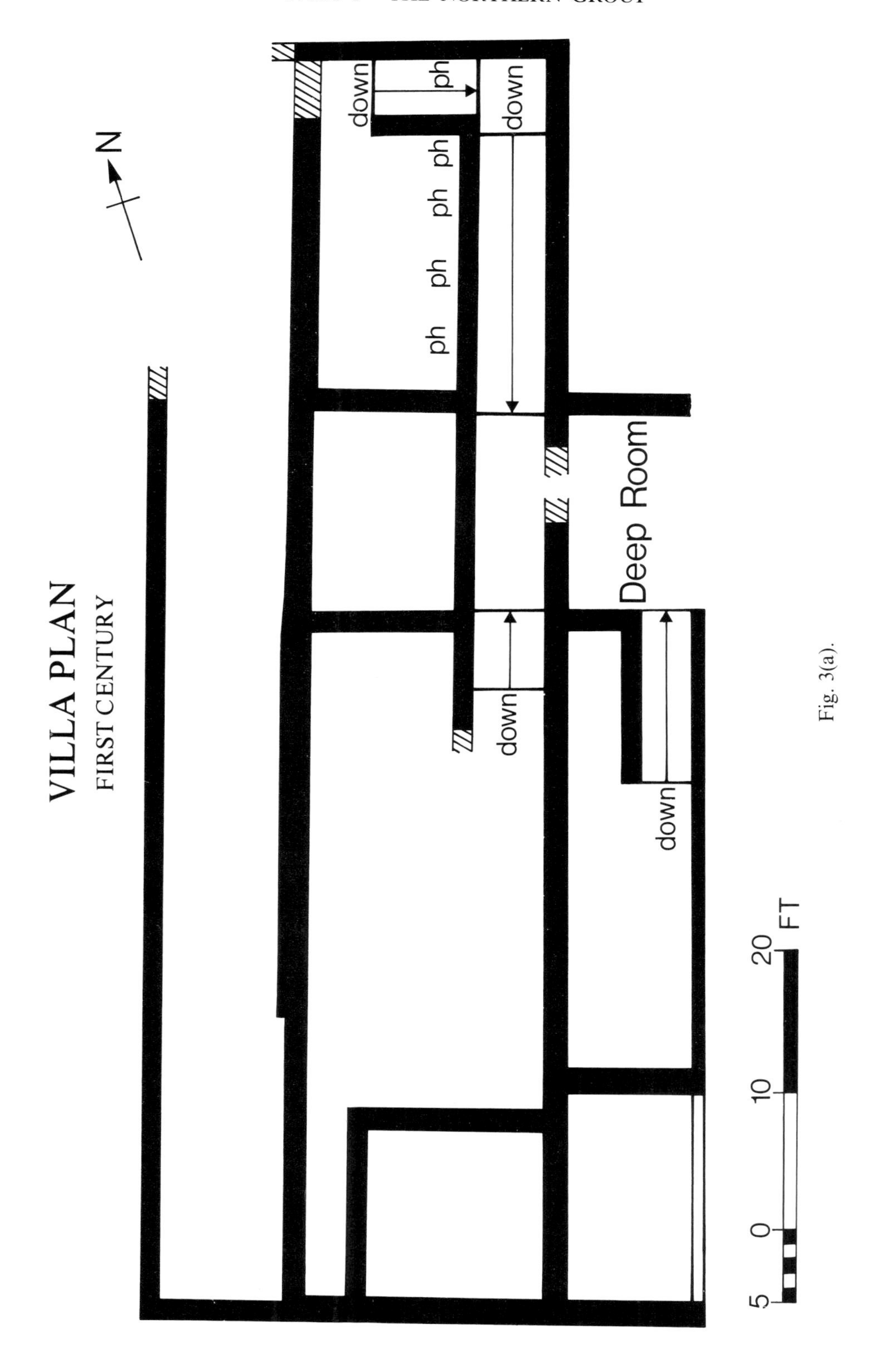
VILLA PLAN
FIRST CENTURY
N
down
ph
down
ph ph ph ph ph
Deep Room
down
down
5 0 10 20 FT

Fig. 3(a).

Deep Room
reconstruction of wooden stair and platform

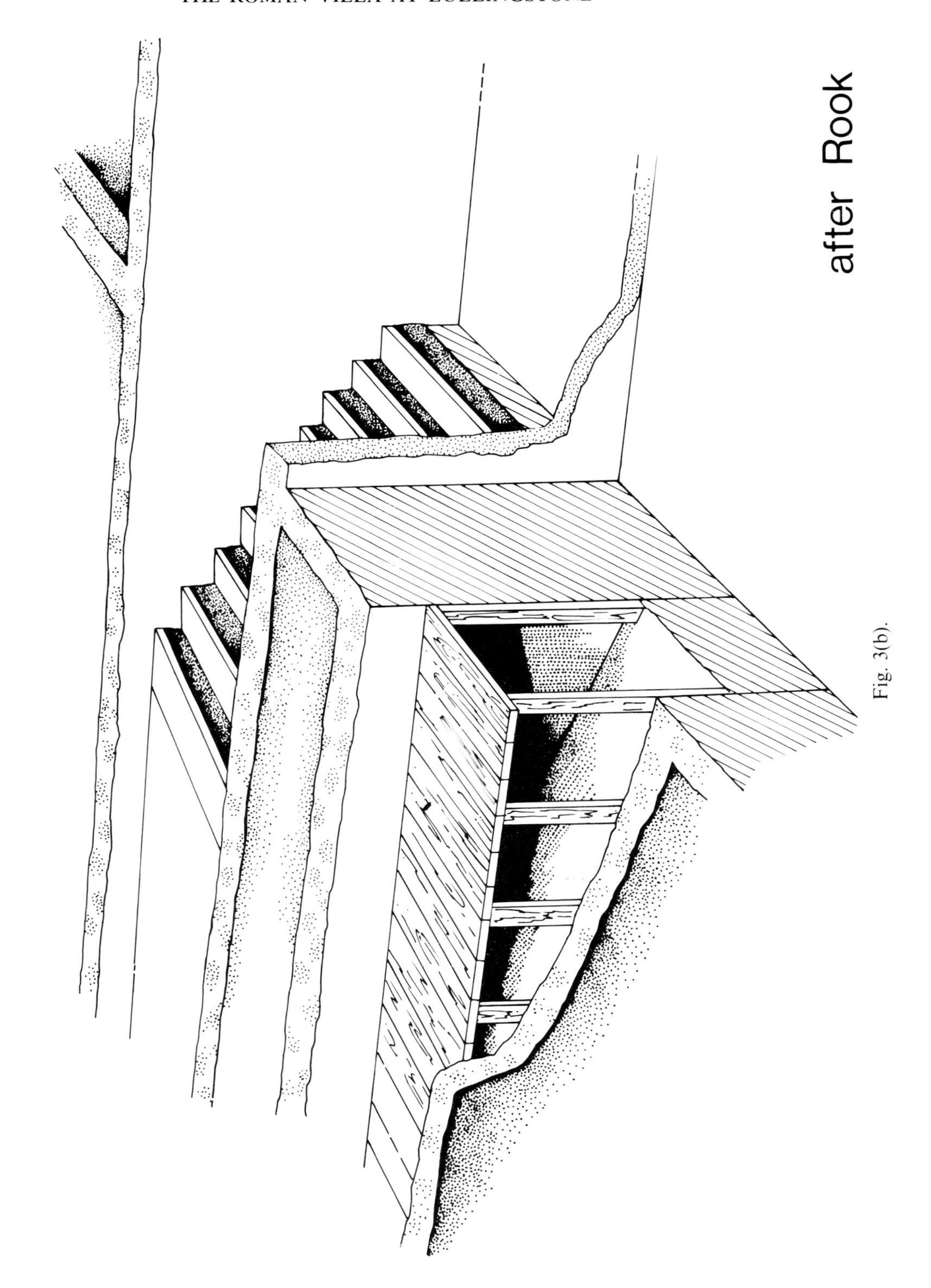
after Rook

Fig. 3(b).

Room. The size and depth of both horizontal and vertical slots also suggest a fairly massive platform, of sufficient strength to bear considerable weight and frequent movement to and from the opening into the Deep Room. The purpose of the slope under the platform is problematical; if it led directly through the wall of the Deep Room, it must have debouched almost 0·45 m. above the floor of the room, with the wooden platform stopping about 0·76 m. above its termination.

Taking (1), (2) and (3) into consideration, all being in use at the same time, the suggestion that the Deep Room was in Period I a very large storage compartment would appear to be the most likely interpretation.

The Deep Room in the second Century

From its initial construction *c.* A.D. 80–90, until the closing years of the second century, the Deep Room remained unaltered, except for the modifications in Period IA, its purpose continuing as a store-room. These modifications entailed a radical alteration to the south wall of the room. The wooden platform was removed, its place was filled up with flint and mortar rubble and the aperture in the wall blocked at the same time. A flight of stairs was then constructed almost central at the north end of the corridor (13A), its steps leading down to the Deep Room, a new opening presumably being made in the wall. Some fragments of tile still remaining mortared into the walls bounding this new staircase, which led up into the house, suggest that the treaders were probably tiled; but subsequent alterations involved their removal when this staircase in its turn became redundant at the rebuilding *c.* A.D. 180. Curiously enough, the west wall that had enclosed the wooden platform was not utilized, being removed, the east wall of the new staircase taking its place, but with its west face continuing the northward line of the east face of the original wall, a large stub of which was left standing towards the south. At the same time, the west bounding wall of the new staircase was constructed 0·60 m. east of the long west wall of the corridor (13A), the space between being packed with dry flints, containing fragments of first-century pottery. Both walls of the new staircase were thus joined to the original walls of the corridor (13A), leaving a flight of stairs approximately 0·76 m. wide, its centre line being 0·45 m. off-centre towards the west. It was not possible to determine precisely the length of time during which this staircase was in use, but its existence was probably a short one (Fig. 5b).

By *c.* A.D. 180, the timbers of the entrance stairway in the south-west corner of the Deep Room must have become weakened and dilapidated; and while there is no evidence of similar deterioration of the flint walls, the house must by then have presented a somewhat venerable appearance when the new owner entered into possession. The alterations he made were radical. The early north–south wall which passed across the Deep Room enclosing the wooden stairway and the walking-ramp, and which probably contained an entrance into the eastern, and much larger, part of the room, was pulled down. This tended to weaken the wall, now unsupported on the south, though the later cracking of it northwards did not occur at this time. The foundations of this wall had been laid in the flood-plain gravel, which up to now had formed the floor of the room. A concrete floor, averaging 0·22 m. in thickness, but tending to thin out as it proceeded eastwards, was laid over the whole room, concealing the wall foundation and the flood-plain gravel; the wooden stairs were removed and blocked off, and a continuous south wall was provided, though for some reason the block sealing off the staircase-well in the south-west corner did not continue the line, but was offset to the extent of its thickness northwards of the wall face. At the same time, the tiled stairs were constructed in the north-west corner; the niche to accommodate the painting of the three water nymphs was cut in the south wall; and the small square well, carefully lined with chalk blocks, was sunk through the concrete floor to the water-table near the middle of the room and in front of the niche (Figs. 4 and 86).

The walls, with the interior of the niche, were then rendered in their entirety with white plaster, upon which the fresco decoration of the room was painted. On excavation, sufficient of this decorative scheme survived *in situ* to allow a comprehensive reconstruction, the west wall providing most of the evidence, the plaster adhering here to a height of 2·20 m. above the concrete floor. This plaster bore the following decoration, all confined to three colours, red, green, and orange-yellow:

At a point 0·25 m. above the floor a dado was painted, 0·40 m. high, consisting of squares and rectangles, the rectangles containing extended lozenges lying horizontally, outlined by red lines. The spaces everywhere were filled by brushwork in the three colours, perhaps intended to depict a marbling effect. The dado was enclosed by thick horizontal bands of orange-yellow, the squares and rectangles being similarly separated by vertical bands of the same thickness and colour.

The whole length of the dado, 3·73 m., from the south wall-block, formed the base upon which were painted two very large panels in perspective. These were outlined in lines of red, green, and orange-yellow, diminishing in distance from each other as they proceeded "inwards", the effect of perspective being obtained by joining up the corners with a line of dots, again in red, green, and orange-yellow, respectively, which had the effect of leading the eye towards the "back" of the panels. The panels themselves were left blank of any decoration, and they were separated from each other by a thick vertical band of orange-yellow, springing upwards from the top of the dado to their top horizontal line. The height of the two panels could be measured, as by a fortunate chance a fragment of plaster still remained *in situ* showing the outer line of red where it lay horizontally. This gave an internal height of the panels of 1 m., which, with their frames, extended upwards from the dado for approximately 1·52 m. Thus, an estimation of the height of the room could be obtained:

Floor to dado	0·25 m.
Dado	0·40 m.
Panels and frames	1·52 m. (approx.)
Top of frames to floor-boards of room above	0·25 m. (approx.)
Total	2·42 m. (approx.)

In length, however, the panels were not exactly equal. That to the south measured 1·62 m. in length between the enclosing red lines, that to the north 1·72 m. With the separating zone of 0·22 m., and the added widths between the outer red lines and the enclosing orange-yellow vertical bands, a total length of 3·73 m. from the south wall-block was thus filled. The remaining 0·38 m. at the north end was filled with a vertical palm-tree in orange-yellow with groups of spreading fronds curving down on either side, from which hung on either side of the stem clusters of red dates, a motif suggestive of the Mediterranean. These were at first thought to represent grapes, but the leaves are those of the date-palm, and near parallels exist in Roman sculptured panels in North Africa, which closely resemble the painted examples at Lullingstone. Similar decoration existed along the north, east, and south walls, with dado and panels, and date-palms rising at either end of the north wall and at the offset in the south wall. These palms were absent from the south-west corner, and from the east wall, where truncated palms only were placed at the ends of the dado, the whole east wall above containing panels, probably as on the west wall, from end to end.

The decoration of the room, with its overall white background, must have reflected all the light that entered, a very necessary matter for a room that was semi-underground. There could have been no windows in any wall, but there is slight evidence of an opening in the middle of the east wall. This was not a doorway, but may have been a high-level aperture beginning some 1·22 m. above the floor and extending nearly to the floor-boards of the room above. Light would therefore have been admitted here from the exterior, with diffused light from the stairway in the north-west corner. Of the room above, nothing is known at this period.

It now remains to consider the niche in the south wall, and the painting that was executed upon its inner face. The niche was constructed 2·75 m. from the east wall, and 0·35 m. deep into the south wall, and was originally approximately 0·76 m. in width. The lehge was horizontal, the back vertical; the height in the centre was 0·91 m., and at a height of 0·50 m. above the ledge the top began to curve, forming a near semi-circle. The sides of the niche were constructed of small chalk blocks, which continued as small voussoirs over the curved top. While the west side of the niche had been later cut away, that side had doubtless been continued down to the ledge with the same chalk blocks. The whole niche was therefore originally outlined in white chalk blocks, all securely mortared into the flint wall. The damage to the west side took place some time in the third century, after the house had been abandoned by its owner *c.* A.D. 200. The niche then no longer bore any ritualistic importance, having been subsequently used as a sort of cupboard, though without any door or shutter; and at the point where the spring of the arch began it had been fitted with a wooden shelf, fixed to a deep wooden vertical plate set in the back and sides, the painting of the water nymphs being destroyed at this point. And later, still in the third century, the wooden shelf was in its turn removed, and the wall on the west side was broken through for some unknown purpose, carrying away almost all of the right-hand seated nymph (Pl. Vd). And finally, on the re-occupation of the house later in the third century, the niche was completely blocked with courses of flints and hard mortar, the courses so accurately continuing those of the wall on either side that no vestige of it was left. Fortunately, on unblocking the niche, it was found that the inmost courses of flints had not been mortared on to the surface of the painting, which therefore was undamaged, except for the previous alterations affecting it and the weathering to which the plaster had been subjected for a considerable time before the blocking. The painting has now been completely restored and made safe, though very properly it has been left untouched by any re-painting, appearing as it did when the niche was blocked, concealing it from view.

The interior of the niche was originally rendered throughout in white plaster, including the shelf or ledge, upon which may have stood some votive object, or perhaps a vessel containing

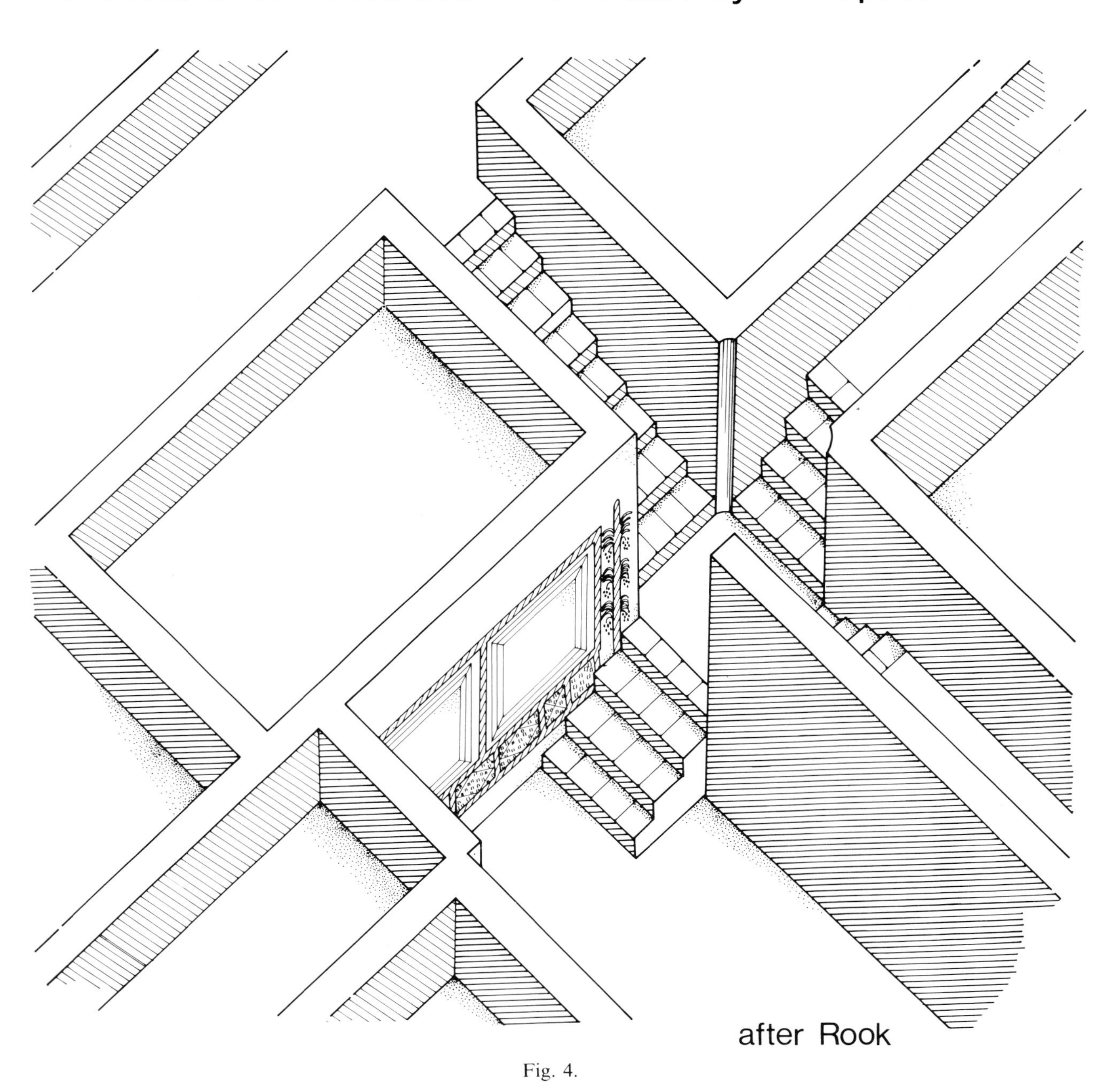

Fig. 4.

flowers and water, frequently renewed, or a votive lamp, though the latter is less likely to have stood before the water nymphs, as no trace of carbon deposit was found anywhere. A continuous red band was painted along the east end of the shelf, being then carried up and over the painting, and down to the west side, where it was doubtless continued along the shelf at this end. A description of the painting by Professor J. M. C. Toynbee is appended[3]:

"The third mythological picture"—the first two refer to wall-paintings at Combe End, Gloucestershire, and at Otford, Kent—"was discovered at the back of a shallow niche cut in the south wall of the basement room at Lullingstone. The complete area of this painting, 0·81 m. high, has survived, apart from a horizontal gash across its centre, where it seems that some Romano-British philistine had fixed a wooden shelf, or similar contraption, just below the spring of the arch of the niche. Since the picture appears to date from the brief, late-second century phase of the villa's occupation, it would seem that this desecration was the work of the reoccupiers of the house in the late third century; and later still, but also in antiquity, the entire niche and its painting were completely blocked up. The subject of the picture is a trio of female figures, the central one standing, the other two seated on either side of her and turned towards her (Pl. LIII, (a)). Of this central figure, who wears a yellow cloak round her lower limbs, the head, face, and torso are well preserved (Pl. LIII, (b)). She has dark hair, crowned by a yellow-and-red diadem, lustrous brown eyes, and red lips, and her face is turned slightly towards the spectator's left. A wreath of green leaves forms a kind of halo round her head; she wears a necklace of light-blue beads strung out at intervals and she holds a green frond; and from her nipples blue jets of water are spurting forth—a feature to which I know no parallel. Of her companion on the left, who is nude save for a dark blue cloak wrapped about her knees, only the outline of the head can be discerned, although her necklace of blue beads, and a curly lock of hair escaping on to her right shoulder, are clearly visible. We can also just descry her right hand resting by her side on an over-turned urn, from the mouth of which a stream of blue water gushes. The woman on the right is lost, apart from her knees, swathed in a partly dark blue and partly reddish purple mantle. It would seem to be certain that the painting represents a triad of Water Nymphs, perhaps regarded as the deities of the River Darent which flows north, just to the east of the villa. The group recalls in its composition a painting of three Water Nymphs from Pompeii and its execution is worthy of an Italian workshop."

The Deep Room in the third Century

From the time when the house became deserted, probably at the very end of the second century, or perhaps in the first decade of the third century, until it was re-occupied late in that century, little can positively be said of its history, or that of the Deep Room within it. Sufficient time elapsed for the re-use of the niche as a cupboard, the cult of the Water Spirits having ceased, and for the weathering and further dilapidation of the painting, before it was finally blocked off to render the south wall continuous. The long flight of tiled steps leading down to the landing just outside the north-west corner of the Deep Room also became concealed from view by the collapse over it of the mortar facing and wall-plaster from the south wall beside it—the fate of the wall enclosing the stairs on their north side is not known as to date of its destruction, which was total. The steps that turned down into the Deep

[3] J. M. C. Toynbee, *Art in Britain under the Romans*, Oxford, 1964, 220–1, illustrated at Plate LIII, (a) and (b).

Room were, however, not so concealed, and the tiles were cut away from their treaders some time while the house remained tenantless.

Late in the third century (a tentative date of *c*. A.D. 280, derived from stratified pottery, is allocated), newcomers came and took over the deserted residence. They made considerable alterations affecting the Deep Room. It may have been now that the niche was finally blocked, and the four steps leading into the room were cut off from the landing outside by a massive wall-block built along the topmost step. The remaining three steps, now bereft of their tiles, thus became as it were projecting shelves. This blocking of the steps was necessary to complete a hypocaust system which was now built north of Room 14 and the Deep Room, the latter losing its entrance up the steps. No entrance from the exterior now remained except possibly by means of the suggested high-level aperture in the centre of its east wall; a ladder through a trap in the floor-boards of the room above could also have been used, though of this there was no evidence.

The deposit of the marble portrait busts in the Deep Room took place at this time (Pls. IIIa, b, c, IVa, b). Already weathered and damaged, they were placed upon the projecting steps within the room, Bust I upon the centre of the top step with its back to the wall-block, Bust II, the head upon a small *podium* beside the steps, leaning against the wall with the face exposed, the damaged torso on the second step against the west wall and wedged for stability against the broken tile treader with a large fragment of storage-jar of first-century date—clearly a suitable surviving fragment chosen for this purpose. The fact that the head and its torso were placed so far apart suggests that the persons who deposited them were unaware that they had once formed a single bust. The absence of marble chippings in the Deep Room, or indeed anywhere else in the house, and the abraded features of both busts, suggest very strongly that they had belonged to the late second-century owner, that they had been left in the house on his sudden departure, that they were damaged before being deposited in the Deep Room, remaining there exposed to weathering and the depredations of men, and that these late third-century newcomers discovered them and desired to place them safely in some part of the house, where the necessary ritual could be paid from time to time to the spirits of the persons whose features were depicted in the marble, although these features may have had an anonymity to these newcomers. Two complete pottery vessels were inserted in holes made for them in the concrete floor of the room, both in a line southwards of the busts. These were, first, a grey cooking-pot of late second-century date, inserted 2·36 m. south of the lowest step (Pl. Vc); second, a metallic-glazed, indented Rhenish ware beaker, decorated with white dots and the word SVAVIS (Sweetness) *en barbotine,* a third-century importation, inserted 0·76 m. south of the same step (Pls. Va and b). This latter vessel contained part of the rib of a sheep, to which a small snail was found firmly adhering, part, perhaps, of a ritual meal taken when the busts were deposited. The lips of both vessels were level with the surrounding concrete floor and open to receive libations. It should be said that there is a possibility that the late second-century pot, situated as it was in the centre of, and only 0·30 m. from the wall-block in the south-west corner of the room, may have been a ritual deposit at the re-construction of the room *c*. A.D. 180, and that the SVAVIS beaker alone commemorated the deposit of the busts. In any event, it is important to note that the busts remained in the Deep Room throughout the subsequent history of the villa, sharing in the final conflagration of the early fifth century.

The "Palm and Panel" wall-decoration of the Deep Room had suffered considerable weathering during the years of vacancy, and the newcomers completely re-decorated the walls of the room, which was now, at least in its western part, a depository for the portrait busts and the two pots in the floor before them, a deposition of pagan ritualistic significance. The small well further to the east was repaired by the insertion of large tile fragments among its lining of chalk blocks, being still useful as a household water-supply. The "Palm and Panel" wall-plaster was pecked all over for the adherence of a fresh coat of white plaster, and this was decorated with horizontal bands of red paint, not fresco, averaging 2·50–3·75 cm. in thickness, which turned vertically in the corners of the room, and with some additional and widely spaced bands of yellow paint applied horizontally. The "Palm and Panel" decoration was thus completely concealed from view. These yellow bands, with the red bands, were most in evidence upon the wall-block behind the busts, to which the third-century plaster was directly applied, there being naturally no "Palm and Panel" decoration upon the wall-block here. The work of painting the room had been inefficiently carried out, as splashings of red paint still remained unremoved from the white background, and the paint had in places dripped downwards from the horizontal bands, again not being erased. This slapdash painting suggests that time and trouble may have been grudgingly given to the decoration of the walls of a room that was, and would remain, dark. The colour red may have a special significance, as it often appears that red was associated with the decoration of buildings devoted to pagan cults. No evidence existed to show whether or not the western part of the Deep Room, containing the busts and the votive pots, had been partitioned off to provide a small, separate compartment for ritual purposes, though this is a possibility, especially as the eastern part probably continued in secular use.

The Deep Room in the fourth and fifth Centuries

The situation in the Deep Room at the opening of the fourth century was as follows. The floor was of concrete, containing within its thickness a level of charcoal, which might be connected with a re-surfacing in past years. The stairs leading into the room, having been blocked towards the end of the third century, when a hypocaust was inserted adjacent on the north, resulted in three remaining steps leading down to the floor; these had lost their tile surfaces and had been used as shelves upon which to place the two marble portrait busts, with the two votive pots in the floor in front of them.

This situation would appear to have obtained until about the middle of the fourth century. At this time, *c.* A.D. 330–350, reconstruction was taking place elsewhere in the house; the "Bellerophon" mosaic floor was laid down in the neighbouring room, at the higher level to the south, and the dining apse, with its "Europa" mosaic panel and wide tessellated floor, was built out from the line of the back north–south wall. The baths were also receiving repair. As regards the Deep Room, its floor was now slightly raised by spreading a clay floor over the original concrete, which had become weathered, together with the three protruding steps of the stairs, during the 150 years or so since their construction. This clay floor was not of a uniform thickness, but averaged 10 cm.; and because the underside of the lowest of the protruding steps had lost a few sertemitnec of its foundation, at the side and front, the clay had been packed into the small space beneath it left by weathering and depredation. This clay floor contained within its thickness four coins of Constantine I, Crispus, *Urbs Roma*, and a minim. While nearer the top of the clay than the bottom, these coins were not connected with the surface, and thus help to date this clay floor towards the middle of the century, when allowance is made for wear and circulation, of the *Urbs Roma* coin in particular. The clay floor was brought up to the small well on all four sides, showing that this was still in use as a source of water supply. It also now covered the two votive pots.

The four piers against the north and south walls were built at this time, those on the north differing in construction from those on the south (Pl. VIa). The south piers were flat-topped and bore strong traces of carbonized wood on their surfaces. Both rose 0·25 m. above the surface of the clay floor, which was carried up to them; but their other dimensions were different, that on the west being 0·30 m. square, the other to the east 0·40 m. square. Both were constructed of flint and mortar, with a little tile. The north piers were each 0·35 m. above the clay floor, which again had been carried up to them, and each was 0·45 m. square. Like the south piers they were constructed of flint and mortar, with tile, but unlike them, they were slotted in their surfaces, the walls of the slots consisting of tile fragments set upright in mortar, which covered their surfaces. The slot in the west pier was rectangular, 0·35 m. by 0·43 m., and 0·11 m. deep (Pl. VIIa); that on the east pier was 0·27 m. square and 6 cm. deep. Each slot contained its wooden plate, completely carbonized. The west pier on the north side had been mortared to the small *podium* upon which rested the head of Bust II, and all four piers were fitted against the third-century wall-plaster, which extended down behind them, already in a decayed condition.

The purpose of these four piers, showing as they did very strong traces of carbonized wooden plates on their surfaces and in their slots, was probably to give additional support to the wooden floor of the room above, which had a free span of 4·42 m.; the uprights bearing down on the wooden plates on the piers would have helped to take the downward thrust of two heavy beams supporting the wooden floor above from off the walls, which were already over 250 years old, being of late first-century construction.

In the north-east corner of the room was a pit of irregular shape, a rough quadrant, extending for 1·22 m. along both north and east walls. It was uneven in depth, generally 0·55 m., descending to 0·68 m. in the corner. Lying on the bottom at its deepest point was a sherd of pseudo-Belgic ware, which might suggest an early date for the pit. It was found to have been filled up with medium-sized flints, some of which had been blackened by contact with water, to within 0·20 m. of the floor, and it had been levelled up in one place with a packing of small flints and chalk fragments in blackish earth, and finally with a flinty upper packing containing mortar and *opus signinum* fragments. Upon this surface lay a fine opal, probably the bezel of a finger-ring. The pit had been dug in its deepest part to the water-table, but the period in which it was dug cannot be estimated, except for the single sherd of pseudo-Belgic ware. By the fourth century it seems to have been levelled up, traces of a carbonized plank being found lying over the filling from north to south, with a thicker stretcher beside the north wall beneath the plank. There was also a line of four very small post-holes containing carbonized wood along the west side of the pit, and these may once have supported a light protective railing (Fig. 7).

When the upper room was consecrated as a Christian house–church, an event which took place *c.* A.D. 380-385, its walls decorated with brightly coloured Christian symbols and praying figures, two more votive pots were inserted in the clay floor of the Deep Room in front of the busts. Their tops stood open for libations some centimetres above the surface of the clay floor, the hole that received the pot furthest from the busts containing a coin of the House of Constantine, *Fel. Temp. Rep.* (A.D. 345–361); and the pot nearest to the busts was provided with a loose lid consisting of a complete segment from a *mortarium* of a typical late fourth-century date (Pls. VIb and c). The clay floor had concealed the first pair of votive pots from view, and therefore from use; but from now on, when Christian worship was taking place in the upper room, pagan libations continued to be made into the second pair of pots to the *manes* of the persons whose features were depicted in the marble, right up to the time of final destruction by fire sometime in the early years of the fifth century. Christian worship and pagan ritual thus continued together.

The small well was in continuous use as a source of water-supply, and indeed, the water still appears in it in accordance with the level of the water-table. Five late fourth-century *mortaria* were found lying on the floor, disposed roughly in a line north to south immediately west of the well, and in one case one *mortarium* rested within a slightly larger one. These *mortaria* doubtless served as balers. Among them lay the remains of a cat, which had been killed by the final collapse of the upper room. This suggests that an entrance did exist into the Deep Room, possibly, as has been said, in the middle of the east wall. There was no evidence of any entrance into the room from inside the house since the blocking of the stairs late in the third century; but this does not exclude a small trap in the floor of the house-church above, with a ladder. This would at first sight seem quite out of place in a Christian church; but when the need for water is considered, for baptistry purposes and for the washing of the ritual vessels, water was already below, and access to it may have been available in this way from within.

Lying with the five *mortaria* was a small grey flagon, resting, originally upright, on a small sheet of much corroded bronze. This little pottery flagon was decorated with the remains of a single wide band of white colour-coat round the girth; it is of fourth-century date, but had already lost its neck and handle, the broken surfaces having suffered abrasion over a long period.

The Limestone Block (Pl. VIIc). An object of considerable interest, indeed of mystery, lay upon the clay floor in the angle between the base of the bottom step and the west wall (Fig. 7). This object had not fallen from the house-church, but had lain upon the floor of the Deep Room, perhaps since the insertion of the second pair of votive pots. It is a large block of oolitic limestone, roughly shaped, but already much weathered before being placed where it was found. In form it tends to be rectangular, but with its sides slightly swelling in curves, both in length and height. The curves turn in on each side to a flat base; the top likewise, though here a large, shallow, ovoid cavity, approximately 0·10 m. in diameter and 37 cm. deep in the centre, had been subsequently moulded. The back is chamfered from base and from top to a horizontal ridge about half-way down. But the two most interesting features are as follows. First, on the left side of the block has been subsequently moulded a second and slightly deeper cavity, roughly circular, 0·13 m. in diameter and 4 cm. deep in the centre. This cavity has been carefully moulded, and its lip at one point shared the lip of the former cavity upon the top of the block; but this part of the lip had disappeared before the block was placed in positionL and as the block had been placed upon its right side, this larger cavity lay upon the upper surface. What was the purpose of the cavity? It had not once been the base of a post-socket of a door, for it shows no sign of wear; both in it, however, and around it, and extending down the original top, which now formed the side, was much reddening of the stone by burning. This almost certainly had been caused by incandescent wood falling upon it from above; but the circular cavity may also have been associated with flame in its own right. As the block lay before the busts, and between the votive pots and the west wall, the cavity in it may have been used as a kind of cresset, with a wick lying in an oil bath. The Deep Room, at any rate at its west end, would have been dark, and a ritual light might thus have been kept burning before the busts, replenished with oil from time to time.

The second interesting feature consists of the appearance of the front of the block. Both sides had been chamfered forward to form a flat face, 0·15 m. wide at the top and 8 cm. at the bottom, its sides being thus inclined regularly inwards from top to bottom. This face was accentuated by curving back above, and sharply cut back below. Upon the face thus made were a pair of identical circular depressions, each 3 cm. in diameter and 1·8 cm. deep in the centre. Their exact symmetry on the narrow face gives a strong impression of a pair of eyes; and across the narrow undercut bottom of the face is a deep incision, 6 cm. long and 1·25 cm. deep, curving down slightly at the extremities, suggestive of a mouth. The gouged-out hollows for the deep-set eyes can be a native, Celtic, method.[4] Taken as a whole, this end of the block is strongly reminiscent of the mask of a large feline, perhaps a lion. The original moulding is clearly primitive, and it has suffered much subsequent wear, including a further small circular depression over the right eye, 7·5 cm. in diameter and 2·5 cm. in depth in the centre. Such treatment of the eyes of Celtic gods is not unusual; projecting, lentoid, eyeballs do not appear to have been obligatory for such Celtic work, though they frequently are shown. The block shows no evidence of having once been attached to any structure, and its original purpose remains obscure.

This interpretation of a feline mask is tentative; but wearing down over a long period can be cited in the case of at least one important object. This is the human head, of marble, found at Bosham near Chichester, and now placed on loan in the British Museum. This head is almost globular in shape, 0·50 m. in height, and the features have been so abraded that nose and mouth have been reduced to a single curve, while the right eye is merely a hole.[5] The sculptured lion appears to have affinity with sepulchral tombstones and monuments. Two examples occur at York, where it is suggested that this creature decorated a tomb or its precinct.[6]

The dimensions of the Lullingstone "leonine" block are: 0·29 m. long; 0·11 m. wide on the underside, curving upwards to a width of 0·205 m., and thence to the top at approximately 0·18 m. The total height is 0·21 m. The width at the back is 0·20 m., and the front is brought to a face whose measurements are recorded above.

Two coins were found associated with the collapse of the house-church into the Deep Room. One, a Theodosius I, lay in the south-east corner, just above the floor and sealed beneath a wattle-and-daub fall of the upper south wall. The other, a House of Theodosius

[4] J. M. C. Toynbee, *Art in Roman Britain*, London, 1962, 146 and Plate 44.

[5] *Antiquaries Journal*, xlv (1965), Plate XLVII.

[6] *Eburacum: Roman York*, i, London, 1962, Plates 63, 123 (a) and (b).

(probably Arcadius), lay in the remains of the carbonized wood upon the surface of the north-east pier. These two coins suggest either the very end of the fourth century or the beginning of the fifth century for the last years of occupation of the Deep Room.

As the collapse of the house-church into the Deep Room is closely related to the history of that room, the question of duration of the house-church may be considered here. The matter cannot depend upon the pottery, though much of this, dating in the second half of the fourth century, was in evidence; it had all been in use for a long period, but any definite length of time cannot be suggested. An exception to this appears, however, when the small *mortarium* from Room 10A on the north side of the house-church is considered. It was found on the floor of this room, sealed by the carbonized remains and structural fall of the final collapse. It is a colour-coated *mortarium* of the second half of the fourth century; but it already had had prolonged use, having been repaired by the drilling of three sets of holes, by which an old breakage had been made good for its secondary purpose, which was to contain a supply of blue paint. Its long use, therefore, probably continued well into the fifth century.

The coin evidence is perhaps more useful. When the northern end of the back corridor of the house was partitioned and re-floored to provide the Vestibule (11) to the Christian Ante-Chamber (10), with a door leading through its end wall to the exterior, the new floor consisted of a spread of gravel. This gravel was thickest and best preserved immediately in front of the doorway that led into the ante-chamber, and nine coins were found here, trodden into the surface. They consisted of three Constantinian, three *Fel. Temp. Rep.*, two minims, and one House of Theodosius. The latter coin, and perhaps the minims, indicate that the doorway was being used as the fourth century drew to its close. In addition, in the ante-chamber itself, which had been floored with boards, was a coin of Arcadius, which had fallen through the boards and lay beneath them upon the under surface. When taken in conjunction with the coin of Theodosius I and the probable coin of Arcadius in the lowest level of the Deep Room itself, these two further coins from the vestibule and the ante-chamber provide strong evidence for a continuance of the Christian house-church to the end of the fourth century, and probably well into the early years of the succeeding century.

The discussion in the Introduction, where the plots of the coins of Gratian and those of the House of Theodosius over the whole site were compared, is revealing. South of a central line taken east–west across the centre of the house, the coinage of Gratian is well in evidence, while north of that line, over the area covered by the Christian establishment, no less than eleven coins of the House of Theodosius were plotted, with a total absence of those of Gratian. These coins of the House of Theodosius span the period from A.D. 379–423; and as several of these were already worn by circulation, the early fifth century is indicated for the latest end of the time bracket, perhaps, indeed, the second decade. This absence of coins of Gratian also suggests, owing to their comparative abundance elsewhere, that the house-church may not have been established until after A.D. 383, the year of his death.

Consideration must be given, however, when dealing with the earliest end of the bracket, to the coins sealed in the pit that occupied the north-west corner of the back corridor before the gravel floor of the vestibule was laid over it; and to the coins sealed in the level beneath the wooden floor of the ante-chamber. In the former case, the pit contained thirteen coins. Excluding a single Tetricus II, clearly a survival, the remaining coins were of the Constantinian period, from Constantine II as *Caesar* to two *Fel. Temp. Rep.* coins. This suggests that the pit could not have been filled in much before *c.* A.D. 361. And in the latter case, on the level, heavily carbonized, but at a time much earlier than the final destruction, and beneath the floor boards of the ante-chamber, two of which actually survived, fallen and sealing some of the coins, were no less than thirty-one coins. These were all of the Constantinian period, and included four of Constantius II as *Augustus,* one of Magnentius, and one of Constantius Gallus. As in the case of the pit below the vestibule, a date not much before *c.* A.D. 361 is indicated for the flooring of the ante-chamber. The total absence in both cases of coins of the Valentinian period, which began in A.D. 364, coins of which are abundant elsewhere on the site, goes a long way to confirm A.D. 361 as near the date for the re-flooring of the west corridor and the room which later became the ante-chamber to the house-church.

The above argument on the basis of the coins suggests a life of the northern rooms, shortly to form the Christian establishment, extending from *c.* A.D. 360 to *c.* A.D. 420, the later date remaining tentative. From forty to sixty years is indicated, with some thirty-five years for the life of the house-church. One small additional piece of evidence may tend to confirm the earliest date. The east wall of the ante-chamber was reconstructed when the Christian rooms were established; and in the small footing-trench of this reconstruction was a coin of Constantius II as *Augustus, Fel. Temp. Rep.,* which gives a date conforming with that obtained from the other sealed coins.

The Destruction. Detailed consideration may now be given to the evidence for the final destruction by fire, the cause of which is unknown. The whole of the northern part of the house was affected, masses of crushed and carbonized wood being found over the mosaic floors of the central rooms, the corridor and room on their northern side, and the house-church with its vestibule, ante-chamber, and the room north of it and east of the latter. The floor of the house-church had burned, then broken, and the planks and small stretchers had fallen. The whole area of the Deep Room was covered with a level, several centimetres in thickness, of carbonized wood, heavily crushed and mingled with silt and soft wall-rendering, which included the masses of painted wall-plaster fallen from the interior walls of the house-church. The crushing and the damp environment had combined to render unrecognizable any fragmentary beams, rafters, or, except in one case to be described later, furniture. But when this level was removed, slightly harder lengths of wood, completely carbonized but showing the grain of the wood, were found in contact with the floor. Nine lengths of fallen planks had thus survived, and they are plotted to scale at Fig. 7. Three lay in a west–east direction, while six lay in a north–south direction, all nearly approximating to a width of 0·30 m. The absence of iron nails over the whole room suggests that the floor of the house-church was constructed with wooden pegs. The position of the four piers suggests a pair of heavy beams spanning the room from north to south, carrying rafters from west to east, which in turn supported the planked floor. Had the two heavy beams fallen early during the fire, their remains would have been recognizable in the débris below; but nothing of this kind was found. They had probably continued to smoulder, being firmly set in the masonry walls, long after the smaller rafters and planks had fallen and been consumed. The two beams may well have remained in a charred condition until the masonry walls collapsed, or they may have been removed; no evidence of them is seen in the subsequent wall-fall.

Two objects of considerable interest fell down from the house-church. The first, a fragment of carbonized wood, 0·20 m. long and of square section, was found lying 1·67 m. from the west wall, and 1·37 m. from the north wall. It was 3·7 cm. square at one end, and tapered regularly to the other end, which was blunt and approximately 1·8 cm. square, this thinner end being damaged. This fragment represents part of the tapering leg of a piece of furniture, possibly a table, which it is tempting to think may have been the small wooden altar. The second object was a large, rectangular slab of pink *opus signinum*, which lay 2·59 m. from the west wall and 1·06 m. from the south wall. It had fallen complete, but had been cracked throughout in all directions on impact and could not be preserved in its entirety. It measured 0·76 m. in length, 0·53 m. in width, and was uniformly 0·10 m. in thickness. This slab lay face downwards, slightly tilted up towards the west, resting upon a few centimetres of crushed rubble (Pl. VIIb). Its original upper face had been rendered smooth and level, with a slight upward flange round the edges, and the impression of wood grain was observable upon the smoothed surface, where a horizontal plate of wood had once been fitted. Assuming that a heavy beam had been supported upon wooden uprights resting upon the two westerly piers, this heavy slab may have been placed upon the floor of the house-church over the beam for greater security. The centre of the slab lay only some 0·25 m. from the east edge of such a beam, while the fragment of tapered wooden table-leg lay 0·40 m. from the west side of the same beam. The two objects certainly lay 1·75 m. apart, but they may well have originally formed parts of one object. It can be suggested with some confidence that here is the *podium* upon which the wooden altar stood in the house-church, with part of one leg of the altar itself. If such be the case, then the altar may have stood towards the western end of the house-church, with a space of some 2·28 m. between it and the west wall, upon which was painted the portico with its row of human figures standing in their attitude of prayer facing the east. This would leave an area some 4·50 m. in length towards the east for the congregation; a western position for the altar would not have been contrary to liturgical custom in these early years of Christianity. Also, this position of the altar would have placed it immediately above that part of the Deep Room which was devoted to the pagan cult of the marble busts, and this may therefore have been intentional.

A third object which had stood in the house-church was found broken where it had fallen beside the steps into the Deep Room. It is a large, wide-mouthed, two-handled flagon of hard red-brown ware with orange burnishing on the exterior, zones of horizontal grooves below the handles, and vertical tooling on the neck. This flagon must have stood in the house-church, probably on the floor, just inside the doorway leading in from the ante-chamber, and may have been a receptacle for water. It is a mid-fourth century type.

A second vessel, also fallen with the collapsed débris of the house-church, is a conical-necked beaker, bulbous in girth, of fine, well-fired pink ware, with an exterior metallic glaze in greenish-brown. The fragments of this vessel lay scattered centrally and downwards from the north side in the thick level containing carbonized wood and painted wall-plaster from the house-church. It is therefore not included in the floor-plan of the Deep Room (Fig. 7); but it is a mid- to late-fourth century type, and may have been dedicated to Christian ritual. The pottery associated with the levels above the lowest, carbonized plank level accords in date with the complete vessels found upon the floor of the Deep Room. All these vessels could have been in use during the last phase of the villa's existence.

Three north–south sections were recorded across the Deep Room, at 0·91 m., 4·42 m. and

6·55 m. from the west wall. They are designated DR(1), DR(2) and DR(3) respectively (Fig. 7), and details of them are below.

Section DR(1) (Fig. 8a). This showed, in succession upwards from the carbonized plank level:

(a) A level, averaging 0·20 m. in thickness, containing carbonized wood, painted plaster, fragments of tile and *opus signinum*, with small lumps of chalk.
(b) A level, averaging 0·25 m. thick in the centre and tailing out to less than 0·15 m. towards the walls, containing clay silt with broken mortar and a scatter of charcoal.
(c) A level, extending for 1·67 m. from the north wall, and averaging 0·10 m. in thickness, containing fragments of wall-plaster.
(d) A mass of broken roof-tiles, 1·22 m. thick, and descending steeply from the south wall to meet (b) in the centre of the room. This mass of tile contained a coin of Constans as *Augustus* (*c*. A.D. 341) near the bottom.
(e) A level, averaging 0·91 m. in thickness, from the surviving top of the north wall to a point 0·83 m. from the south wall, and 0·30 m. from the surviving top of that wall, where it met (d). This level consisted of wall-fall.
(f) An upper filling of post-destruction date, its lowest point, in the centre, being 1·06 m. above the carbonized plank level, and rising 2·36 m. to wall-top level at the north, and 1·52 m. on the south, rising to 0·15 m. below wall-top. It contained large tile fragments with scattered sherds of late fourth-century pottery.

Section DR(2) (Fig. 8b). This showed, in succession upwards from the carbonized plank level:

(a) A level, averaging 0·30 m. in thickness, extending across the room, containing carbonized wood and painted wall-plaster.
(b) A level of decomposed wall rendering averaging 0·22 m. in thickness at the north and tailing off 1·37 m. from the north, and 0·91 m. thick against the south wall, falling steeply and tailing off 1·22 m. from the wall. This level contained, against the south wall, an iron tempering anvil and hammer, both lying parallel with each other as if originally tied together.
(c) A level, 0·61 m. thick, consisting of wall-fall. It extended to within 1·22 m. of the south wall, where it met the tail-end of (b). It contained a large number of chalk bodies, consisting of 43 voussoirs of an arch, three of these still remaining as a block, with thick mortar between the voussoirs. Three large semi-cubical blocks were also present. These voussoirs indicate a doorway, of which they formed the hemispherical arch, in the north wall of the house-church, a doorway giving access from the room immediately on the north. On assembly of the voussoirs, an arch of between 0·91 m. and 1·22 m. diameter is suggested, the chalk arch fitting into the flint and mortar wall and surmounting a doorway of that width.
(d) A level, averaging 0·30 m. in thickness, from both north and south wall-tops, but descending to a point 0·94 m. from the south wall, where the bottom of the level was only 0·30 m. above the carbonized plank level. It contained black silt, with some carbonized wood, painted wall-plaster, and fragments of two red colour-coated bowls

with painted scroll-work on their exteriors. This level may represent a short period of rest before the remainder of the house-church collapsed.

(e) A level of wall-fall, some 0·76 m. thick in the centre of the room and descending towards the south, meeting (d) 0·91 m. from the south wall.

(f) A level of decomposed wall rendering with abundant tile fall, descending from the continued vertical line of the south wall to a thickness of 0·91 m. Above this lay a level of large flints, suggesting a levelling-up subsequent to the final collapse.

Section DR(3) (Fig. 8c). This showed, in succession upwards from the carbonized plank level:

(a) A level of burnt wattle-and-daub, with charcoal, containing small fragments of timbers, with chalky silt, 0·27 m. thick against the south wall, and tailing off to a point 1·98 m. northwards. Also, a level of unburnt daub, showing abundant traces of wattle strengthening, forming a large slab 1·83 m. long and approximately 1·22 m. wide at its greatest, with an average thickness of 0·12 m. This level began 0·25 m. from the north wall, and extended southwards to approximately 0·61 m. from the tailing-off of the southern wattle-and-daub level. A study of this slab shows a partition of daub approximately 0·12 m. thick, containing two vertical rows of 12·5 cm. wattles 0·25 m. apart. Both these daub levels had collapsed from above, and suggest that at the eastern part of the house-church, while the east wall remained a masonry one, both north and south walls may have had wattle-and-daub partitions resting upon the original masonry walls of the Deep Room.

(b) A level, whose surface was roughly horizontal and approximately 0·30 m. above the carbonized plank level. It contained many large fragments of *opus signinum* and chalk lumps, with painted wall-plaster, mostly unburnt, fallen from the walls of the Deep Room, and from the east wall of the house-church. Among these many fragments, found fallen centrally, were a number showing parts of a large *Chi Rho* monogram and its surrounding floral wreath, together with the lower legs and sandalled feet of at least two persons. Such a monogram is thus suggested to have occupied the centre of the east wall of the house-church. A number of flints from the next level above had sunk into this level.

(c) A level of wall-fall, containing also fragments of *opus signinum* and painted wall-plaster. This level descended sharply from a thickness of 1·06 m. at the face of the north wall, to an average thickness of 0·30 m. in the centre of the room, and gradually rising to the face of the south wall at a thickness of 0·38 m. The wall-fall contained some sherds of colour-coated and rilled wares, all of the late fourth century, with the remains of a burnt and crushed glass vessel with folded, three-ribbed, handle, probably again of fourth-century date. The surface of this level was found to have been compacted with pebble-mortar and small flints, extending as a surface from the south wall for a distance of 2·16 m.

(d) A level, 1·37 m. thick in the centre and rising to 0·25 m. from the surviving north wall-top, and to 7·5 cm. from the surviving south wall-top, consisting of quantities of roof-tiles, the majority sloping downwards from south and east, all embedded in brown silt, containing painted wall-plaster. In the top half of this level were a number of chalk blocks, and three large masonry blocks from the upper east wall, one block showing successive levels, all mortared together in courses—flint, mortar, flint, tiles in two courses, flint, and mortar, with chalk blocks mortared in. This block measured 0·83 m. in length, and 0·30 m. thick at its surviving maximum. This level also contained sherds of red colour-coated, rilled, and hand-made wares, all of mid- to late-fourth century date. The most important object, however, contained in this level was the capital and part of the shaft of an oolitic limestone column (Pl. VIId). It lay 0·45 m. above the bottom of the level, and 1·67 m. from the north wall, and had come to rest top downwards at a steep angle from the east wall, as if it had been thrown in from that direction. The column is 0·50 m. in height, the abacus of the capital 0·28 m. square when complete, the depth of the abacus being 0·10 m. The circular shaft narrows in a gentle curve from a diameter of 0·26 m. at its junction with the abacus to a diameter of 0·19 m., and shows four horizontal mouldings placed at regular intervals, the lowest protruding 1·8 cm. with a flat upper surface. The shaft has been broken across, leaving a flat section at approximately 20 degrees from the horizontal. Some two-thirds of the upper part of both shaft and abacus has also been broken, again at an angle in the same direction, but at a slightly steeper angle than where the shaft is broken; enough of the dowel-hole in the centre of the top surface remains to give its approximate dimensions—5 dimensions—5 cm. square and 7·5 cm. deep. A near parallel in form and mouldings occurs at York,[7] where the dimensions are similar, and the shaft is broken at much the same angle. The date cannot be obtained from the Form. Such a column is suggestive of a town building; but it can also find a place in a country villa. Both at the end of the second century, and during the fourth century, the villa was sufficiently luxurious to have had such columns incorporated in its construction; there is no reason to suppose that it was brought from elsewhere and dumped among the fallen débris of the house-church. Its original position is unknown; it may have formed part of one of a pair of columns flanking the main entrance.

Fallen near the column was part of a large *tegula*, 0·43 m. long, and 3·7 cm. thick. One of its long sides had been roughly cut in a long arc of diameter approximately 0·28 m., but its original purpose is obscure. Also in this level was a number of large slabs of thick, white mortar, some of which fit together. They show a flange at an angle of 60 degrees, with a gradual inward curve on the side of the flange. Both the flanged face and approximately 6·8 cm. of the flat face are painted red, the latter face having a further band of yellow beyond the red. The undersides of the slabs are flat, and the long curve had been mortared to a background of wood. These slabs had fallen from the east wall of the house-church, and may have formed part of a shallow, curving recess in which the central *Chi Rho* monogram may have been painted.

A study of Sections DR(1), (2) and (3) shows, immediately above the carbonized plank level, which extended over the entire floor of the Deep Room:

(a) That the thick level of carbonized wood and painted wall-plaster tended to give place, except at the south, to an area at the east end where the carbonized wood tends to be substituted by wattle-and-daub, but still with abundant painted wall-plaster, though smaller in quantity than over the rest of the room, again except at the south. This

[7] *Ibid.*, Plate 40 (116).

suggests that at the eastern end of the house-church both the north and south walls may have had wattle-and-daub partitions, though still carrying painted wall-plaster, at least on the southern partition. The fallen plaster throughout the southern part of the Deep Room shows that it had been applied to a wooden wall, incorporating wattle-and-daub, which may have extended for the whole length of the south wall of the house-church. Both the south-west and the south-east angles of the house-church were obtained from the surviving fragments of angle-plaster, and at the south-east the whole decoration was re-assembled, being found to extend from the south-east angle along the east wall for a distance of 0·56 m., where it turns into the decorated splay of a window. The dimensions of this window are uncertain, but it is likely to have been small and narrow, perhaps not more than 0·30 m. in width at the opening. No evidence remained of a companion window towards the north end of the east wall, but if the arrangement was symmetrical, then a similar window must have existed there. A tentative reconstruction of the east wall of the house-church, based upon the fallen wall-plaster and the painted mortar from Section DR(3), level (d), suggests a pair of windows, each 0·56 m. from the ends of the wall, with a blank space between them of 2·36 m., assuming the width of the window openings to have been 0·30 m. This central portion was occupied by the *Chi Rho* monogram within its floral wreath, centrally placed; and as the fragments of this conformed in size with the *Chi Rho* monogram upon the south wall, its diameter would have been approximately 0·91 m. This would have given a distance between its outer edge and the flanking windows of 0·72 m. on either side.

Except in Section DR(1), level (c), the fallen wall-plaster lay thickest against the west and south walls and over the centre of the room, and tended to lessen considerably in quantity along the north wall and in the north-east corner. This may suggest, either that the north wall of the house-church was for the most part undecorated, or that this wall stood for a sufficient period after the destruction for its plaster face to have become mostly disintegrated by frost and general weathering. As west, south and east walls were lavishly decorated, the north wall probably conformed. The chalk voussoirs in Section DR(2), level (c), provide strong evidence for an arched aperture in the north wall, about 4·57 m. from the west wall. The entrance in the north-west corner leading from the ante-chamber was probably at least 1·22 m. wide, so the remainder of the north wall was blank, with the arched aperture, between 0·91 and 1·22 m. wide, in the centre. This would leave some 2·13 m. on either side of the aperture for decoration.

(b) That a short interval occurred between the collapse of the rafters and floor-boards, with the west and south walls of the house-church, which were timber-framed with wattle-and-daub, and the collapse of the north and east walls, which were probably for the most part carried up in masonry, especially the east wall, which was probably entirely built in this manner. Both the north and east walls were of original first-century construction, and while no doubt they had been repaired from time to time, they are unlikely to have been cut down in any part to receive timber-frames. Also, the archway of chalk voussoirs would have been set in a masonry wall; a timber wall would have had an aperture spanned at the top by a horizontal beam.

Part of the roof fell from the south part, before and after the falls of the masonry walls (Sections DR(1), level (d), and DR(2), level (f)). The wall-fall of flint and mortar is shown in all three sections as descending in the main from the north towards the centre of the Deep Room; and at the east, the descent is indicated from that direction as well. No such masonry wall-fall is shown descending from west or south, where the lower part of the original masonry walls continued to stand. The three large blocks of masonry near the east wall suggest that here the remnants of the wall had been deliberately demolished, these blocks falling into the Deep Room while the remainder was pulled down on the exterior ground level. This would explain the comparatively small quantity of wall-plaster from the east wall that was recovered from the Deep Room; and the backings of this wall-plaster show that it had adhered to an irregular flint surface. It would seem that a purposeful levelling-up was effected some time after the destruction.

Room 10

A study of this room presents a comprehensive picture of this part of the villa, from the insertion late in the second century of the tiled stairs leading down to the remodelled Deep Room, through the alterations effected late in the third century, to the final destruction of the Christian house-church, of which this room formed the ante-chamber.

The first-century construction has already been dealt with, when the approaches to the Deep Room were considered. The west wall of the descending ramp had been destroyed during subsequent alterations, but a stub of it appears in Room 10, showing in it a recess for an upright wooden post. The wall had also been cut away south of this to allow the insertion of the tiled stairs late in the second century. The lower portions of the south and west walls of Room 10 are of first-century date, the former being rebuilt in the second and fourth centuries. The latter was rebuilt in the third and fourth centuries, the third century wall being carried over the disused stairs. The re-building *c.* A.D. 180 involved much destruction at the north end of the house. As in the case of the new baths, tiled stairs were inserted, passing through Room 10 down to the landing, and thence northwards into the ambulatory round Room 8, rising in two steps at this point. The earlier ramp was now concealed by these steps, by the landing, and by the steps leading from it down to the new concrete floor of the Deep Room. The main flight of steps leading up to the back corridor probably consisted of nine tiled treaders, of which six remain, the upper three having been removed when the footing-trench was dug in the further re-construction late in the third century. Each step was constructed of flint and mortar, the risers averaging 0·20 m. in height, the surface of each step bearing four *tegulae* with their flanges removed, providing treaders 1·22 m. wide and 0·38 m. in depth. Many of these *tegulae* remain intact, except on the north side and on the fifth treader, where the tiles have been broken away (Pl. VIIIa).

The south wall bore one large slab and one small slab of painted plaster *in situ,* showing a yellow trellis between descending handrail and skirting in red, the whole 1·06 m. in height. The angle of descent conformed with that of the stairs. This south wall ended at the landing, where it turned through a right-angle to its continuance with the west wall of the Deep Room, with a coigning of small bricks at the angle, which remained to a height of some 1 m.

The north wall of the stairs, and where it had originally turned northwards to form the west wall of the ambulatory, had been completely destroyed at the late-third century re-construction, and it is not possible to say of what material it had been constructed or of the character of the decoration, if any, that it had borne upon its inner surface. It is not possible either to say whether these two destroyed walls had been exterior walls; they were probably interior walls, as foundations of further walls of their date were found further to the north. No indication survived to suggest how the stairway had been roofed. The concrete landing had never been tiled.

A section was cut across the fillings of Room 10 (Pl. VIIIb, Fig. 10), and a study of this showed a period when the plaster facing and rendering of the south stairway wall had weathered and fallen over the steps, remaining 0·30 m. in thickness at the wall, and tailing northwards for 1·42 m., where it met the stub of the north stairway wall. The tiled treaders of the steps were thus concealed from view by the late third century, and this may explain the intact condition of many of them. An *as* of Antoninus Pius lay in this fallen wall-rendering, 5 cm. from the south stairway wall and 5 cm. above the tiled surface of the neighbouring step. The coin was in fair condition and bore on the reverse a figure of Britannia, a coin minted in A.D. 144–145; it may well have been circulating towards the end of the second century. This level also contained sherds of late-Antonine pottery, with samian dated from *c.* A.D. 185–200. The coarse pottery included a fragment of *amphora* bearing the stamp ACIRCI, which is of second-century date.[8]

The tiled stairs having been concealed by the fall of plaster and wall-rendering, a deposit resulted sloping down northwards and eastwards towards the landing. The south wall itself had broken along a roughly horizontal line from a point 0·40 m. above the fifth step to a point 1·27 m. above the landing; the coigning of bricks at the corner above the landing had completely fallen away down to approximately 1 m. above the landing. All this is strong evidence of a dilapidation over a period of abandonment of the villa, a dilapidation which had to be repaired by newcomers late in the third century, and was so repaired.

These newcomers decided upon a radical rearrangement at the north end of the house. The remains of the square Cult Room 8 with its ambulatory were demolished nearly to ground level, and the long west–east wall, bounding Rooms 10 and 11 on the north side, was carried eastwards across the site of Room 8. The house was thus shortened from north to south by some 4·27 m. The northern end of the back corridor was retained as such, but the remainder of the space east of it was now designed as a hypocaust system. To enclose Room 10 completely, a wall-block was inserted at the south side of the landing, where the stairs continued down into the Deep Room, and another wall-block was inserted across from north to south, roughly on the line of the original east wall of the west ambulatory and upon the lowest step leading up to the south ambulatory. This wall-block formed the eastern limit of Room 10. In the block, which is strongly built in horizontal courses of alternate flints and mortar, was centrally constructed an arch completely turned in brick. It is of "key-hole" design, 0·45 m. wide at the bottom, the sides sloping slightly inwards to the spring of the arch to a width of approximately 0·40 m., the arch itself being depressed, the height to its crown on the inside being 1 m. The key-stone bricks were slightly cut down when the upper portion of the block was rebuilt *c.* A.D. 360–370 (Pl. IXa).

The compartment (10A) immediately east of Room 10 was 5·18 m. long and of the same width, and across it, 2·74 m. east of the arch, was constructed another block crossing the compartment, with a second, and probably similar arch in the centre, an arch which had

[8] J. P. Bushe-Fox, *Excavations of the Roman Fort at Richborough, Kent,* IV, Oxford, 1949, 242.

subsequently been completely robbed out. The east wall of the compartment contained a third arch, of which a few broken bricks remained at the base. All three arches lay on the same central axis, and beyond the eastern one was situated a small room, floored with rough concrete, 3·66 m. long and the same width as Room 10. This small room was designed for the furnace. Between the two easterly arches the compartment (10A) had been filled up on either side with rubble and clay rammed down, leaving an open channel on the axis of the arches, concealing the south ambulatory of the square cult-room, the concrete floor of the ambulatory being revealed on excavation. The fallen rendering from the walls of the ambulatory included slabs of the second century "Palm and Panel" wall-decoration, with portions of its north clay wall, where the plaster had been keyed on to the clay with "herring-bone" impressions made by a roller.

The fallen wall-rendering on the south side of Room 10, covering the steps from view, was surfaced with a thin level of clay, averaging 5 cm. in thickness, sloping eastwards to the first arch and northwards towards the bounding wall in that direction, thus providing a channel running south to north at the bottom of the block containing the arch, and turning westwards along the base of the north wall. The hot air would therefore be directed from the furnace through the three arches, meeting the clay slope, being drawn round to the north along the channel and thence to the west. Four box flue-tiles were fitted into the north wall, one at each end with two between them, all at the same distance apart (Pls. IXb, Xa). The earlier west wall was rebuilt to contain in addition one box-flue 0·30 m. from each end, with a further pair placed together in the centre. The south wall did not contain any box-flues.

Room 10 thus became an apartment with under-floor heating. No trace or impression of any piers was found that might have supported the floor, and this could not have been constructed of concrete or bricks. The distance from the furnace to Room 10 was 6·40 m., a distance probably considered of sufficient length to allow a wooden floor to be fitted in the room with safety from fire, though again no evidence survived of such a floor except for two long carbonized beams lying west–east with many iron nails, described in more detail below. These beams seem to be associated with a later floor; in this third-century reconstruction a wooden floor may have been provided, but there was no evidence of any ledge or inset in the walls upon which the rafters could have rested. Such evidence may have been destroyed when the later reconstruction was made which turned Room 10 into the ante-chamber to the house-church.

It is uncertain whether this heating system was ever put to use. There was no sign of heat action upon the remaining arch or upon the flints of the wall of the furnace, and carbonized material was absent from the appropriate third-century level in Room 10. The clay baulk also showed no signs of hardening or discoloration by heat. No carbonized material was found even at the site of the furnace, where evidence should have been abundant to indicate prolonged fire and rake-back, as in the case of the furnace of the baths, which was in use for a long period. There was also an absence of such material from the channel between the second and third arches, where it would certainly have tended to collect.

It seems that Room 10 began to receive a deposit of rubbish very soon after the clay baulk and its east and north channels had been made. This deposit was greyish in colour and sharply contrasted with the yellowish late-Antonine level sealed beneath it. It consisted of earthy silt with small flints and fragments of tile, and contained third-century pottery sherds, including flanged bowls with incipient rims, an indented beaker, with a little samian dated *c.* A.D. 200, which again was present in the channel beside the north wall, in the form of fragments of a samian "cut-glass" beaker, likewise dated *c.* A.D. 200. A *denarius* of Alexander Severus (A.D. 222–228) was recovered from this deposit at a point 1·11 m. from the north wall and 17·5 cm. above the underlying floor level. This coin was in fair condition, but may have had a long circulation before being dropped into the deposit. Another *denarius* of Julia Maesa, contemporary with Alexander Severus, was recovered from the surface of the concrete floor of the furnace-room. This coin was also minted early in the third century, but its state of wear suggests a lengthy circulation period. Both coins had lost much of their silver coating. A much clipped and worn *sestertius* of Faustina I (*d.* A.D. 141) was also recovered from the decayed mortar of the east wall of the furnace-room, a coin that had been circulating for a very long time before being dropped in the mortar. Two similar clipped and worn *sestertii* of Faustina II (A.D. 141–175) were found stratified in the granary, which on abundant evidence was constructed about the time of Allectus (A.D. 293–296), or a little earlier. The long persistence of such coins is clear.

The floor of the furnace-room was composed to a concrete consistency of fine mortar and pounded fragments of painted wall-plaster. This plaster was largely pink, white, red and green, and had been brought from elsewhere; it bore no resemblance to that from the clay walls of the ambulatory (2). But much of the ambulatory wall-plaster was found next to the furnace-room, fallen or thrown down, together with the remnants of wall to which it had adhered. It is wall-plaster to which allusion is made in the section describing the Northern Complex—plaster that was painted possibly to simulate stonework; it was lying as a slab, some 0·91 m. by 0·76 m. in size (Pl. XIIIa). A thin silting became deposited over this fallen plaster next to the furnace-room, and in the room, and it was upon this that the floor had been laid, varying in thickness from 5–15 cm., with a smooth upper surface, and sloping up towards the furnace-flue at a gradient of approximately 1 in 6.

In Room 10 two ox-skulls were found deposited with third-century rubbish, one against the north wall of the room, the other beside the arch. They probably had no ritual purpose, unlike the horse-skull found outside the north wall of the square cult-room 8, which had been deliberately placed there (see Northern Complex (Pl. Xc)).

Towards the middle of the fourth century a new activity was observable in Room 10. A level, not extending eastwards through the arch, was deposited over the southern half of the room, 0·25 m. thick at the wall face, thickening to 0·30 m., and descending to a trough running west–east, with rounded ends, in the centre of the room, approximately 0·30 m. wide with a shallow curving base (Fig. 9). This level consisted of tightly-packed laminations of charcoal, burnt clay and reddened sandy material, and indicates much incandescence in this part of the room over a lengthy period. The level continued upwards from the trough to the north wall, where it was 0·25 m. thick and rested upon a quantity of broken tile immediately below the box-flues, indicating that they had gone out of use before this deposit began to accumulate. This part of the deposit, north of the trough, appeared to be the result of rake-back from the southern part, the site of the incandescence, and in the north-east corner was an area of rough concrete which had perhaps formed a small standing. This area of concrete sealed a badly burnt coin, probably Constantinian. The whole deposit, from wall to wall, contained thirty-one coins—2 Constantine I, 3 Constantine II *Caesar,* 1 Helena, 2

Theodora, 7 *Urbs Roma,* 1 Constantinopolis, 2 Constantine II *Augustus,* 1 Constans *Augustus,* 4 Constantius II *Augustus,* 5 House of Constantine, 1 Magnentius, 1 Constantius Gallus, and 1 minim. These coins date from *c.* A.D. 330–354, the terminal date being fixed by the Magnentius and Constantius Gallus coins, both of which lay on the surface of the deposit near the south wall.

The purpose of the combustion that took place during this period is uncertain. However, a thin, hard level was encountered over the major portion of the southern burnt area, at a few centimetres beneath its surface; and this hard level contained 71 small circular post-holes, all confined to an area next to the south wall, an area approximately 2·44 m. from west to east, and averaging 1·06 m. in width (Pl. Xb and Fig. 9). With the exception of a few outliers, these post-holes formed an irregular arc around an empty space next the south wall, the centre point of this rough semi-circle being marked by a single large post-hole. The post-holes were of two sizes, fourteen having an average diameter at the top of 7·5 cm., the remainder of 3·75 cm. All were conical, descending to blunt points, and the maximum depth of the fourteen larger post-holes was 0·33 m.

The pattern is not so haphazard as it appears at first sight, and the following explanation is suggested. If a movable framework is postulated, this framework having from time to time been lifted and placed in different positions, but with its centre point unchanged beside the wall, the legs of such a structure might well have produced such an apparently chaotic pattern of post-holes. Signs of such a framework are suggested at Fig. 9, where the large post-holes 1, 2, 3 and 4 seem to be centred on post-hole 5, the distances being 0·94 m., 1·04 m., 0·96 m. and 1·14 m., respectively. Of the remaining large post-holes, the distances from post-hole 5 are:

Post-hole 6 at 0·81 m.
,, 7 ,, 0·76 m.
,, 8 ,, 0·83 m.
,, 9 ,, 0·86 m.
,, 10 ,, 0·76 m.
,, 11 ,, 0·83 m.
,, 12 ,, 0·66 m.
,, 13 ,, 0·66 m.
,, 14 ,, 1·67 m. (an outlier)

The distances of post-holes 6 to 11 lie nearly on an arc, centred again on post-hole 5, approximately 0·23 m. inside the arc upon which post-holes 1 to 4 nearly lie. Post-holes 12 and 13 do not as closely conform.

These two arcs of the main post-holes may indicate the supports of a semi "bee-hive" type of framework, with its diameter of approximately 2·21 m.[9] The chord then lies along the face of the wall. Had this been the sort of contrivance used, it may have been placed over incandescent material, for drying, airing, and possibly bleaching garments spread over the framework, confining the heat and partly excluding the air. This was scarcely a fuller's establishment; but it is possible that part of the laundry work of the household may have

[9] *Archaeologia,* lix (1905), 209, Plate LV.

been carried out here in the fourth century. There is no evidence of any kind of smelting or foundry work.

This activity, whatever it may have been, ceased during the period suggested by the coins, the post-holes being covered by a further deposit of burnt material, the top surface of which became hardened down with a dressing of clay to the trough, and across to the north wall. The purpose of the trough is unknown.

The room was once again altered *c.* A.D. 360-370, shortly before becoming the ante-chamber to the house–church. A small gravel ramp was laid in the south-west corner, leading from the back corridor down to the hardened surface of the burnt material. This ramp covered the southern box-flue and half of the double box-flue in the west wall, and the walls were then rebuilt, starting from a level about 0·33 m. above the tops of the box-flue apertures, involving the destruction of what remained of their upper portions. As has been mentioned, the upper portion of the brick arch was cut down, and the small footing-trench at this point, inside Room 10, contained a coin of Constantius II *Augustus* (A.D. 337–361). A wooden floor was constructed at the new, higher, level and the interior of the walls received the coating of plaster which bore the new Christian decoration. This consisted of a large *Chi Rho* monogram in red within a wreath of leaves and buds, situated approximately in the centre of the south wall, between panels outlined in purple on either side, and with borders of zig-zag panel design in a variety of colours. The doorway leading into the house-church itself was moulded in very thick plaster, painted grass-green, to a width, from top to bottom, of 0·10 m, and then turning into the doorway, where it showed the impression of the wooden door-frame. The *Chi Rho* monogram was equal in size with the two in the house-church, and it incorporated the *alpha* and *omega*. The reconstruction of the painted decoration was obtained not only by fitting together many of the fragments of painted plaster, but also by dividing the room into fifteen zones, to each of which was allotted a colour. Spots of the appropriate colour were placed upon the backs of the plaster fragments as they were found, and the overall position of the fall, when colour spots were equated with the painted decoration, decided the position of the *Chi Rho* monogram and other features of the overall design, which included the panels outlined in purple on either side of the monogram. The original scheme of decoration on the south wall of the room was thus obtained.

The west wall of the room was reconstructed with an entrance into the ante-chamber, which was now its character, the whole wall being slightly set back from the original wall containing the truncated box-flues. This latter wall was not properly levelled, the mortar base of the new wall curving up towards the north wall over the uneven and broken surface of the earlier wall. The treader and sides of the entrance were found on excavation to retain their mortar rendering almost entire, and the sides were not straight, but had each a curious angled portion jutting out and then splaying outwards to the inner face of the wall; the wooden door-frame probably occupied the western part of the entrance. The clay and gravel floor of the Vestibule 11 abutted upon the entrance.

The ante-chamber shared in the final destruction of the house-church. The wooden floor burned, collapsing upon the Constantinian level below with its disused central trough, and two long planks or rafters were found lying completely carbonized upon its surface. This pair of rafters had probably supported the thin planks of the floor, to which they had been attached by iron nails, unlike the pegged floor of the house-church, many of these nails being recovered. The rafters lay west–east, the centre of one being 0·55 m. from the south wall, the centre of the other 0·73 m. from the north wall. They both averaged 0·25 m. in width, and 5 cm. in thickness, and were 1·60 m. apart, edge to edge. The western end of the southern rafter lay upon the small area of gravel slope leading inwards and downwards from the west wall. A coin of Arcadius (A.D. 395–408) lay on the carbonized surface, and had fallen either with the collapse of the burning floor or previously through the floor-boards; it is associated with the period during which the Christian rooms were in use. A level of carbonized wood and many fragments of painted wall-plaster lay over the whole width of the room, compressed to a thickness of from 0·22 m. at the face of the south wall, to 0·12 m. about the centre, and thinning to 7·5 cm. at the face of the north wall. Above this was a massive wall collapse across the room of flints and mortar, 0·30 m. in depth on the south, thickening to 0·76 m. in the centre, and diminishing to 0·45 m. to the north. It included a mass of mortary rubble against the north wall. Only a little tile was found in this fall. If the roof had been tiled, as is probable, in conformity with the roof of the house-church, then the tiles had slid downwards to the exterior level, to be subsequently removed.

Room 10A

The history of this room, as an occupied apartment, is concerned only with the later years of the fourth century and the first decade or so of the fifth century. Little can be said of the room upon the scanty evidence available. It was, however, intimately connected with the house-church, having in its south wall an entrance, arched with chalk voussoirs, that led directly into it. All the second and third century levels had been successively sealed by a make-up of clay and mortary rubble, which provided an uneven floor 0·55 m. below both the south and north wall-tops. Three rectangular slots appear in the south wall extending throughout its width, which may have received strengthening timber uprights for the wall. They seem, however, to be sited too low for the latest treading levels on either side of the wall, and are unlikely to have enclosed the ends of floor rafters; they probably belong to an earlier period, especially as they were found to have been carefully packed with flints, being almost unobservable.

The latest floor-level in Room 10A continued along the top of the brick arch in the centre of its west side, almost concealing the bricks from view, and equating with the rebuild of the wall above the arch which had resulted in cutting off the tops of the bricks. The absence of fragments of painted wall-plaster shows that the interior of the room was not decorated.

It was upon this floor that a complete red colour-coated *mortarium,* dated by form to the second half of the fourth century, was found lying beside the west wall. Having been broken and repaired, it contained a blue frit, such as might have been used for fresco painting. It had been laid down by its user, who may have been engaged in touching up the decorations on the walls of the house-church when the final fire occurred.

The floor bore a level of black ash, associated as elsewhere with the final destruction, averaging 0·22 m. in thickness on the north and tailing off to some 7·5 cm. at the south wall.

A small deposit of rubble and clay occurred between this black ash and the north wall, and in this was found a coin of Arcadius; and on the surface of the black ash was another coin of the House of Theodosius, both coins attesting the period of the fire. This deposit was succeeded by roof and wall fall; the whole was found on excavation to be interrupted in the middle by a wide robber-trench of medieval date, which in turn had been dug into in modern times (Fig. 13b).

A small oven or kiln was found to occupy the south-east corner of the room (Pl. XIb). It had been constructed upon the level of the latest rubble and clay floor of the room, and it may have been contemporary with the house-church. But as no black ash occurred above it, it is more likely to be of post-destruction date. This is also suggested by a fragment of painted wall-plaster, believed to have come from a destroyed wall of the house-church, a fragment which was found in the carbonized level beneath the oven; and some of the *opus signinum* used in the oven's construction appeared to overlie the broken wall-top of the east wall of the room. The evidence is, however, very tenuous, but a contemporary date for the oven with the house-church is less likely than a date subsequent to its destruction; the matter remains uncertain. However, fragments of a rough, barbaric copy of a folded beaker, bright orange-red on the interior, with an exterior slip of dark purple, and with scale decoration, were found in the make-up of the oven. This vessel appears to be similar to one from Silchester, and there dated by analogy to the reign of Honorius (A.D. 395–423).[10] The hard, bright red clay is similar to the Lullingstone example, but the Silchester specimen has a crimson slip. If this identification is correct, then the oven can with some confidence be dated *c.* A.D. 400, or perhaps a few years later. There is, however, a further and more positive aspect to this dating problem of the oven. In the north-east corner of the room, the heavy carbonized destruction level caused by the final fire bore upon its surface a flat, rough paving of broken tiles, which exactly agrees with the top surface of the oven in level; and beneath this rough paving were found the coin of Arcadius and that of the House of Theodosius mentioned above. It would seem, therefore, that the oven was sited upon the final destruction level, and was in use after that event, and not during the life of the house-church.

The oven structure was packed against the south and east walls of the room, its dimensions being 1·06 m. from south to north, and 0·91 m. from east to west, with an average height of 0·40 m. It was roughly constructed of flints and tiles bedded horizontally in clay, which was heavily reddened by heat where it formed part of the sides of the central cavity. This was rectangular with vertical back and sides, 0·61 m. long from the north face, upon which it opened, 0·20 m. wide, and averaging 0·17 m. in depth throughout its length. The top surface of the whole structure comprised, in addition to two areas of reddened clay, two large slabs of *opus signinum,* thirty-one tile fragments, and seventeen flints, all small, unlike the usual construction of ovens and kilns, where the tiles often tend to be either complete or in large pieces. Little carbonization was present, and no pottery sherds appeared, and the purpose of the structure is unknown, except that, if it is post-destruction, it may have been an oven for baking bread or simple cooking for persons who survived the destruction of the villa.

Room 10A is likely to have served as an undecorated sacristy or priest's room to the

[10] T. May, *Silchester Pottery,* Plate III, type 90.

house-church, with which it was, as has been stressed, closely connected. Finally, it probably served merely as a convenient place in which to build a simple oven.

Room 11 (Pl. XIa)

The first-century house had a long west corridor whose northern limit was probably reached a further 7 m. beyond the south wall of Room 11, though positive evidence of this is no longer apparent. This corridor continued in use when the tiled stairs were inserted late in the second century, providing access from within the house to the Deep Room and its associated cult-room. Evidence for the use of the corridor is provided by a thick deposit of Antonine rubbish which had accumulated outside the west wall. The west entrance in this wall may be of this date; it was certainly used in the fourth century, and was blocked when the room became the vestibule to the Christian rooms. This entrance is of curious construction. In length 1·09 m., its treader consisted of two horizontal wooden beams, each 0·17 m. wide, lying against a longitudinal mortar core of the same width. When made obsolete in the late fourth century, the wooden beams were removed, and their places filled each with a regular course of heavy flints carefully selected and mortared together and to the central mortar core.

In the late third-century reconstruction, however, the corridor was truncated, the new north wall of the house now forming its northern end, the house having been shortened from north to south by some 4·27 m. It remained a corridor until the wall-block, which eventually formed the south wall of the room, was inserted when the Christian complex was designed.

In the first half of the fourth century the end of this corridor was used as a kitchen or preparation-room and was floored with sandy clay; and a large, circular, refuse-pit was dug in its north-west corner (Fig. 11b). This pit was 1·22 m. in diameter, its sides straight but slightly inclined inwards to a flat bottom 1·06 m. in diameter and 0·68 m. in depth. The primary silting contained a sherd of red colour-coated, rosette-stamped ware, and the general sealed contents included three specimens of small, thick cooking-pots roughly hand-made, indicating local manufacture and use of such very coarse hand-made pottery during the period when the pit was in use. The contents also included animal bones and portions of animal skulls, showing knife-cuts when the flesh was removed, and also the iron knives themselves, all strongly suggestive of the purpose of this part of the corridor at this time, as a kitchen or preparation-room.

The primary silting of the pit consisted of dark gravel, 0·10 m. deep in the centre and rising up the side to an average height of 0·30 m. Above this was a deposit of blackish silt containing much decayed organic material, with small flints and tile fragments, no doubt to facilitate soakage. This deposit was some 0·25 m. in average thickness, and it was from it that were recovered the cooking-pots, animal bones, iron knives, with thirteen coins. These were: 2 Constantine II *Caesar*, 1 Helena, 2 Urbs Roma, 1 Constantinopolis, 1 House of Constantine, 2 Constans *Augustus,* and 3 House of Constantine *Fel. Temp. Rep.,* with 1 Tetricus II, which was a survival. These coins suggest that the pit was dug shortly after *c.* A.D. 330, and continued in use to *c.* A.D. 345–361.

An early third-century drainage-pit outside the west entrance to Room 11 was re-lined with clay, in which two geese were deposited (see Part III), about the same time as the pit was dug inside the room, and it probably served as an additional refuse-pit for a time, though it seems to have been filled up and levelled over before the inside pit received the same treatment.

The coin-bearing deposit in the inside pit was covered with a thin level of wood-ash, upon which was spread a clay seal 7·5 cm. thick in the centre. This in turn received a covering, averaging 0·12 m. in thickness, of black silt with charcoal; and above this again was a make-up of earth and mortar fragments, 0·81 m. above the bottom of the pit. The surface of this was roughly levelled off with gravel and clay to provide the floor of the vestibule to the Christian rooms. A footing-trench next the east wall, probably associated with the late fourth-century rebuild, was filled up level with this floor with mortar and chalk rubble, amongst which appeared a few fragments of painted wall-plaster, not associated with this part of the house, but brought with the rubble from elsewhere. The gravel and clay floor sloped gently up to the entrance into the ante-chamber, and trodden into the surface of this floor were found nine coins: 1 Constantine I, 1 Constans *Caesar*, 1 House of Constantine (A.D. 341–345), 1 House of Constantine (A.D. 345–361), 1 Constantius II *Augustus*, 1 Constantius Gallus (A.D. 351–354), 2 minims, and 1 House of Theodosius (A.D. 379–395). The Constantinian coins are survivals in circulation late in the fourth century, while the Theodosian coin joins with the Arcadius coin in Room 10 and with the other Theodosian coins in the near neighbourhood, to attest the long survival of the Christian house-church. The date of the minims is uncertain; they may be either Constantinian, or they, too, may be contemporary with the Theodosian coins (Fig. 11a).

At the same time as the entrance was constructed in the east wall of Room 11, the corridor was blocked by a wall, forming its south limit, whereby access to the residential portion of the house was denied. An entrance was also constructed in the north wall, giving access from the exterior, through the vestibule and the ante-chamber, to the house-church; this was no doubt for the convenience of Christians living in the neighbourhood, who could now enter the Christian rooms to participate in the ritual. They could not, owing to the new wall-block, proceed southwards into the privacy of the house itself. This exterior entrance was 0·91 m. wide on the outside, widening halfway to 1·14 m on the interior. It was found on excavation to have been rendered on both treader and sides with mortar, which bore on the former the impressions of wood.

A small quantity of tile was found on the floor level, including the major part of an *imbrex*, and this suggests that the roof was tiled; but the absence of carbonized wood may indicate that the final fire did not destructively affect this part of the building. Above this intermittent tile-fall was a 0·40 m. thickness of flint and mortar wall-fall, with fallen mortar rendering from the walls on east and west. The whole was levelled off from one wall-top to the other, providing a surface which was still exposed in the fourteenth century, attested by a silver penny of Edward I which lay just above the surviving top surface of the west wall.

Room 14

This room was part of the original construction of A.D. 80–90, but its purpose is unknown until the early years of the fourth century, when the Constantinian occupation began. The room containing the Bellerophon mosaic floor was bounded both on south and north by short corridors running west–east and floored with red-brick *tesserae*; and Room 14 lay immediately north of the northern of the two corridors (Fig. 12). It was not therefore directly associated with the rooms containing the mosaic floors.

Its floor consisted of clay and gravel, rammed to a fairly hard surface, and occupation is attested by two small, shallow, circular pits which were scooped out rather than dug at this time. They were exactly equal in diameter, 0·55 m., and of the same depth, about 0·20 m. in the centres. They lay together along the west wall, the centre point of the southern 0·30 m. east of it, that of the northern 0·45 m. east of it. The centre of the southern pit was 0·55 m. north of the south wall, the centre of the northern pit being 2·33 m. north of the same wall. The two pits were thus 1·78 m. apart centre to centre.

The southern pit contained eighteen coins: 4 Crispus (A.D. 320–324), 9 Constantine II *Caesar* (A.D. 320–324), 4 Constantius II *Caesar* (A.D. 324–326), and 1 Constantinopolis (A.D. 330–337); 1 Urbs Roma (A.D. 330–337) lay just 0·15 m. east of the pit and clearly belonged to the group. These coins were in a remarkably uniform condition, appearing as if fresh from the mint; and had the Urbs Roma and Constantinopolis coins not been directly associated with the others, a date somewhat earlier than A.D. 330–337 would have been indicated. But the latter date must govern the deposit of all nineteen coins.

The northern pit contained four coins: 1 Constantine I (A.D. 320–324), 2 Crispus (A.D. 320–324), and 1 Constantine II *Caesar* (A.D. 320–324). Again, these coins were in remarkably good condition; they suggest perhaps a slightly earlier date for their deposition in this pit. But both pits were almost certainly dug at the same time, and used for the same purpose, and for the same duration.

Each group of coins was concentrated, each in its pit, and the positions of the pits relative to the south and west walls suggest that they may have been excavated in the floor under the heads of two narrow beds, both extending towards the east, their heads against the west wall. The distance apart, 1·78 m., is suggestive of a "barrack-room" layout, giving two 0·91 m. widths for the beds, with a 0·91 m. space between, and leaving a space of 1·22 m. on the north side. And when it is remembered that even in modern days the occupants of such a room usually place their personal belongings in containers under the heads of their beds, the human reaction is clear. Under each bed-head, safely in a shallow pit, and probably in a cloth bag, lay the spare cash or savings of the two persons who, by the evident poverty of their weath and the Spartan aspect of their shared room, were probably household servants.

The room continued in occupation into the Valentinian era, two coins lying upon the floor, one of which was a Valens (A.D. 364–378), the other a House of Valentinian (A.D. 364–375), by which time the pits had probably been levelled over. And when the inhabitants of the villa embraced Christianity and the house-church was established *c.* A.D. 380–385, the flooring of the rooms of this part of the house was reconstructed in wood. Not only were the house-church and its ante-chamber so provided, but Room 14 also. Beneath a fall of roof-tile, thickest towards the west wall-partition of the house–church, was a spread of carbonized wood, among which could plainly be recognized the remains of two thick planks, each averaging 0·30 m. in width. They lay west–east, parallel to each other, 2·13 m. apart centre to centre, and each was distant approximately 0·91 m. from the north and south walls. They represent large, rafter-like planks upon which the thin floorboards had been laid, fixed, as in the house-church, by wooden pegs rather than iron nails, which were absent. A coin of the House of Constantine lay sealed beneath the carbonized remains of the northern plank, and this attested the mid-fourth century at the earliest for the insertion of the planked floor. Two coins of the House of Theodosius were also present in the room, one near the south-east corner, the other above the northern of the two Constantinian pits. Both these coins, and those of the Valentinian period, had fallen upon the planked floor and were found in the level of carbonized wood.

The total absence of burnt wattle-and-daub, and of any trace of painted wall-plaster, in the room suggests that its north, west and south walls had been carried up in flint and mortar and without decoration. The partition between the room and the house-church, however, consisted of a wooden frame with daub, having the Christian painted decoration on its far side; this partition had burned and fallen forward into the Deep Room, and not back into Room 14. The room continued in use to the final destruction, but its purpose in the last period is unknown. No evidence appeared of any entrance through the north wall into the ante-chamber, nor through the east partition into the house-church; and indeed, the Christian wall decoration on the far sides of both wall and partition has been sufficiently restored to preclude any such entrances.

THE NORTHERN COMPLEX—ROOMS 3 AND 8, AMBULATORY (2) (Figs. 14 and 15a–d)

The removal in 1956 by the Kent County Council of the obstructing road that covered the east frontage of the villa allowed the plan of the complex to be ascertained, except where the valley sewer-trench had destroyed it.

From the Landing (1) on the north-west exterior of the Deep Room two tiled steps, 0·91 m. wide, led up to a corridor floored with concrete, proceeding north for 5·18 m. Here it turned eastwards, continuing for 6·40 m. to a small rectangular room, with a tessellated floor in red and yellow and an *opus signinum* quarter-round moulding, which was built on the north-east exterior of the complex as part of the original layout. Through this room and southwards, the valley sewer-trench had destroyed much, but slight evidence remained of a continuation in that direction of the corridor for 3·35 m. from the small room, to a point where it turned westwards, proceeding for 6·10 m. to another pair of tiled steps, 1·11 m. wide, which led down to the original landing. This corridor or ambulatory therefore enclosed a rectangular room, 4·88 m. from west to east, and 4·27 m. from north to south, producing a plan strongly reminiscent of the Romano-Celtic temple type, of which some thirty-seven examples are listed in Britain.[11] A possible entrance may have existed in the east wall immediately south of the small room, Room 3, a pair of large circular post-holes being found on the exterior here 1·83 m. apart; but it is more likely that these post-holes were associated either with the third-century reconstruction, or perhaps with the late fourth-century occupation; the point is obscure. The true entrance was inside the house, by way of the tiled stairs leading down from the long back corridor. The reason why the steps leading up to the ambulatory were designed to rise may possibly lie in an attempt to simulate a low *podium* for the temple.

[11] M. J. T. Lewis, *Temples in Roman Britain*, Cambridge, 1966, 13.

That it probably was designed as a temple of Romano-Celtic type is suggested not only by its physical connection with the Deep Room but by the overall wall-decoration of both its walls and those of the latter, consisting as it did of panels, dadoes, and palms, in red, green and orange. Slabs, large and small, of exactly similar wall-plaster, alike in design, colours and technique of painting, were recovered from the collapsed walls of the ambulatory and the room it enclosed, and also from the walls of the small room on the north-east corner. These slabs occupied positions on the north, east and south sides, fragments of the same dado, the same panels, the same yellow palms, together with new ones in green, all appearing. A close study of this plaster placed the matter beyond all doubt. Here, and only here, in the house, embellishing the fourfold stairways, the Deep Room, and the temple with its ambulatory, was the same exotic decoration, a decoration with a distinct, perhaps Mediterranean, "date-palm" bias.

One unit, therefore, of the second-century house had been planned for pagan cult purposes, involving approach from within the house, down to the landing, and thence further down to the Deep Room, and slightly upwards to the ambulatory surrounding the temple. This plaster, in the Deep Room only, had been "pecked" all over as a key for the showed small yellow palms forming the ends next to the corner of the "lozenge and square" dado, and exhibiting exactly the same technique as the tall palms with their bunches of red dates beside the steps, and as the palms on the fallen plaster from the clay walls of the temple. This plaster, in the Deep Room only, had been "pecked" all over as a kay for the subsequent third-century plaster, while the fallen plaster in the neighbouring temple had not been so treated; the clay walls had here fallen or been overthrown before the Deep Room was redecorated in the third century. The religious significance, if any, of the "date-palm" motif, especially when applied to so curious a complex within a country residence of the second century, is not known.

Construction

The construction of the square complex, together with the reconstruction of the Deep Room as a *nymphaeum,* was preceded by a Flavian-Trajanic occupation of the site, when the floor of the Deep Room had been approached by wooden stairs on the south, and by a walking-way of gentle gradient on the north, the latter leading up to the exterior surface. Here, at the surface, the somewhat steep natural slope down from the west and north-west tended to level out, and upon this piece of ground was founded the square complex. A considerable amount of Flavian-Trajanic material had accumulated over the area as rubbish survivals, and when the site was levelled much of this was cast aside while some remained undisturbed; and because a proportion of this earlier material lay upon the higher slope, in course of time, especially when the complex became deserted, it accompanied the hill-wash creep and became deposited above the late second-century material which is contemporary with the square complex occupation. This simple dilemma posed itself during excavation of other parts of the villa, where indeed in one place Roman lies over medieval, in another, Flavian over Antonine, and it is clearly due to hill-wash creep depositing earlier rubbish over later deposits.

Having levelled the ground, the builders proceeded in the following sequence:

(1) The Flavian wall of flint and mortar bounding the Deep Room on the north was

already standing when the flight of steps were inserted *c*. A.D. 180, as was also the west wall with its stout, square timber uprights (Fig. 13a), but this latter wall was not used. A continuous flint and mortar wall was added along its inner face, the corridor that was to become the west ambulatory being reduced in width to conform with the steps.

(2) The ambulatory was planned out, and it was decided to use walls of clay for the remainder of the complex, with the exception of the small tessellated room, which was designed to occupy the north-east corner and whose walls were built of flint and mortar. Such clay walls have been found at Verulamium, Canterbury, and in Villa II at Farningham, Kent.[12] They seem to be of an early date, though at Verulamium they may be a late reversion to an earlier practice. At Farningham they are Flavian, at Lullingstone late-Antonine; the technique may well have been of native persistence, generally disappearing by *c*. A.D. 200. It should be noted that at Lullingstone the clay does not contain any trace of wattle strengthening, and in consequence the walls were probably designed to bear only their own weight, the roof, possibly of thatch rather than of the heavier tiles, being supported on a somewhat widely spaced wooden framework. These clay walls were placed upon flint and mortar footings, as at Farningham, where the post-holes in these footings were designed for wooden uprights, not only to support the thatched roof but also to clasp at short intervals the clay baulks. The Lullingstone posts were more widely separated, only four post-holes being discernible; and these were somewhat irregularly disposed along the north clay wall, the two towards the east being indeed possibly associated with the exterior entrance rather than with the clay wall. A fourth was sited at the north-east corner of the inner room, at the meeting of north and east clay walls. The positioning of these uprights seems to have come later in the sequence of building.

(3) A curious drainage system (Pl. XIIIc) was next laid out at the northern exterior of the projected building. Two small gullies of square section were cut into the natural clay-with-flint, their sides consisting of selected flints and chalk blocks packed in clay, their flat bases provided with a skim of pebbly mortar. Much of this rendering was found to have perished, and indeed, owing to the sides being of clay, silting must have been rapid. The westerly gully, having left the line of the wall at right-angles, turned north-east at once and proceeded in that direction, meeting the easterly gully 5·80 m. north of the exterior. The latter gully, however, having also left the wall at right-angles, proceeded in a straight line northwards to its junction with the westerly gully. Both gullies having joined and formed a single, wider gully, this latter then descended steeply beneath the modern road, presumably to a sump; it was not possible to investigate this. This drainage system is of unusual design, the gullies proceeding outwards at right-angles to the wall and not appearing within the building. While the westerly gully received surface water from the slope on the north-west, the fact that both gullies were laid out at right-angles to the wall suggests a pair of vertical drain-pipes, perhaps of wood, connected to a horizontal gutter at roof level, thus providing roof drainage of modern pattern. The fact that such roof drainage has not been usually observed in Romano-British buildings does not vitiate so sensible an arrangement.

(4) Substantial flint and mortar foundations, which included a proportion of rough chalk blocks, were laid in shallow footing trenches sunk into the undisturbed clay and flint sub-

[12] *Archaeologia Cantiana*, lxxxviii (1973).

soil. These foundations were employed for the outer north and inner east clay walls of the ambulatory, the inner north ambulatory wall being devoid of any such foundation. This latter clay wall was built directly upon the natural clay-with-flint, which was not countersunk to receive it. The north wall foundation passed over the ends of both gullies, which ended beneath it.

(5) The next step was to found the wooden framework of the rectangular complex. A span in either direction of some 7·93 m. was needed. This is by no means too long for single beams resting upon corner posts and strengthened by an occasional upright. But, as has been said, the post-holes, though carefully sought, proved elusive. A simple wooden construction of the type suggested can, however, safely be postulated, bearing a roof that was probably of thatch rather than tiles—very few tile fragments were recovered from the area. At the same time as this framework was being built, the flint-and-mortar footings around the small tessellated room were laid and tied in to the clay wall footings; the joints are bonded with the same mortar and no straight joints exist. The tessellated floor was not yet laid down.

(6) The clay walls were then built (Pls. XIIa, c–d). A slightly sandy clay, remarkably free from flint and other extraneous matter, was used. At Lullingstone, the walls were unusually thin (the Farningham walls averaged 0·40 m. in thickness), being not more than 0·15 m in thickness, and no support, either of wattle or reed, was included. The clay was carefully packed, its verticality being continually adjusted as the layers were added; and gradually the walls rose between the wooden uprights that supported the roof, being clasped between them. They could either have risen to rafter level or could have been left at breast-height to give an open verandah effect. If the latter, a light wooden sill could have rested on the clay; or, if the walls did rise to rafter level, light window-frames of wood could easily have been inserted to admit light to the interior. In any event, window-glass was not used—no fragments were found. It has been suggested that the clay may have been placed in position in the form of soft bricks. There was no sign of this; lumps of soft clay, perhaps indeed roughly shaped, were doubtless used, and then smoothed off to a finish. It is possible, but unlikely, that the walls of the small tessellated room may have been partly built of clay; but the destruction to which this room had been subjected when the valley sewer was inserted through it and its position on the exterior of the building have obliterated any certain evidence, though the position of the large fallen slab of painted wall-plaster and its backing, south of the small room, is suggestive (Pl. XIIIa). This plaster, exhibiting as it does a curved flange in red, may once have decorated the south face of the room, the flange being then vertical at the corner; it might be regarded as exterior decoration, to which its worn condition on the face would conform. The painted simulation of stone panel-work may also here suggest exterior equally with interior for its original position. After falling flat, the slab was covered by a thick layer of mortar from a flint wall, the flints having been robbed away, which points to the south wall of the small room having been thus constructed, the east and north walls conforming; but the evidence is uncertain.

(7) The clay walls having been raised straight and trim, were keyed when still soft to hold the plaster facing; this keying was of a special kind. A wooden die, in the shape of a roller, perhaps some 0·30 to 0·37 m. in length, was operated in an upwards direction, impressing the clay with a "zig-zag" or "chevron" pattern, together with groups at intervals of vertical grooves. This pattern is strongly reminiscent of those sometimes impressed on box-flue

tiles.[13] An example of plaster, bearing on its inner face such a pattern, was found *in situ* and recovered from the west clay wall of the inner room. This method of using a wooden die, so similar to that in use with flue-tiles, may provide a valuable method of dating this plaster—the dating in regard to the tiles being suggested by A. W. G. Lowther in his paper as from A.D. 80–150, and in no case later than A.D. 200.

(8) The plaster having been applied, was then painted. Most was found in a very fragmentary state; but many slabs of some size were found where they had fallen, and their positions were plotted. The painting was without exception confined to the three colours of the *nymphaeum*, i.e. red, green and orange-yellow; and the same design and technique were employed. Fragments from the dado indicated a similar design of lozenges and squares, and the mode of suggesting perspective in the large panels was identical with that used in the great panels of the *nymphaeum*; each panel was outlined in the three colours, with rows of dots in the corners to give the illusion of a deep frame. In every case the panels were left blank.

In addition to the foregoing scheme of decoration, the "date-palm" motif played an important part; the spreading fronds were depicted either in yellow, confined to the *nymphaeum*, or in yellow or green in the adjoining temple. The palms in the latter agree with the smaller palms in the *nymphaeum*, where they terminate the north and east dadoes, and they were similarly positioned, below the panels but at the ends of stretches of wall. They probably marked doorways and corners. This is especially so where the north and east ambulatories debouched into the small tessellated room, "palm" decoration being found at both these points. The panel-work already alluded to upon the large slab of fallen plaster on the south side of this room, where the panels are small and appear to simulate stone-work, is the only example of such decoration associated with the temple, and while the "palm and panel" motif certainly provided inside decoration for both ambulatory and inner room, this "stone-work" may have been an exterior design as already suggested; its possible position as a re-entrant perhaps protecting it more than the rest of the exterior decoration, which, if once existing, had perished.

The fact that so much of the second-century plaster was found in slabs, often laminated face up and then face down, with much fallen clay from the walls, provides an interesting side-light upon the action of the third-century people who came to re-occupy the derelict house. They found that the plaster had already suffered prolonged and severe weathering while it remained clinging to the walls; but the clay of these walls would prove useful for new structures and purposes. The plaster was therefore sliced off the faces of the remaining walls, each slab being deposited alongside in the roughly horizontal position in which it was found, but face up or face down, depending on how the slicing was made.

The importance of this second-century plaster cannot be over-estimated. Interesting in itself, without it the unity of the *nymphaeum*, the stairway complex, and the temple, could scarcely have been demonstrated.

(9) The next procedure was to lay down the concrete floor of the ambulatory. First, a narrow board was placed horizontally against the base of the painted plaster to receive the

[13] A. W. G. Lowther, *A Study of the Patterns on Roman Flue-tiles and their Distribution*, Research Paper No. 1, Surrey Archaeological Society.

thrust of the concrete—the slots, filled with dark silt, were evident on excavation, the wood having rotted *in situ*. The quarter-round mouldings were found to overlie the slots.

(10) A spread of clay and flint packing was then put down, and on this was laid a heavy concrete floor, composed of rough pebble concrete, some 5 to 7·5 cm. thick, the sides being shaped into shallow mouldings as indicated above. These ambulatory floors came to light in a virtually undamaged state, and a few sherds of samian ware sealed by them are of critical value, dating the floors to after *c*. A.D. 160.

(11) The entrance into the inner room from the north ambulatory was then made. A light door-frame of wood was inserted in the clay wall, and the treader securely founded. When in later years the wood was removed, the clay preserved the dark stain of this treader, and it was from observation of its position that the position of the doorway was confirmed. Post-holes were naturally absent, as the frame had been inserted as a complete unit. There were no signs of hinges or bolts to suggest a swinging door, and the aperture was likely to have been provided with a curtain.

(12) The doorway having been constructed, the inner room was floored with a level deposit of crushed and broken red brick, extending in uniform thickness throughout the room. Some of this crushed brick had been extended into the doorway to serve as its top treader surface, even projecting for some 0·45 m. out into the north ambulatory. It formed a sort of "mat" at the entrance to the room.

A circular depression was cut in the crushed brick floor in a significant position. It did not occupy the centre point of the room, being 3·35 m. from the west clay wall and 1·83 m. from the east clay wall; but it was equidistant from the north and south clay walls, and its centre lies on the north–south line that exactly bisects the doorway into the room from the north ambulatory. Of diameter 0·81 m., and 0·15 m. deep, it contained no brick fragments. It may have been the prepared seating for a circular receptacle, perhaps for water; but no trace of impressions was visible on its clay and flint floor, and no signs of carbonization or drainage. Whatever it had contained had been removed at the third-century reconstruction or before; the third-century west–east wall conceals half its area, the wall foundation descending into it.

At the same time as the inner room was receiving its floor, the tessellated floor of the rectangular room at the north-east corner was laid. It consisted of coarse brick *tesserae*, but in this case the proportion of yellow brick was much higher than usual. These yellow *tesserae* had been cut from roof-tiles, and at Lullingstone the use of yellow tiles is confined to the late-first and second centuries only; they never occur in any later construction. It may be permissible, therefore, on the evidence of these yellow *tesserae* in quantity in this small floor, to suggest a date for it somewhere in the latter part of the second century and not later. These *tesserae* may have come from the floor of the circular shrine (Part IV) which, first built *c*. A.D.100, may have gone out of use by the end of the second century. The proportion of yellow to red in both circular shrine and this small room is closely similar, and the area of tessellation removed from the former roughly agrees with that of the latter. In the north-west corner the quarter-round moulding of *opus signinum* that sealed the junction of floor and wall all round, is taken round the flint and mortar footing upon which stood one of the timber uprights.

(13) The type of roof cannot positively be determined; the extreme rarity of tile

fragments, which would otherwise be expected, is suggestive of a roof of thatch or wood; but how such a roof was tied in to the rest of the building is not clear. The clay construction of the walls and the few posts concerned—if this is indicated by the dearth of post-holes—do suggest the lightest type of roof, one of the simplest design. It may have been of pyramidal form with pentices on the sides, customary with Romano-Celtic temples; and part of a finial of yellow brick, which was found on the floor of the north ambulatory, suggested that the finial may have crowned the apex of the roof.

Purpose of the Complex

Because the square room and its ambulatory were allowed to fall derelict, to suffer weathering and human depredation, and because at the third-century reconstruction it was finally destroyed almost to floor level, the significant evidence for any sort of religious or cult use is sparse; and except possibly for the "palm and panel" motif adorning the walls, the few objects that might be deemed significant cannot definitely be said to have been connected with the square inner room during its use, though their find-spots within the ruined complex suggest that they may have been. They are listed and described as under:

(a) A rectangular deposit of short carbonized sticks upon a rough surface of *opus signinum,* lying immediately on the exterior of the north clay exterior wall, and with a small, roughly rectangular, cemented level just north of it.

This deposit covered an area roughly 1·98 by 0·61 m. and rested upon *opus signinum* covering the same area. It consisted of short lengths, from 5 to 15 cm., cut from willow and hazel. The sticks were at first thought to represent the remains of a length of wattle fencing lying on the ground; but on a close examination this was found not to be so. The sticks were disposed in all directions and formed no recognizable pattern. They exhibited no sign of crushing and appeared to have lain undisturbed since being placed in this limited area. It is not impossible that we have here the discarded fuel from a dedication-sacrifice, to which the horse-skull ((b) below) may also refer. No examples of the seeds of *Pinus pinea* occurred in the deposit, though several portions of this imported species were recovered from the well (24) outside the south end of the house—a well which began to silt up *c.* A.D. 200 when the whole building was abandoned. The following quotation is of interest in this connection: ". . . the pine had associations with Dionysius (Bacchus), but it is particularly connected with the Phrygian Cybele and her son Attis, whose cults enjoyed a wide vogue under the Roman Empire."[14] The late Professor Sir Ian Richmond found carbonized cones of the Mediterranean pine prepared for altar fuel in the *mithraeum* at Carrawburgh.[15] The Lullingstone examples were submitted to Dr Alvin, of the Department of Botany at Birkbeck College, and were stated by him to be *Pinus pinea.* Thus, at a time contemporary with the Northern Complex, such cones were being imported to Lullingstone and presumably used there.

(b) A horse-skull deposited among the burnt sticks at the west end of the carbonized deposit, and parallel to the north exterior wall.

[14] R. E. M. and T. V. Wheeler, *Verulamium,* Research Report No. XI, Society of Antiquaries of London, Oxford, 1936, 119–20.

[15] R. L. S. Bruce-Mitford (Ed.), *Recent Archaeological Excavations in Britain,* London, 1956, 84–108.

This skull was devoid of its lower jaw, and no teeth remained in the upper jaw. In spite of its appearance of age when deposited, its position among the carbonized sticks does suggest some connection with them. It shows no sign of burning; it was put among the sticks after they had lost their heat. Indeed, the earth and *opus signinum* showed no sign of scorching; the wood seems to have been spread out when cold, together with the skull. A number of snail-shells were found in the skull cavities, and they might suggest that flesh may still have adhered to the skull when it was deposited. This isolated skull, much mutilated, may have a votive significance in connection with the foundation of the building outside which it was found.

(c) A close scatter of bone fragments over the north concrete ambulatory floor.

These fragments number one hundred and fifteen (Pl. XIIIb). They show no sign of calcination and were found scattered above a thin silt layer over the surface of the floor, and below the fallen clay and plaster wall. Their interest lies in their shape. They consist of lengths cut from the leg-bones of animals, probably oxen, from which the marrow had been extracted by longitudinal splitting—lengths that have afterwards in most cases been cut at angles at the ends to form rough points. The following table gives their lengths:

Length in cm.	*Number*
26	1
17·5	1
16	1
13	1
12·5	3
11	6
10	5
8·75	23
7·5	25
6	27
5	15
3·75	7
Total	115

The usual length will be seen to vary from between 8·75 and 5 cm. accounting for 78% of the total. The number, their lengths and curious shaping have been recorded here, though no explanation is offered, if in fact they possess any significance. But, taken with the other objects from the complex, they certainly are a find that should not be disregarded.

(d) The top of a yellow brick roof-finial, or perhaps of a "votive lamp", found immediately outside the inner clay wall and in the north ambulatory.

The following information in regard to votive lamps is extracted from these sources:[16] Belonging to a class of "lampshades" more common in the Mediterranean world than in the North, and occasionally found in Britain, they seem to have been used as objects to which some religious significance was attached, such as votive lamps or lamp chimneys, possibly for use upon open-air altars. They seem to be associated with both burials and temple

[16] A. W. G. Lowther, *Surrey Archaeological Collections*, xlii (1934), 61–6; *op. cit.* in n. 14, 190–1, and Plate LVIII; *Antiquaries Journal*, lvi (1976), 41.

worship. Built in tiers, but in one piece, and with apertures cut in the sides of each tier, these chimneys resemble, and no doubt were founded upon, the classical light-house. They appear usually to have been made of red or yellow brick. In the first and second centuries A.D. the normal shape is cylindrical (as at Lullingstone), being replaced after the close of the second century by a quadrangular tower. In addition to the fine examples from Verulamium, and from Ashtead, Surrey,[17] and the fragment from Lullingstone, these objects are recorded from several sites in Britain and from the Continent. At Xanten, a grave deposit included one of these chimneys, resting on the ground and surrounded by a number of small votive pots, much of the type as that listed under (e) below. The Lullingstone object is, as has been said, of circular section, the solid "roof" portion being of a cylindrical shape, conical from the base upwards. There are indications of six openings in the top tier or stage, alternatively flat-headed and arched, though their placing is not quite symmetrical. There is no sign of a circular frill above the openings, though there appears to have been a narrow row of notching around the top, reminiscent of rough rouletting. It is not possible to estimate the length of the openings. The spike, or similar finial at the top, has been broken off. There is, however, a fragment of red brick, apparently moulded, embedded in a hard deposit of puddled chalk that now fills the interior. This is a subsequent deposit, and the fragment of brick may have formed part of the finial. A tentative and approximate suggestion as to the original height of the Lullingstone object may perhaps be arrived at by comparing the proportion of this fragment with the complete example from Ashtead, which it may have resembled:

	Diameter of roof excluding frill	*Total height, base to top of spike*
Ashtead	0·14 m.	0·61 m.
Lullingstone	0·06 m.	?0·28 m.

This object has been included because of its possible votive significance. It is more likely, however, to have been part of a roof-finial; yet, its fineness does not suggest an exterior position, open to weathering. Again, the rarity of such objects on villa sites, even in a fragmentary state, suggests that they were not in common use for the exterior decoration of houses.

(e) A miniature pottery vessel of light-brown fabric (Pl. XIIb) which may have a votive significance.

It was found embedded in the mortar of the east wall of the east ambulatory, positioned low down in the side, with its mouth upwards, open and accessible, scarcely the result of chance. The examples from Xanten have been mentioned, and this may be such a relic. Its position in the wall was secondary; it had already interesting characteristics. One part of the circumference had been pierced near the rim by a hole 4·6 mm. in diameter; and an area, averaging 1·25 cm. wide, and extending down to the bulge of the pot from the hole, shows evidence of wear by friction—it may originally have been tied fairly firmly against some upright object, harder in material than the pot. Some such deposit, again as at Xanten, may have been involved, and the little pot could have had a votive connection in its primary use. The usual suggestion that such small vessels were merely children's toys does not seem fully

[17] *op. cit.* in n. 16, 61–6.

to explain their occurrence. At Verulamium, such pots were certainly used as votive objects in the Triangular Temple.[18]

(f) Three objects of shaped chalk, found at the east, south, and north parts of the inner room.

Their shapes are remotely phallic in appearance. The first object was found within the inner room, close to the line of the east clay wall. It consists of a block of chalk, roughly circular in section, but with one flat face planed longitudinally, of diameter 0·05 m. and length 0·14 m. In addition to the flat face, the block has been planed to five other faces, the base slightly tapered, the other end fashioned to a blunt point. The second object was found again within the inner room, close to the line of the south clay wall. It also consists of a block of chalk; but instead of having a circular section with one main face, its section exhibits a pair of near-parallel faces with a further two pairs of smaller planed surfaces between them. The result is more rectangular than the first example. The base has been broken away, so that the original length is unknown, though the surviving length is 0·10 m. The point, however, has been carefully shaped by planing the chalk to eight faces, the point itself being slightly worn. The main flat faces on both these examples served to prevent them from rolling when set down. It cannot, of course, be said that they were contained in the inner room during its period of use; but their likeness to objects of phallic type may suggest their association in some pagan activity. The third object, also of chalk, is much smaller and is shaped rather like a small dumb-bell, one bulge of which is conspicuously larger than the other. The object could be mistaken for a small pestle; but chalk is not a suitable substance of which to make such a tool, which should be of much harder material. It, too, might have some phallic significance, its shape being susceptible of other interpretations than that of a pestle or pounder. It was found on the exterior line of the north clay wall of the inner room. There are no signs in this case of planing of the chalk; it appears to have been rubbed into its generally curved shape of a miniature dumb-bell.

These three objects, when taken as a series, do suggest some activity in or about the area where they were found, an activity that does not seem to be an attribute of the ordinary domestic life of the house.

(g) A nearly circular hole was found in the north-east corner of the inner room, at a distance of 0·81 m. from both the north and east clay walls. It was found to contain large fragments of various pottery vessels, mainly dating in the second half of the second century. These fragments included the base of a large Patch Grove vessel, with the underside upwards, occupying the most prominent position in the hole. The position of this Patch Grove base and its accompanying pottery in and about the hole was reminiscent of the ritual foundation-deposit found inserted in one of the rooms in the Farningham II house[19] where it, too, occupied the north-east corner of the room. The date of the Farningham II deposit was, however, Flavian, and consisted of a complete bead-rim vessel of native manufacture, dated to A.D. 60–80, and containing a *dupondius* of Vespasian.

The foregoing finds (a) to (g), that may be thought to point to some religious cult, have been considered fully, because they have a cumulative effect. The plan of this temple, its wall decoration, and the objects found within it, few as they are, do provide something more than

[18] *op. cit.* in n. 14, Plate LIX.
[19] *Archaeologia Cantiana*, lxxxviii (1973), 7.

a suspicion that here might have been a place devoted to the practice of some pagan cult, which its Romano-Celtic plan, and its association with the *nymphaeum,* certainly suggests.

The Third-Century Reconstruction (Figs. 13b and 13a)

As has been elsewhere recorded, during the greater part of the third century, up to *c.* A.D. 280, the house remained abandoned to the elements and to the occasional depredations of man. Its reconstruction involved the destruction almost to floor level of the temple with its ambulatory, the blocking of the tiled stairs leading down into the Deep Room, and the construction of a hypocaust system on the north side of the latter. This is described under the sections dealing with Rooms 10 and 10A. A gully was dug north-west and north of the new exterior wall of the house, at the foot of the hill-slope, for diversion of rain-water. It covered the northern side of the ruined temple. At the same time a shallow hearth 0·91 m. long and egg-shaped was constructed in the concrete floor of the west ambulatory.

The Fourth Century

As has been elsewhere recorded, the third-century furnace-room and the hypocaust system were probably never taken into use, and sherds of fourth-century pottery soon found their way into the rooms. Fragments of red colour-coated vessels and typical fourth-century *mortaria* were found in the silt immediately above the furnace-room floor, together with much evidence of destruction. But, except for this, there is nothing to show that the furnace-room was used for any other purpose. No connection could be observed between it and the Christian re-arrangements which took place late in the century; by then it had been dismantled. During the excavation of Room 10A particular attention was paid to any possible connection it might have had in the late fourth century with the Christian rooms beside it on the south and west. Room 10A was certainly connected to the house-church by a doorway, arched with chalk voussoirs, and may have served as a priest's room or sacristy, though its walls were devoid of any decoration from which a Christian purpose might have been deduced. This room is described in detail under the section, Room 10A, together with the small oven or kiln that was inserted in its south-east corner, perhaps after the destruction of the house early in the fifth century.

That part of the clay wall complex that lay north, and exterior to, the new third-century west–east masonry wall had been destroyed almost to floor level; but the northern and eastern areas some distance from the fourth-century house did, however, provide a few Constantinian coins and fragments of pottery of mixed date, for the most part lying on a patch of very worn white cement. Also, two large post-holes had been dug, sited along the eastern face of this part of the exterior, but their purpose is unknown. Three further post-holes, narrow and ill-made, were found cut into the collapsed clay of the clay wall complex; but they provided neither dating evidence nor coherent plan, though they may be of late-Roman date.

Dating

Four levels which provide dating evidence can be distinguished in the temple and its ambulatory. They are as follows:—

(1) The prepared level upon which the complex was founded.

(2) The occupation level.

(3) The destruction level lying directly upon (2).
(4) The subsequent level of clay-with-flint hill-wash.

An overall picture is provided of a late first-century occupation, subsequently modified towards the end of the second century, and falling to ruin before destruction by the third-century re-building. This late third-century re-occupation is a subsequent event and need only be touched on here; it only directly affected the southern part of the complex.

Before analysing the contents of these four levels in detail, the dating summary from coarse pottery is as follows:

(a) Flavian–Trajanic—below the clay walls and corridors of the complex.
(b) Last quarter of the second century—contents and surface of the crushed brick floor, and of the burnt level on the north side of the complex.
(c) Late-second to early-third century—contents of levels containing fallen clay walls and plaster.

This indicates a building erected towards the close of the second century upon a late-first century to early-second century site, and falling into ruin *c.* A.D. 200, not late enough to include typical third-century material (the metallic-glazed wares must be placed in the last decade or so of the second century, coming, as they do, from levels containing second-century coarse pottery exclusively); and this building, being connected by the tiled stairways with the Deep Room, and comprising with the latter a single unit within the house, can be used to date the Deep Room. Indeed, pottery fragments found sealed behind the late-second century wall-blocks in the Deep Room confirm the dating of the whole complex to the decade or two at the close of the second century.

The following is a Table of the coarse pottery contents of the four levels:—

Average representation by fragments	Level (1) Pre-build	Level (2) Occupation	Level (3) Destruction	Level (4) Hill-wash	Totals
Pompeian red platters	1	1			2
Vessels of native fabric	15	33	36	36	120
Patch Grove vessels	3	4	11	8	26
Native bead-rims	3	4	5	3	15
Romanized bead-rims	2	3	1	1	7
Mica-dusted vessels	1	1	2		4
Rough-cast vessels		2	4	2	8
Poppy-head beakers	3	8	17	9	37
Second-century flagons	8	21	26	8	63
Second-century *mortaria*	1		3		4
Typical late-first to second centuries vessels	8	41	55	18	122
Trajanic-Hadrianic pie-dishes	5	9	7	2	23
Late-Antonine pie-dishes		12	18		30
Late-second century Castor		3	6	1	10
Metallic-glazed Rhenish		4	17		21
Totals	50	146	208	88	492

Note: Level (2) above mainly consists of the contents of the crushed brick floor of the temple, together with the contents of the burnt area immediately exterior to the north ambulatory.

In the above Table the governing items are:

(a) The late-Antonine pie-dishes.
(b) The late-second century Castor ("Hunt cup") vessels.
(c) The late-second century Rhenish wares.

These provide an unassailable dating for occupation and destruction, in spite of the large quantity of fragments of vessels dating earlier in the second century. Indeed, without this late-second century material in the occupation and destruction levels, a false picture of early- to mid-second century would be provided. This earlier material is of rubbish survival value, much of it from wares that could easily have had considerable time-span. On its own account it suggests a Trajanic-Hadrianic occupation of the house; the amount of recognizable Hadrianic-Antonine material is slight.

Of the total recognizable sherds, numbering from this area, small as it is, just on 500, no less than one-third consists of native wares of coarse fabric, including a small amount of Patch Grove ware. These wares are definitive of a Flavian occupation, of a non-luxury type, persisting well into the second century—Patch Grove ware in particular has not infrequently been associated with samian and coarse pottery of Antonine date; it is not at all unusual to find a long persistence of these native types with their "backward-looking" tradition.

Pompeian red platters have been mentioned, and a word must be said in regard to these. Several of such platters have come to light, notably at Colchester; but as far as is known, the clean, high-grade finish of the Lullingstone examples is unique. It might first be supposed that they are an imported type from which the far rougher and larger Colchester examples derive; but it is difficult to accept this. The Lullingstone platters were taken to Colchester and compared directly with those in the Colchester Museum, and the late Mr M. R. Hull, while acknowledging the finer quality of the former, expressed his opinion that they could scarcely be later in date than those in the museum, placing them thus at *c.* A.D. 65 at the latest. However, unless we are confronted with a specially imported type of second-century date, perhaps hitherto unrecognized either in Britain or on the Continent, it is necessary to place these extremely interesting platters in a context not earlier than Flavian at Lullingstone. A discussion of this type of red-coated platter appears in *Camulodunum,* 221 and in D. P. S. Peacock (Ed.), *Pottery and Early Commerce,* London, 1977, 147–62.

Another example of imported Roman ware, other than flagon and amphora types, was recovered during the excavation of the granary (Part IV). It consisted of part of a samian platter, Form 15/17, and is dated to the reign of Nero (A.D. 54–68). It came from a ditch of first-century date long pre-dating the granary, a ditch that also contained a quantity of first-century native and neo-Belgic wares, with which it was stratified. The Pompeian red platters are therefore not alone as importations in the second half of the first century.

The iron brooch does not affect the dating of the Northern Complex. It is dated towards the end of the first century, and this relates it to the earlier Flavian-Trajanic occupation; and its position in the clay-with-flint deposit covering the destroyed complex, in company with contemporary sherds, is the result of subsequent hill-wash downward creep.

No coins were found in any of the critical levels of the temple and its ambulatory, though the positions of the *denarius* of Julia Maesa, and the worn *sestertius* of Faustina I in the third-century furnace-room help to secure the post-destruction rebuild in the third century. The remaining coins of fourth-century date have no connection with this particular dating problem, but further confirm the strong fourth-century occupation of the villa.

PART II

THE CENTRAL UNIT

The Mosaic Rooms (12) and (13), and their North and South Corridors
The Entrance Corridor (13A)
Room 15

The Mosaic Rooms 12 and 13, with their north and south Corridors

Before embarking on a comprehensive consideration of the mosaic rooms (as they may be described), it is convenient first to deal with their north and south corridors, which form a single unit with them, the whole constructed within the three decades A.D. 330–360.

The north Corridor

This corridor is 4·88 m. long and 0·91 m. wide, and received a tessellated floor, traces of which still remained *in situ*. Its eastern end extended for 1·14 m. over the filled-up Period I staircase-well that originally contained the wooden stair leading down to the Deep Room; but the corridor stopped 0·22 m. short of the east wall of the staircase-well. At this end the corridor was thus laid upon the tightly packed clay-with-flint filling of the staircase-well, its immediate foundation being composed of compacted blackish rubble and earth, averaging 0·20 m. in thickness, upon the surface of which the *tesserae* had been laid. Its east bounding wall ran north of the Room 13 north partition for approximately 0·91 m.. This east wall had been of light construction, almost certainly of wood and daub, and rested upon a foundation of chalk blocks 0·45 m. in width, which was found to have sagged downwards towards the north (Pls. XIVa and c, and Fig. 16), the chalk blocks having been placed in the blackish rubble and earth, into which they had partially sunk. The levels between them and the surface of the chalk ramp 1·67 m. below at its higher end, sloped downwards towards the north at an approximate angle of 20 degrees. The south end of this chalk wall foundation abutted on the *tesserae* next to the drain in Room 13, forming one unit with it and thus demonstrating that the corridor is contemporary with that room.

At a point 2·44 m. east of the west end of the corridor (Pl. XIVb), the coarse *tesserae* on the north side of the mosaic floor in Room 13 had sagged downwards, and a small excavation beneath the *tesserae* and the line of the south partition wall of the corridor revealed a small hearth containing ash, oyster-shells, and the major part of a bulbous, metallic-glazed beaker with a high and narrow base. This vessel is probably a Castor-ware product, and in form it dates well within the fourth century. The *tesserae* sealing it were laid continuously and showed no signs of a later patching. This vessel, together with the Urbs

Roma coin found sealed below the pink cement of the foundation of the east wall of Room 13—see below—confirms the construction of the mosaic rooms and the corridors to have taken place after *c.* A.D. 330, and the wear of the coin suggests a date later still, perhaps as late as *c.* A.D. 360. The latter would appear to be the latest dating, as the mosaic floors contain no obvious Christian symbols in their design, and the neighbouring house-church was erected not long after this.

There were slight signs of a narrow doorway from the north corridor into Room 13 at its north-west corner, but this remains uncertain. No iron-work or fragments of window-glass were found in this north corridor.

The south Corridor

Like the north corridor, this was 4·88 m. long, but it was 1·22 m. wide, 0·31 m. wider than the former; it also had received a tessellated floor. At its west end a single step 0·91 m. wide and faced with tiles led up to the Corridor 17 leading southwards to the baths. The partition separating this corridor from Room 13 had been constructed of wood and daub from floor level, the daub being rendered with painted plaster on both sides, the bottom portion of which facing the corridor being found *in situ* at the north-west corner of the corridor where it turned southwards at a right-angle to embrace the northernmost of the three brick piers or pillar-bases along the east face of Corridor 17 (Pl. XIVd). This pier formed part of the foundation of the northern upright of the door-frame over the step, and all three piers were of equal size, 0·25 m. square, and disposed at equal distances. This painted decoration had been in part discoloured by burning, but in the main it had escaped the flames, surviving in its original colours.

The decoration was exceedingly free, almost barbaric in character, and showed a series of pillars painted brown, with wide edgings of red, the white spaces between being filled with intermittent daubs of orange and thin freehand scrolls in purple. This paintwork having been executed towards the middle of the fourth century, it is interesting to observe an evident deterioration of artistic perception when compared with the excellent work of the late second century, as shown by the classical treatment of the water nymphs, and the careful panel-work of that time. It might be due to the withdrawal of Continental artists and the employment of native decorators, in whom the Celtic urge, now less inhibited by Roman artistic pressure, was coming to the surface. Even when one considers the slightly later Christian paintings, from the artistic standpoint it can scarcely be said that the conception of the artist contained much of classical tradition. The architecture depicted looks back to classical style, but severity has been lost, and an exuberant display of decoration for its own sake almost afflicts the eye, so bright, and indeed clashing, are the colours used. All this may be thought to reflect a lack of discretion and discrimination both in the artist and in the recipient of his work. A sense of serenity has been lost.

This loss of a sense of fitness and control is also apparent when the state of the south corridor is considered. Its floor was found to have been a dumping-place for rubbish, with decayed animal and vegetable refuse, trodden down upon the surface together with a coin of Constantius II *Augustus* and a minim, which help to date this squalid level; and while the floor of Room 13 on the other side of the partition had certainly been clean when the destroying fire occurred, the state of the corridor outside points to a slatternly disregard for order and cleanliness by the last occupants of the house.

An examination of this corridor revealed, at a point about 3·05 m. from its west end, and along the line of the partition, two large iron door-hinges, a number of heavy iron bolts, and a fragment of an inward splay of plaster *in situ*. An entrance from the corridor into Room 13 is thus inferred, the door of which had been consumed in the fire. Along the line of the partition were numerous fragments of window-glass, grass-green in colour, some smashed as the panes had fallen, others contorted by heat as they had become viscous, sliding down in the heat of the fire. A line of small windows facing south had been inserted in the partition, probably high up, as the glass was translucent but not transparent. The absence of iron cleats suggests that the small panes were fixed in wooden frames by mortar, traces of which, pink in colour, remained adhering to many of the glass fragments. It is interesting to consider that, when the doors of the mosaic rooms were closed, the daylight transmitted through the glass would have flooded them with a greenish light, a prevailing atmosphere that must have radically affected the aspect of the mosaic floors within.

The Mosaic Rooms 12 and 13 (Pl. XVa)

A complete photographic survey of the mosaic floors was made by the late Mr M. B. Cookson, of the Institute of Archaeology. This consisted of thirty-four overlapping exposures, all taken from the same height above the floor, and enlargements at a scale of one-quarter of the complete survey were mounted in a large volume, specially bound and entitled by Mr Bernard Middleton, F.S.A., and presented by the late Mr C. D. P. Nicholson, F.S.A., and the writer to the Library of the Society of Antiquaries, where it may be examined. Every detail of the composition and laying out may here be studied.

The Reception Room 13 is separated from the apsidal Dining Room 12 by a mosaic step 3·05 m. in length between returning flint and mortar walls at either end. The top edge of this step was found on excavation to have been broken away, except at the ends, where the small mosaic *tesserae* still remained curving over to meet the edge of the mosaic in the dining room. The design had consisted originally of two rows of white triangles, twenty-one in each row, one above another, upon a background of red mosaic. The bottom row remains complete (Pl. XVIIc).

The apsidal Dining Room. This had been built out westwards, over-sailing the original west wall of the house by 2·13 m. in the centre, and the original wall was found to underlie the apse; the discovery of this part of the wall was made possible by excavating a fourteenth-century plough-furrow which extended over it. This was one of a series of furrows which had been caused by driving a plough from a northerly direction towards the hidden floor. The surrounding foundation of the apse wall, however, had caused the coulter to jump up at each approach, so that the furrows did not extend far, thus causing only small damage to the tessellated surround of the Europa mosaic panel. The plough had been turned each time, and the scratch made by the coulter appeared in the floor between the furrows as the plough proceeded northwards again after each abortive attempt to cross the hidden apse. The dating of this ploughing was established by the discovery of a silver penny of Edward I and two silver halfpennies of Edward II in the large furrow and in a line with it over the west wall-top of Room 11.

Some 1·52 m. of clay-with-flint hill-wash had been deposited over the surface area of the ploughing, indicating the rate of slip downwards towards the flood-plain since the fourteenth century, no doubt accelerated from time to time by contour-ploughing in later times further up to the west.

The wall of the apse was of flint and mortar, and was strengthened by two external buttresses. Its south part overlaid the earlier coarse red-brick *tesserae* of the Corridor 17 leading to the baths; this tessellated floor had not been repaired since it had been laid at the end of the second century, and perhaps re-laid in the third century—it contains no yellow *tesserae*. It was found to be in a bad state, parts of it needed patching and many loose *tesserae* were scattered over it.

The apse is not strictly an exact apse; its eastern ends on the interior begin to curve inwards along the perimeter of a circle whose centre lies at the most westerly point of the *guilloche* surrounding the Europa panel, giving an interior radius of 3·20 m. A small, squared moulding of red *opus signinum* sealed the joint between the *tesserae* and the internal wall-plaster, the latter not surviving to a height of more than 5 cm., and therefore exhibiting nothing of the original painted decoration of the interior. The exterior wall of the apse, while curving round outside the west wall of the house, was laid in straight lengths to form the ends of the southern and northern corridors. The original east wall of the long back corridor lies uninterrupted beneath the mosaic step. The exterior part of the apse was without windows.

The focal point of the apse is the Europa panel, but the rest of the area was provided with a floor of coarse red-brick *tesserae,* many having been cut from box-flue tiles bearing the combed indentations of such tiles. *Tesserae* of other colours are absent, and the small squares are larger and shallower than the coarse *tesserae* of the second and third centuries, the former also often including a quantity cut from yellow tiles. The *tesserae* were not laid to any particular plan, except where they outlined the Europa panel. Here they enclose it by carefully fitted concentric curves forming a band just over 0·30 m. wide. This in turn is enclosed by a wide curving zone 0·81 m. wide, with a regular outer edge; beyond this, however, up to the *opus signinum* moulding, the laying of the *tesserae* ceases to conform and becomes haphazard. This may be explained by the probable disposal of furniture in the Dining Room. Over this latter area, backing against the curving wall and for the most part concealing from view the *tesserae,* were doubtless placed the permanent couches, thus making further careful laying of the *tesserae* unnecessary.

The Europa panel (Pl. XVb) lies centrally when viewed from the couches. Semi-circular in shape, though slightly extended on either side towards the step, it is 2·44 m. across at the step, and at its widest part extends into the room for just over 1·52 m.. It is enclosed as far as the step by a blue band bearing a simple twist in white, containing thirty-two discs of alternate red and white, the whole having the appearance less of a true *guilloche* than a jewelled chain. The ends of this chain show on the south side a red disc, on the north a white one, somewhat spoiling the symmetry, as does also the occasional inaccuracy in the positioning of the discs. Between these ends, running along the edge of the step, is an inscription in blue on white, set in two lines, each underlined by a narrow strip of red extending across the whole width of the panel to the interior edges of the blue band Containing the chain. The inscription is 1·95 m. long, the letters being 7·5 cm. high, and is intact except for the third word in the top line, which has been supplied in consultation with the late Sir Mortimer Wheeler and the late Dame Kathleen Kenyon. No spacings occur between successive words, but the letters themselves, while starting in both lines on the left in regular spacing, have been spread out to the right as if to fill the space, especially noticeable in the lower line. It would seem from this that the mosaicist was not copying direct from a prepared drawing, but may have been inserting the letters from dictation. It is interesting to note that the lettering at the southern end of both lines has been further baked by a smouldering beam fallen from the roof, so that the blue *tesserae* have become red.

The inscription forms an elegiac couplet:

INVIDA SI TA(VRI) VIDISSET IVNO NATATVS
IVSTIVS AEOLIAS ISSET ADVSQVE DOMOS

(If jealous Juno had seen thus the swimming of the bull she would with greater justice have repaired to the halls of Aeolus)

In Virgil (*Aeneid*, I, 50) Juno, espying Aeneas at sea with his fleet, visits Aeolus in his cavern to demand a storm to overwhelm him. The reference is here jestingly transferred to her faithless consort Jupiter, who is depicted below the couplet as a bull, bearing Europa through the waves. Two other direct references to the *Aeneid* occur in Roman Britain. In the mosaic at Low Ham, Somerset, the story of Dido and Aeneas is presented continuously; and a fragment of quotation appears on a wall-painting found in the Roman villa at Otford, Kent (part in the British Museum, part in Maidstone Museum). It is clear that the inhabitants of all three villas were well acquainted with Virgil, which is likely to have been the case in the higher strata of society generally in Roman Britain. It suggests a high level of education and a ready understanding of historical and mythological allusions, at least among the more prosperous inhabitants of the province.

The scene is executed most successfully in red outline on a white background, the deep blue of the sea being filled in below with a straight horizon. The blue *tesserae* are fitted together in lines which slightly converge to the centre, thus carrying the eye to the horizon and the figures depicted above it. The bull is shown in spirited action, swimming towards the right and breasting the waves, bearing Europa on his back. She is seated facing the bull's tail, with her right leg raised, but with her head turned in the forward direction, her gaze being directed over the bull's horns. In her hands she holds part of the diaphanous drapery which covers her left leg, and the wind billows it out behind her head as the bull progresses through the sea, the thicker folds of the veil being blocked in with yellow. She is otherwise nude, except for necklet and armlets. Her expression is remarkably serene. The designer of the panel has shown artistic perception by setting the hind hooves of the bull and the left foot of Europa against the deep blue of the sea.

This central group is accompanied by two flying *amorini,* one leading, the other firmly grasping the tail of the bull; he is not trying to retard the progress of the bull, but is more likely to be guiding him in the direction of his destination. The foremost *amorino* looks back, raising his right hand in encouragement, and bears in his left hand an upright torch whose red flame burns beside his head. Parts of the wings, and the hair, of both *amorini,* and of Europa herself, are blocked in with minute *tesserae* of variegated colours, some of which may be of foreign marble. Otherwise, the whole scene is set in outline. It is interesting to observe that the nakedness of the *amorini* is treated in a modest fashion, unlike the usual treatment in the depiction of such infant figures, the right leg of the leading *amorino* moving forward, the bull's tail passing across the body of his companion.

A point of some interest arises as regards the drawing of the Europa figure, which, when observed vertically from above is much elongated. What was its approximate presentation to the eye of a diner reclining on one of the couches? Assuming the height of the couch above the floor to be about 0·45 m.,[20] and the mattress a further 0·15 m. when the height of the forearm is taken as 0·25 m., and the eye-level about 0·10 m. above the wrist, a total height from ground to eye-level would be approximately 1·10 m.. When observed from this height above the floor, and at an appropriate distance from the back wall of the apse, the figure of Europa appears in normal proportions. This may be fortuitous; but it may be evidence of a successful attempt to give the figures perspective.

The rectangular Reception Room. This apartment measures 6·10 m. from north to south and 5·18 m. from west to east. The west–east centre line of the room is not, however, a prolongation of the centre line of the apse, but lies 0·30 m. to the south, while the red tessellated surround is 0·91 m. wide along the south and only 0·38 m. wide along the north. Along the east it is 0·68 m. wide, except where it continues into the opening of the main doorway in the east wall. As has been said, an Urbs Roma coin (A.D. 330–337), in somewhat worn condition, was found sealed by the pink cement of this east wall foundation, a valuable indication of the date of construction of the central unit.

The remainder of the floor is covered by a large "carpet" of mosaic, 4·88 m. from north to south and 3·96 m. from west to east. This is arranged in four panels, with a wide meander border based on the swastika or Greek key motif on three sides; the mosaic step and the internal walls close the fourth side. These panels comprise:—

(1) A rectangular panel lying north–south next the step and joining with it.
(2) A square panel, with figure subjects, placed centrally east of (1).
(3) and (4). Narrow rectangular panels bordering (2) on north and south, their exterior edges conforming with the north and south ends of (1).

Detailed descriptions of these panels are as follows:—

(1) This panel is 3·05 m. long and 0·91 m. wide (Pls. XVIIb and c). It contains four rows of ten motifs each, bounded on the east and south only by a narrow border of single leaves and simple rectangular designs, with two small *guilloche* twists on the south. Looking from the south, the four rows contain, from west to east:

Row 1. 5 Heart-shaped leaves without stalks, one of which only points to the north, all the others to the south.
2 Swastikas, black on white and bordered by black, rotating in opposite directions.
1 Triangles.
1 Self-closing *guilloche*.
1 Four-fold leaf with common centre.

Row 2. 5 Heart-shaped leaves without stalks, pointing south.
5 Crosses.

[20] J. E. A. Liversidge, *Furniture in Roman Britain*, London, 1955, Plates 9 and 10.

Bellerophon and the Seasons.

Row 3. 2 Heart-shaped leaves without stalks, pointing south.
1 Two-handled vase, base to south, top to north.
1 Swastika, black on white and bordered by black, rotating anti-clockwise.
2 Triangles.
1 Squares.
1 Lozenges.
1 Self-closing *guilloche*.
1 Four-fold leaf with common centre.

Row 4. 3 Heart-shaped leaves without stalks, pointing south.
4 Crosses.
1 White cross.
1 Squares.
1 Lozenges.

Of the three swastikas in the panel, one revolves clockwise, the remaining two anti-clockwise.

The placing of these forty motifs appears at first sight to have been haphazard; but of these no less than fifteen are heart-shaped leaves—which might be taken as hearts, being bereft of their stalks. A further three motifs are the black swastikas. Dr W. H. C. Frend points out[21] that swastikas and hearts were designs, worn as amulets, to avert the evil eye; in this case to protect the house itself, and therefore presumably the inhabitants. There may thus have been a very real intent in the inclusion of these motifs in the floor.

Another possibility in connection with this panel has been advanced. It may have been intended as a species of games-board, the diners casting dice, while a servant moved pieces from motif to motif in accordance. Such a game has in fact been worked out for this floor; but it is not difficult to devise any method in such a case. The suggestion cannot be proved; but certainly the panel was intended to be looked at from the south and not from the apse—indicated by the position of the two-handled vase and the directions that the "hearts" are pointing, fourteen towards the south, one towards the north, the latter in the extreme south-west corner. It is a suggestion, though in the absence of proof or of any known parallel it cannot be given much credence. The finding of a single bone-dice on the mosaic floor can have little significance; but the possibility must be recorded.

(2) This panel is finely executed and shows another mythological scene (Pls. XVIa and b). The background is white, and a large, cushion-shaped, three-strand *guilloche* surrounds the spirited scene. The winged horse Pegasus flies towards the right, in the same direction as the bull is swimming in the Europa panel, and is ridden by Bellerophon, seated between the horse's wings. The hero wears a red *chlamys* and red boots, and is holding a long lance of alternate red and white *tesserae,* with which he is thrusting down at the Chimaera below, upon which his gaze is fixed, while he controls the horse with red reins and bridle. As with Europa and the Bull, Bellerophon and Pegasus are drawn in outline, only the *chlamys,* boots, and hair of Bellerophon being blocked in with colour, the mane and the wings of Pegasus partially so. The *tesserae* with which the head of Bellerophon is made up are minute, some not more than 3 mm. in size, and cut to fit the features of the face. The Chimaera is blocked

[21] W. H. C. Frend, "Religion in Roman Britain in the fourth Century A.D.", *Journal of the British Archaeological Association,* Third Series, xviii (1955), 15.

in with yellow, outlined in red, with red lion's mane and three streaks representing red fire proceeding from its mouth. The end of the tail is intended to depict the head of the serpent, while the goat's head and neck protrude upwards from the back, with two ears, the jaws gaping wide, into which the iron barb of Bellerophon's lance strikes. Both the serpent's head and that of the goat are so badly executed that it might seem that the mosaicist was not fully acquainted with the mythological composition of the Chimaera. Otherwise the action and details are correctly displayed.

Four dolphins surround this scene. One is deep-blue, one lemon-coloured, two orange-yellow. In each case the tail fins are shown in red, as are the ears, while the eyes are white with a black central dot, and the whiskers black. They are shown in pairs, each pair face to face, the tails curled round quite unlike dolphins as seen on other mosaic floors. Indeed, as with the Chimaera, the mosaicist seems not to have known the true appearance of a dolphin. Between the heads of each pair is a curious little openwork figure in red, which is intended to represent an opened-out shell.[22] This marine association of Bellerophon may, as Professor Toynbee points out, comprise within a single picture two successive episodes of the same story: Bellerophon crossing the sea to slay the Chimaera, and his rôle as a maritime hero.

The cushion-shaped *guilloche* enclosing the whole is uncommon, but it can be paralleled in the floor at Brislington, Somerset. Its shape allows space in the corners of the whole panel for four red circles enclosing representations of the seasons. Of these three survive, Summer (presumably) having been destroyed by post-hole diggers in the eighteenth century. These seasons apparently progress in clockwise order. Spring is depicted as a girl against a white background, wearing an orange-yellow dress to the throat, with a red cloak thrown over her left shoulder (Pl. XVIIa). She gazes at a dark-blue swallow which has alighted upon her other shoulder. This swallow is particularly interesting. Not only has it the two long tail-feathers, but its throat is reddish-brown, showing that the mosaicist was well acquainted with the appearance of a swallow, as opposed to that of a swift or a martin. The girl's hair is intricately braided in masses of different colours.

Proceeding clockwise, Summer has been almost entirely destroyed, and only part of the enclosing roundel survives, with a fragment of dress, which would appear to have conformed with that of Spring and Autumn. Summer may have been wreathed in flowers.

The next season, Autumn, shown against a white background, is robed like Spring, but an older woman is suggested (Pl. XVIa). Her hair is also intricately braided, with strands of corn and straw extending from it. Though her dress is light in colour, and with the same red cloak over the left shoulder, on excavation much of the figure was found to be encrusted by hard, black, carbonized material. A burning roof-beam had fallen across it, and had lain smouldering, thus discolouring the *tesserae*. One *tessera* was removed, and the underside proved to be near-white, suggestive of the dress having been originally of a pale colour.

The last season, Winter, has been slightly damaged by the eighteenth-century work, but nearly all of it survives (Pl. XVIa). A still older woman confronts us, this time against a yellow background, her face white, her head and shoulders covered with a deep-blue hooded cloak of thick material, rising conically above the face, the folds indicated by lines of still deeper blue, almost black. Unlike the mild expressions of Spring and Autumn, Winter exhibits a stern, unsmiling aspect, which she directs across at Spring.

[22] *op. cit.* in n. 4, 201.

(3) and (4). The two narrow panels bordering (2) on north and south have been much damaged by the eighteenth-century excavations. They appear each to have consisted of two rectangles with a narrow rectangle between, the latter containing in each case a two-handled vase, facing inwards, with thin leaves rising from it. The two large rectangles on the north were composed of white right-angled triangles on a red ground, set each in seven even lines east–west. The pair on the south, however, was composed of two rows in each of saltire-crosses, alternately blue on white, and white on blue. Except for the small central rectangles containing the vases, of which scarcely anything on the south side remains, these north and south panels do not therefore exhibit symmetry when the whole floor is considered.

Panels (1) to (4) are enclosed within an intricate meander or Greek key design in red. The widths of this border and its background colours are not, however, the same. The north side is 0·83 m. wide, but shortly before it reaches the north-east corner the outer band of white is turned in to make a width of 0·76 m., which is carried on along the east side. At a point 2·74 m. southwards, the outer white band on this east side ceases abruptly, giving way to a broad patch of red mosaic, which continues to the southern end of this east side. This patch is close to the south end of the wide doorway in the east wall and suggests that persons were accustomed over a considerable period to turn left on entering, thus in time causing an extensive patch to become necessary at this point, which for some reason did not include a continuation of the original white band. Both north and east sides have a white background, and the red meander is continuous but complicated along these two sides. The south side is different. The meander does not continue into this south side, but begins again, the background is yellow, and the width is reduced to 0·61 m.. The number of lines in the meander is the same on all three sides, but they are necessarily set closer together on the south side. The reasons for these differences are unknown.

Along the north side of the room, the tessellated area had been slightly curved downwards to provide a shallow gully leading to the drain passing through the northern end of the east wall, where the curve is well pronounced, the better to channel away the water from floor-washing towards the drain (Pl. XVIIIa).

The materials from which the mosaic *tesserae* were cut are of tile, the deep-blue from the semi-baked cores of red tiles, and of hard chalk, with a large number from the Greensand ridge in the northern Weald. The latter ranges from purple to near-black, and is usually of crystalline structure. It is likely that some of the smaller *tesserae,* as from the hair of Europa and her attending *amorini,* may be from foreign marble of varying colours; but this is exceptional. In the meander border, especially along its east side, a small number of blocks of *tesserae* are included from an earlier floor, though not necessarily a Lullingstone floor. No samian or glass *tesserae* are included. After laying, the whole floor received a thin wash of watery pink mortar, which remained between the *tesserae* here and there as a slight film or ridge on their surfaces.

In regard to the foundation of the mosaic floors, the two eighteenth-century post-holes proved useful, allowing some slight investigation. Without undercutting, it was clear that no hypocaust or other space existed under the floors, the slight sinkage here and there being due to earth movement. The concrete in which the *tesserae* were set was founded upon the natural clay-with-flint, levelled for the purpose. The Bellerophon panel was found on excavation to be bowed over vacancy, the underlying clay having been slowly washed away by water entering by way of the neighbouring post-holes; this was grouted and made safe. The Europa panel is almost as flat as when first laid; indeed, the mosaic floors are in a remarkable state of preservation, especially when it is remembered how shallow was the earth-covering towards the east, where it was only just 0·30 m. above the remains of the east wall.

Significance of the Mosaic Designs

The discovery in September 1963, of the mosaic floor at Hinton St. Mary, in north Dorset, has provided a striking parallel to Lullingstone. This newly discovered floor bears not only the *Chi Rho* monogram, against which is set the presumed head of Christ, but also includes in the same layout a representation of Bellerophon killing the Chimaera. And at Lullingstone appears the Bellerophon motif again in mosaic, with the three *Chi Rho* monograms painted on the walls of the house-church and its ante-chamber immediately north of the room in which the motif appears. This is unlikely to be fortuitous, and if the *Chi Rho* monograms and the Bellerophon motif have significant connection, which they certainly would seem to have at Hinton St. Mary, the latter motif may well be of Christian relevance. Professor J. M. C. Toynbee, in her paper on the Hinton St. Mary mosaics, writes as follows:—[23]

"It is important to remember that by the fourth century the representation in art of the traditional Graeco-Roman myths, gods, and personifications, and of many motifs from daily life (such as hunting scenes) had increasingly tended to assume an allegorical and quasi-religious meaning. This is particularly evident in the sphere of funerary iconography. But there can be little doubt that the selection of themes for domestic paintings, mosaics, and other forms of decoration was not infrequently determined by ideas concerning death and the life beyond the grave, to which a spiritual rebirth in this world forms the prelude. Such ideas are likely to have lain behind the choice for the Hinton St. Mary mosaic of the Bellerophon story, of the Wind Personifications, of the great tree, and of the hunting scenes; and it is in the light of its place in a context of this kind that we should interpret the most important and the most impressive of all the figure-subjects on the pavement—the bust with the *Chi Rho* behind his head."

And she thus continues (p. 14)

"Bellerophon slaying the Chimaera would be an allegory of the overcoming of death and evil, a Christianized pagan allegory drawn from that traditional storehouse of Graeco-Roman mythology that was the fourth century Christian's cultural heritage. And it is of interest to remember that in the Lullingstone Villa the Christian paintings (the three *Chi Rhos* and the *Orans*, etc., figures) were in a room adjacent to that in which was laid the Bellerophon mosaic and that the paintings and the mosaic were probably contemporary."

Dr W. H. C. Frend forms the same conclusions in considering the Lullingstone mosaics, where he writes in regard to the evil eye:—[24]

"At Lullingstone, for instance, the great mosaic, probably of Constantinian date, in the east room contains three elements, each with a magical or religious significance. The principal panel contains in the four corners roundels of the Four Seasons and within a curving *guilloche* zone is a picture of Bellerophon mounted on Pegasus slaying the Chimaera with his spear. Secondly, there is the rape of Europa by the Bull, with which is associated the inscription . . ." (which he quotes with translation). "Thirdly, there are the swastikas and hearts and floral designs which form the border round the whole mosaic. The Four Seasons occurs also at Brading in the Isle of Wight, Chedworth, and Bignor. They are the symbol of the continuance of life here and hereafter

[23] *Journal of Roman Studies*, liv (1964), 7–14.
[24] *op. cit.* in n. 21, 14–5.

after the pattern of the seasons, and also of the essential harmony of the universe." He continues, "The panel representing Europa and the Bull seems at first sight to be an ordinary copy of a mythological scene, but note the choice of verse in the couplet. It opens with the word for jealousy, *invida*. The Evil Eye was 'jealous', and on half-a-dozen Christian and pagan sites in Africa of this period, we find verses in mosaic beginning with this word. They were to prevent the Evil Eye from possessing the house. The same may be said of the swastikas and hearts. Both designs are found worn as amulets which have turned up on sacred sites from one end of the Roman world to the other. The object was to banish evil from the wearer."

Professor Toynbee underlines these comments:—[25]

"Such scenes of rape and the overthrow of evil monsters could allude to death and the Soul's victory over it."

And in reference to Bellerophon and the Seasons:—

"If the slaying of the monster denotes the Soul's victory over death, the Seasons would be an allegory of its everlasting bliss in paradise."

These interesting and authoritative interpretations might suggest that at Lullingstone the mosaic floors were laid down at the same time as when the Christian rooms received their wall-decoration. On consideration, however, this seems unlikely. A family, suddenly converted to devout Christians, would surely be thoroughly imbued with Christian ideas, which ought perhaps to have been directly reflected in the design of the mosaic floors. But these floors bear no positive Christian symbols, only pagan mythological scenes from which Christian allusions may have been drawn. As with the mosaic floors at Hinton St. Mary, in Dorset, and at Frampton in the same county, where a *Chi Rho* was prominently displayed in the mosaic scheme, the Lullingstone floors might have been expected to incorporate such direct references to Christianity. But this does not occur; the suggestion that the floors were already laid before the Christian wall-paintings were begun depends largely upon this difference between the mosaics and the decoration of the house-church.

It was important to discover whether or not the central rooms showed signs of occupation when the final destruction took place; excavation showed that these rooms were empty of furniture when fire destroyed the building; no fragments of carbonized wood that might have been shaped for furniture, nor any bronze finials or domed studs for upholstery, were found. This fact suggests that these two rooms may already have changed from secular use to a Christian assembly-room towards the end. The pagan mythological scenes, therefore, could indeed at this late time have provided religious thought complementary to that derived from direct Christian symbols displayed in the house-church.

The Entrance Corridor (Fig. 5b)

This corridor, 9·95 m. long and 2·44 m. wide, lies north–south on the exterior of the Reception Room 13. It is treated separately from the mosaic rooms and the north and south corridors, as it exhibits evidence of successive phases of occupation from the first to the fifth centuries. Its northern end is of particular interest as it was here that successive entrances to the Deep Room were constructed, remains of all being found to underlie the upper levels contemporary with the laying down of the mosaic floors in the rooms to the west of it. These earlier constructions are described under *The Deep Room in the First Century* (Part I).

When the Deep Room was reorganized to provide a *nymphaeum c.* A.D. 180, the Period

[25] *op. cit.* in n. 4, 14, 201.

IA staircase at the north end of the entrance corridor was wrecked and filled up with rubble, the aperture in the wall of the Deep Room being filled with coursed flints. The corridor received at this time a concrete surface, rising at a slight gradient from the east wall to the west wall, completely sealing the remains of the Period I and IA constructions. This concrete surface led down to a newly-built entrance in the east wall, the foundation piers for its wooden portico having been built out at right-angles, where they joined the remains of a wall further east and parallel with the east wall of the corridor. This fragmentary wall appears by construction to belong to the Period I plan. Nothing is known of its purpose, but it may have been merely for a verandah facing the river. These foundation piers were 0·61 m. thick and set 2·89 m. apart. It is likely that the main reception room was situated at this time where the large mosaic floor was later sited, though for obvious reasons it has not been feasible to excavate beneath the mosaic floor or the tessellated surround to check the late second-century level.

No positive evidence of any third-century work was found in this entrance corridor, but considerable additions were made in the fourth century. The second-century concrete floor had become very dilapidated, and patches of red clay were inserted to level up its surface. A further rendering of *opus signinum*, in places nearly 7·5 cm. thick, was laid down over this old surface, again sloping slightly downwards towards the east, where it met the top of the east wall of the corridor. This new floor continued upwards to an entrance into the Reception Room 13, an entrance 3·05 m. wide, certainly too wide for a single door, and even for a double door. This wide doorway was carefully investigated. Burnt débris from the final destruction of the house lay upon the wall foundations on either side of the doorway and directly upon the tessellated floor, which here had been laid within the doorway, bounded on north and south by the outward curves of the *opus signinum* surround of the room. It was noticed that the *tesserae* sloped downwards towards the east all along the doorway, and had become disinarticulated, indicating that an existing wooden sleeper-beam had either been subsequently robbed out or had been destroyed by the fire. The former is more likely, as the amount of carbonized wood *in situ* was quite insufficient for a complete beam. The upper part had no doubt become charred, but in the main the beam, being bedded down, would have been little affected by the fire, and might have still proved suitable for use elsewhere.

This beam had been approximately 3·66 m. long, 0·15 m. high, and 0·175 m. wide, and it had extended for 0·30 m. at either end beyond the entrance, terminating in two roughly circular, shallow, post-holes, each approximately 0·15 m. in diameter (Fig. 5a). These post-holes had served as sockets for wooden uprights, probably mortised into the sleeper-beam, and the absence of iron hinges at either end suggests that doors were not hung upon them. The entrance, being within the house, may simply have been provided with heavy curtains only; there was no indication of sliding doors.

There was a suggestion of a blocking of the entrance towards the end of the occupation of the house; a loose, dry flint packing was observed along the entrance in prolongation with the walls, and this may have supported a flimsy wood and daub partition. But the evidence for this was slight, and the point is recorded merely as a possibility.

The laying down of the mosaic floors is well dated to *c.* A.D. 330–360, and these additions, doorway and *opus signinum* surfacing, were effected at the same time.

The new reception room was provided with a drain in its north-east corner, made of pairs of *imbrices* (Pl. XVIIIb), and this drain passed through the west wall of the entrance corridor, being continued across it, and apparently ending upon the top of its east wall foundation, or perhaps originally penetrating the wall, thus carrying away water from washing-down the mosaic floor to the east exterior of the house, where it probably fell directly upon the garden level. This continuation of the drain *imbrices* over the surface of the corridor at a slight downward gradient extended for 1·67 m. from the west wall, two of the covering *imbrices* being still *in situ*; but eastwards of this point the covering *imbrices* were found to be missing. It is probable, also, that this drainage proved insufficient for the volume of water, or that it leaked—the *imbrices* were not mortared together—for a large patch of chalk had later been spread over this part of the corridor to facilitate disposal of the overflow, a patch of irregular shape, approximately 1·67 m. by 0·91 m. This inefficient arrangement underlines the curious squalor that is seen round the reception room as the fourth century drew to its close, especially in evidence in the south corridor. This highest and latest surface of the entrance corridor had here and there been further patched with poor concrete and was found to be in a very worn and dilapidated condition, unrepaired and apparently uncared-for by the time of the final fire.

Room 15 (Figs. 17a and 18)

This room is situated immediately south of the south corridor of the reception room. On excavation, it was found to be floored throughout with white concrete, varying in thickness from 7·5 cm. to 0·15 m. There were signs that the top surface of this concrete floor had been rendered with an *opus signinum* finish, but the whole floor showed extensive disintegration, probably by long exposure to the open air, and was much patched with chalk and rubble. It had probably been laid down as part of the extensive alterations to the house at the end of the second century, being re-surfaced when the fourth-century mosaic rooms and corridors were constructed, and subsequently patched as necessary during that century when it was an unroofed open space. The floor was level, contrasting with the courses of flints in the earlier south wall, which had been built on a slight gradient downwards from west to east, the original excavation of the natural slope having been made only approximately to the horizontal.

The Corridor 17 leading to the baths remained a covered way, its east side becoming an open verandah with three square brick bases, each 0·25 m. square, within the open area of Room 15. These brick bases or piers were not the remnants of pilasters rising to roof level, but originally supported three stout timber uprights forming part of the corridor structure during the fourth century. The centre brick pier was found to cant slightly towards the east, pointing to an outward thrust of the corridor roof at this spot; beneath it was a post-hole, 7·5 cm. in diameter and 0.30 m. deep, slightly tapered at the bottom, where a wooden support had been driven in when the concrete floor was laid down, to give further strength. This weakness was apparent from the late second century onwards, both post-hole and brick pier showing this, the former having been an attempt to correct it.

The concrete floor extended up to the south wall of the south corridor of the reception room, covering an area 4·57 m. from north to south, and 4·88 m. from west to east. Before considering the levels sealed by it, it is convenient first to detail its history in the fourth century, when, as has been said, it was an open space. It was notable that, unlike the

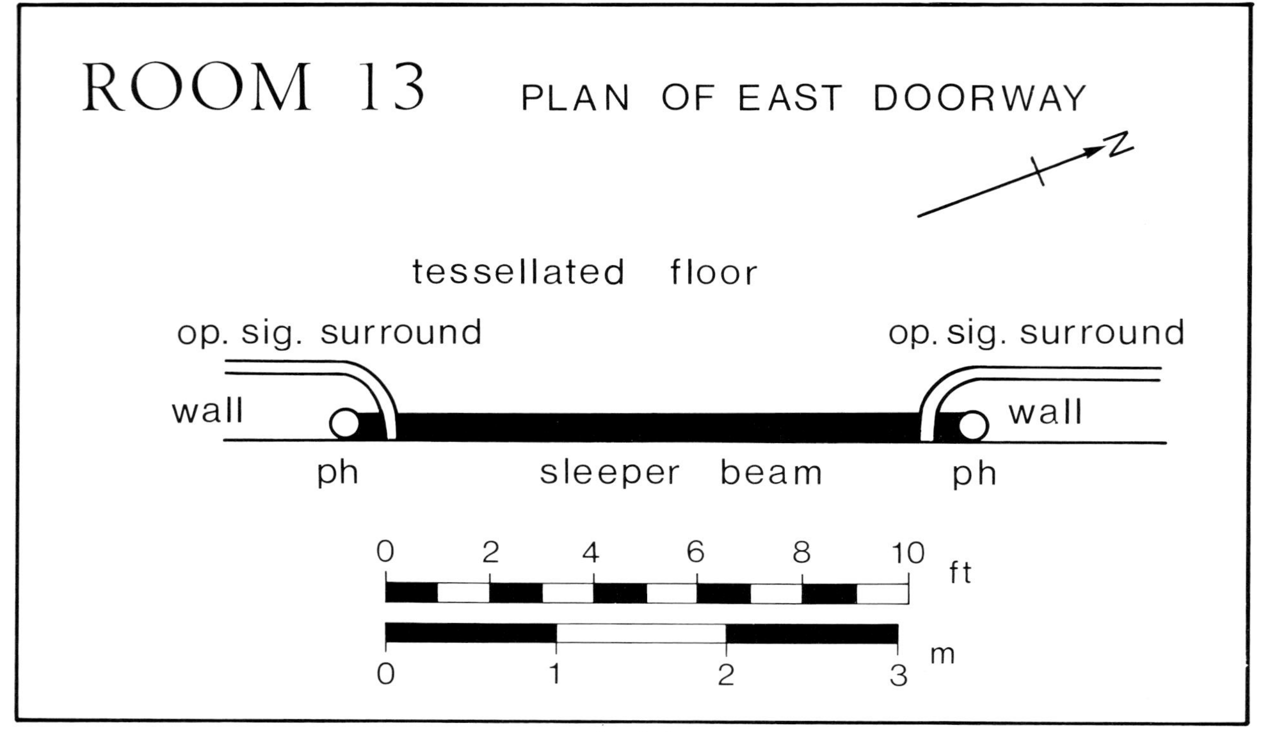
ROOM 13
PLAN OF EAST DOORWAY
N
tessellated floor
op. sig. surround
op. sig. surround
wall
wall
ph
sleeper beam
ph
0 2 4 6 8 10 ft
0 1 2 3 m

Fig. 5(a).

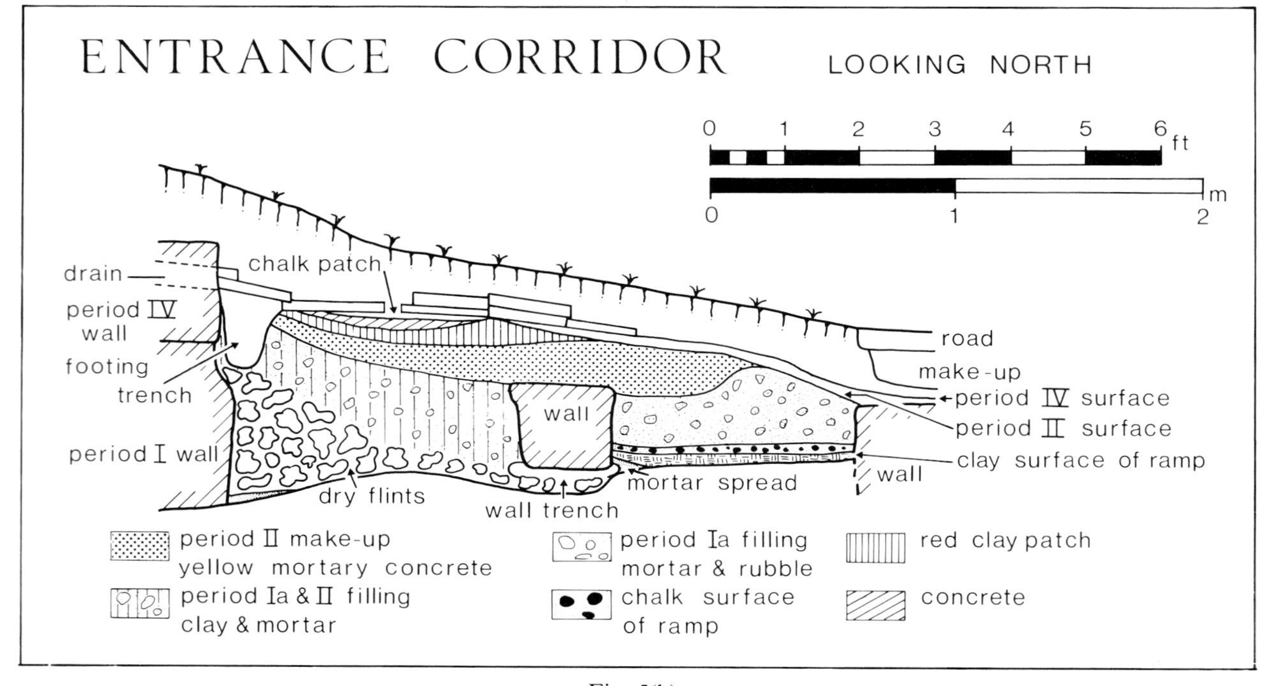
ENTRANCE CORRIDOR
LOOKING NORTH
0 1 2 3 4 5 6 ft
0 1 2 m
drain
chalk patch
period IV wall
footing trench
period I wall
dry flints
wall
wall trench
mortar spread
road
make-up
period IV surface
period II surface
clay surface of ramp
wall
period II make-up yellow mortary concrete
period Ia & II filling clay & mortar
period Ia filling mortar & rubble
chalk surface of ramp
red clay patch
concrete

Fig. 5(b).

neighbouring mosaic rooms and their corridors, no destruction level lay upon the concrete floor, with no tile fall, which was abundant elsewhere, and which would certainly have been in evidence had the room been roofed. Room 15 was a diminutive courtyard or semi-peristyle within the house.

During the fourth century a small, roughly semi-circular, pit, 1·22 m. wide, was dug through the concrete floor against the south wall, 1·98 m. from the west wall and 1·67 m. from the east wall, and in it was placed a large storage jar, inclined at an angle of 30 degrees from the vertical towards the north, its top broken away to provide a wide opening, and its base thrust downwards to facilitate drainage (Fig. 17b). Earthy rubble was filled in round the lower portion of the jar to stabilize it in this position, and it was further wedged in place by large fragments of brick and with the major part of a colour-coated bowl, probably an import from East Gaul. The storage jar was made at the potteries in Alice Holt forest, near Farnham, Surrey, and is one of four such immense jars which the house possessed during the fourth century. This was its secondary use; its interior showed a horizontal, circular stain caused when it had previously stood elsewhere in an upright position, probably as a receptacle for water.

This pit, with the storage jar, was intended for use as a latrine, being, as it was, conveniently close to the dining apartment. It has been described as a kitchen pit, but a further assessment of the coins it contained shows that it was dug at the same time as the kitchen pit at the north end of the back corridor of the house, Room 11, going out of use and being filled in *c.* A.D. 350, some few years before the pit in Room 11. Both pits contained sufficient coins to provide datings as follows:

Room 11.	13 coins	*c.* A.D. 330–361.
Room 15.	20 coins	*c.* A.D. 330–350.

It is possible that the dining apartment no longer served this function when the kitchen in the back corridor ceased to be used after *c.* A.D. 361, though the life of the coins may extend this time. But the absence of Valentinian coins points to its end before *c.* A.D. 364–378. The Christian house-church and its associated rooms having been constructed not long afterwards, *c.* A.D. 380–385, secular use of the dining apartment and reception room may have changed in character or even ceased altogether.

The twenty coins in the pit in Room 15 consisted of: 5 Constantine I, 1 Helena, 4 Crispus, 2 Constantine II *Caesar,* 1 Constans *Caesar,* 5 House of Constantine, 1 Constans *Augustus,* and 1 minim. One Constantine I lay beneath the storage jar; the Constans *Caesar* lay low in the filling beside the base of the jar; the Constans *Augustus* was within 0·15 m. of the top of the jar filling; the five House of Constantine lay within 5 cm. and 0·37 m. of the surface of the pit filling; the minim was recovered from a second examination of the jar filling, and it is clear that such minims were in use in the Constantinian period. No *Fel. Temp. Rep.* coins were found.

Besides the coins, which were well scattered throughout the pit filling, the latter contained a bronze "Lion Mask" axle-cap, a circular iron padlock and chain, fragments of at least four small, thin glass beakers, and parts of a glass bowl, decorated with a draped female figure holding a long staff and standing amid trees and foliage. This decoration was made with a buffing-wheel operated vertically, and is typical of such decorated glass bowls imported from the Rhineland in the earlier part of the fourth century. The group of pottery from the pit includes the East Gaulish bowl previously mentioned, a typical *mortarium,* and two examples of metallic-glazed and rouletted Castor-ware box-lids. This group can be closely dated by the coins to the twenty years *c.* A.D. 330–350, as can the glass bowl and beakers, and the other objects of metal.

The latrine may have been provided with a light partition placed around it, but no evidence of this came to light in spite of a close examination of the surrounding concrete floor. From this floor were recovered the following coins: 1 Carausius, 1 Constantine I (sealed by patching), 1 Constantius II *Caesar*, 1 Constans *Augustus*, 1 Constantinopolis, 1 House of Constantine, 1 Gratian, 1 Arcadius, and 3 minims. Both the Gratian and the Arcadius coins lay upon the concrete floor, which clearly continued in use as an open space until the final destruction of the house.

Some modification appears to have taken place during the fourth century. An intermittent line of cement and plaster lay west–east, about 0·30 m. south of the south corridor of the reception room, and three small post-holes were found along this line, 1·29 m., 1·67 m., and 3·96 m. respectively from the west wall of the room. A light partition is indicated, which may have existed only for a short time. In the filling of the centre post-hole was a minim. It is not possible to assign this slight construction with any certainty either to the Constantinian period or to the late fourth or early fifth centuries; the latter may be the more likely.

To this last period of the occupation of the house is assigned an infant burial, cut through the concrete floor. Roughly circular in shape, 0·43 m. long by 0·38 m. wide, it had been cut at a point 1·67 m. west of the east wall, by chance over an earlier wall (see below), concealed by the floor, which formed its base. The hole was therefore very shallow, and the major part of the infant had been removed after burial, leaving the skull, some ribs, with a few fragments of the arm and leg bones. The burial was accompanied by 4 minims, 2 minimi, a fragment of figured bronze from a large vessel, a sherd of undatable pottery, and a handful of carbonized wheat. Neither the sex nor the age of the infant is known, but the age might lie within the last month of pre-natal life and the end of the first month of infancy. If, as the minims and minimi suggest, the burial took place towards the end of the existence of the house, when Christianity had been adopted for some time by the inhabitants, it is at first sight a curious reflection upon the early Christian mind and practice. But a suggestion may be offered. The burial, with its accompanying objects, including the handful of grains of wheat, would seem to be pagan; and it will be remembered that in the Deep Room, beneath the Christian house-church, libations were still being made to the *manes* of the persons whose features were portrayed by the marble busts, right up to the end. A second manifestation of paganism is indicated by this infant burial. It seems likely, therefore, that some of the people connected with the villa still preserved their paganism, possibly the workers and menials rather than the owner and his family; and the burial was probably made by the former. Again, as it is likely that towards the end secular habitation had given way to an establishment predominantly devoted to Christian worship, the burial would have been made outside the rooms so devoted; the ritual connected with the marble busts may also have been considered to take place outside, though below, the Christian house-church. Pagan practices and Christian ritual were running side by side, and it is even possible that the propinquity of the pagan infant burial to the Christian establishment may have been considered as a prophylactic against Christianity by those who made it. We do not know how integrated, if at all, were the villa inhabitants in religious matters, nor how those who still followed paganism regarded those who had been converted to Christianity, nor the attitude of the latter towards the conservatism of paganism, which was evidently very strong when we consider the policy of the emperor Julian (A.D. 360–363), and the widespread building of pagan temples in Roman Britain late in the fourth century.

On removal of the concrete floor of the room, the hidden wall, briefly referred to above, was revealed. It extended northwards for 3·50 m., and then turned at a right-angle eastwards, continuing for 3·66 m. until it joined the main north–south wall. It thus enclosed a virtually square apartment. All four bounding walls of this apartment are of Period I (*c*. A.D. 80–90), and both lengths of the hidden wall, which was 0·45 m. wide, showed a top surface smoothly finished in yellow mortar, slotted and bevelled to take large horizontal timber beams, the mortar showing many impressions of studded sandals or boots and the paw-marks of dogs. This suggests wooden internal partitions within the Period I house, and the absence beneath the concrete floor of Antonine pottery, which is abundant wherever the late second-century alterations were made, demonstrates the level below the concrete floor to have been of the earlier period. This is confirmed by the presence of first-century pottery in a clay and gravel level averaging 0·22 m. in thickness bounded by the hidden wall; and in addition, a brooch of Hod Hill type, dated to the period Tiberius–Nero, was found in this clay and gravel level. Also, in the clay-with-flint packing immediately east of the main first-century wall bounding Room 15 on the east, was found a brooch of Colchester type, of Flavian date, at the same level as the clay and gravel level inside the room. The footing-trench, sealed by the concrete floor, contained first-century pottery of Belgic derivation. The wall itself was well-built and finished, with offsets on either side, in the excellent style that may be associated with professional surveying and building in the first century. This footing-trench, extending downwards for 0·17 m. to the offsets in the wall, and thence a further 0·48 m. to the bottom of the wall, impinged upon flint rubble on which the wall had been built in a shallow slot, on either side of which was an extensive horizontal mortar spread. The faces of this wall were cleanly finished, the mortar smoothed by some form of shuttering. Owing to the slope of the ground, the wall was found to lean very slightly out of the vertical towards the flood-plain. The west wall of Room 15 still stood firmly founded in a vertical position.

The clay and gravel level of Period I within the hidden first-century walls contained in places a very thin, horizontal band of carbonized wood; but this was not sufficient to indicate that this part of the house had been burnt at an early date; the carbonized remains may have been those of thin horizontal planks, either of a floor, or used to level up and stabilize the clay and gravel level.

A further interesting discovery was made on removal of the concrete floor in the south-west part of the room. A compact deposit of four large ingots and a roughly circular casting, all of a mixture of copper and lead, accompanied by a large pottery vessel of Patch Grove type, had been placed in a small pit dug for their reception, between the hidden wall and the west wall of the room, and about 1·37 m. north of its south wall. The pit was roughly rectangular, some 0·61 m. north–south and 0·5 m. east–west, and dug to a depth of approximately 0·61 m. down from the underside of the concrete floor which covered it. The ingots were placed on edge in front of one another, with the casting behind them, also standing on edge and nearly vertical (Pl. XVIIId). The Patch Grove vessel had been placed upon the ingots at the north end, and partly rested against the north end of the casting, the whole closely packed together (Pl. XVIIIc). The upper 0·10 m. of the vessel, however, had been broken away when the concrete floor was laid over the deposit, though parts of the rim and shoulder lay broken off the vessel; and this has allowed it to be completely reconstructed. A further packing of clay and small flints had been laid over the whole deposit as a foundation for the floor at this point. The disposition of ingots and casting shows that they were deposited between the walls when the latter were already built, and their stratigraphical position places them in the first century, the accompanying Patch Grove vessel reinforcing that time for the burial of the deposit. As we know that the house was not constructed in flint and mortar until *c.* A.D. 80–90, the deposit must have taken place not long after this.

All four ingots are of the same size, 0·35 m. by 0·12 m. by 0·03 m., the casting having a mean diameter of 0·50 m. The composition of both ingots and casting is the same, 60% copper and 40% lead. The large proportion of lead makes the objects extremely heavy for their size. No marks or *graffiti* are visible upon their surfaces, which are uniformly corroded, and it is not possible to explain positively for what purpose they were to be used, or the reason why they were buried. The relative content of copper and lead might indicate that the area from which the objects came may have been North Wales, where both copper and lead were apparently being mined in close proximity. But this is pure conjecture. In any event, in their final form they had probably been part of the stock of a bronze-smith, using a large amount of lead in his mixtures. They could, again, have been acquired by the owner of the house for local manufacture of household objects and ornaments, and he may have hidden them at some time of danger or disturbance in the countryside; the fact that they were never recovered would therefore suggest that this owner did not survive or return. In any event, a deposit of this size and importance is rare in the civil zone of Roman Britain, especially within a house.

PART III

THE AUXILIARY STRUCTURES

The Baths—Rooms 16–23 and Well, 24
The Kitchen Area
The Tannery and Drainage Pit

The Baths (Pl. XIXa, Fig. 19)

As with so many Romano-British villas, the Lullingstone house contained a large and extensive baths. Its proportions were more than ample when regard is made to the probable size of the family, and indeed it accounted for almost 25 per cent of the total area of the residence. It was also very compactly designed. The original house of the late first century was not, it seems, provided with an adjacent bath suite; if one did exist, it must have been well separated from the building and still awaits discovery.

In the last quarter of the second century, the reconstruction and enlargement of the whole house transformed it from its more modest aspect to one of impressive size and arrangement. The natural slope westward from the flood-plain had already been utilized for the siting of the Deep Room at the north; and advantage was taken of this natural feature to create a shallow terracing at two levels. Flights of tiled steps were inserted at both the north and south ends of the house, the former to conduct the inhabitants down to the Deep Room which was now transformed into a shrine for the cult of the water spirits; the latter, exterior to and adjoining the south wall of the house, to lead down to the new baths which was now added here. This flight of steps was found on excavation to have been largely robbed of its tiles, but the flint courses that separated the treaders were still in place, and as the photograph shows (Pl. XIXb) the steps were clearly indicated though only the lowest two treaders retained their tiles intact. The steps, seven in number, do not appear all to have had the same widths though their lengths were the same, namely 1·14 m., each being faced with four re-used *tegulae* in a line, the risers being of well-smoothed pink cement. At the level of the third step from the bottom a doorway spanned the flight, its posts founded upon cemented tiles. No actual door is likely to have swung here, but thick curtains may suitably have been suspended to exclude the draught from the house-corridor, Room 17, which would otherwise have proved inconvenient to the bathers in the rooms below.

Before discussing the baths in detail, it is convenient shortly to summarize the different types of rooms it contained and to provide a series of dates for its construction, reconstruction and final destruction. The rooms consisted of a Cold Room 19 leading directly to a large Cold Plunge Bath 23, a Tepid Room 20, a Hot Room 21 with Hot Bath 22 leading off it, and with a small Cold Plunge Bath 23 at its eastern end and next to the large cold plunge bath. The heat was generated in a large Furnace 16 at the west end, and north of this, abutting on the staircase, was an additional room with an open side on the west, whose purpose is unknown. Westwards of the furnace was an extensive levelled area, probably for the storage of fuel which would have consisted of cut logs and heavy brushwood. For the first period of its use the baths was supplied with water from a Well 24 situated 4·27 m. to the southward.

The dating for the construction of the baths is obtained by a study of the earliest levels in the cold room, of the exterior drain of the hot bath, which contained a Colchester-type brooch of Vespasianic date, of the filling beneath the stairs, and of a long westward section which was cut immediately outside the furnace. The dating for the reconstructions is obtained from a study of the superimposed floors of the cold room, and the dating for the final period and disuse of the baths is obtained from a study of the late fourth-century fillings within the various rooms. The filling of the well also provides confirming evidence for the earlier use of the baths; but it should be said here that after the abandonment of the house *c*. A.D. 200, the flint lining of the well having collapsed, it speedily became filled to the surface. No site for subsequent water-supply has as yet been discovered.

The dating thus obtained are:

Construction of the baths	*c*. A.D. 180
First reconstruction	*c*. A.D. 280
Alterations	*c*. A.D. 300
Second reconstruction	*c*. A.D. 340
Disuse and destruction of the baths	*c*. A.D. 380–390

At the bottom of the stairs, where the doorway opened into the baths at the floor level of the rooms, a narrow corridor stretched towards the east; its extent cannot be estimated, but it was found to have led into the area occupied by the cold room and the cold plunge bath. The south wall of this corridor was built of clay, probably revetted with wattles and supported upon a flint and mortar base in a shallow trench. The clay wall probably began at floor level, and it was decorated with painted wall-plaster depicting an attempt at marbling on a pink ground with occasional narrow green bands edged with black upon a white ground, which may have formed part of painted panelling resting upon a marbled dado.

The Cold Room 19 (Fig. 21a)

This room measured 4·70 m. north–south and extended for 5·33 m. to the point where it descended by concrete steps into the large cold plunge bath. Here the modern sewer-trench has destroyed the connection, which can only be assessed by step levels, which in turn depend upon a consistent height and width of each step based on the dimensions of the remaining one (Fig. 22b). The floors of the narrow north corridor and of the cold room had been tessellated with red-brick *tesserae* very cleanly cut and showing little sign of wear. They are generally smaller and of nearer cubic shape than the red-brick *tesserae* of the later floor, which was subsequently laid at a higher level. The *tesserae* of this first floor also include a few made from yellow tile which occurs at Lullingstone in contexts not later than the second century. At the junction of this floor and the walls was a quarter-round moulding of pink cement which sealed the *tesserae* next to the walls (Pl. XXa). Towards the south side of the room a large number of white and grey mosaic *tesserae,* with a quantity cut from samian vessels, suggests that a mosaic panel may have occupied part of the floor here. They are, however, loose and out of place and furnish no idea of the subject of such a panel. That the *tesserae* of this first floor has been for the most part removed after a short period of use is suggested by very evident lack of wear. At a point very nearly central in the room was placed a complete samian bowl (Form 18/31) with the stamp of PATERATVS upon the basal interior, and a small knob of cement beneath the bowl appears to have been so placed to keep it in position. The working life of this potter lay within the Antonine period, probably after A.D. 150 rather than before that date, and the presence of the bowl upon the floor suggests an Antonine date for the construction of the floor, and by implication for the foundation of the baths. Many fragments of samian vessels were subsequently found mixed with a loose mosaic *tesserae,* and included fragments of a second identical bowl also bearing the PATERATVS stamp, which was probably from the same die. Much of this material still remains sealed beneath the later re-flooring of the room.

The floor of the cold room extended eastwards to the cold plunge bath which formed an extension of it. The bath, 2·44 m. wide from north to south by 3·20 m. from west to east, was constructed with walls of flint and yellow mortar averaging 0·45 m. in thickness west–east and 0·81 m. along the east side, where the alluvium of the flood-plain required a stouter wall with brick coursing at the corners. The floor was of cement averaging 0·25 m. in thickness and was floated over a foundation of flints and cement. The surface of the floor was 1·06 m. below that of the cold room, but whether there existed steps or whether there was a vertical drop into the bath is uncertain. The outlet was not discovered, and no evidence of internal rendering of the walls or of any quarter-round moulding was found.

The reconstruction of *c.* A.D. 280 involved a new floor to the cold room and the insertion into the cold plunge bath of a tiled floor with a step with moulded edge extending the full width. The narrow corridor before referred to was now disused and its painted clay wall on the south was removed, a new floor being laid overall. Rubble make-up was inserted over the remains of the earlier floor, and the new floor was also of red-brick *tesserae* with a small angular pink cement moulding against the wall, which received a second plaster rendering of plain pink slightly speckled with red. The complete PATERATVS bowl may have been centrally placed in the middle of the earliest floor for ritualistic purposes before it was covered by the new rubble foundation for the later floor; the presence of fragments, however, of the second PATERATVS bowl with much other smashed samian towards the south does not seem to confirm this—the bowl in the centre of the room, though clearly specially placed there, has no positive significance. The mosaic panel, if such existed, was taken up before the later floor was laid, many individual *tesserae* being left. The samian *tesserae* found in the granary (Part IV), which was built *c.* A.D. 280, may have come from this cold room. The floor of the cold plunge bath was heightened by 0·25 m., flints were packed over the existing floor, white cement being floated over them, the surface of which received a floor of tiles 0·30 m. square. A quarter-round moulding of *opus signinum* was fitted round the sides and the walls were rendered with the same material smoothed to a finish and painted red. This floor did not serve for long. A second level of tiles was fitted upon the first and a second quarter-round moulding, also of *opus signinum* and slightly larger than the one it now concealed, was also provided. The walls retained their first rendering. This second floor lay some 0·91 m. below the level of the later floor of the cold room, and a step the whole width of the bath was constructed to lead directly down into the bath from the floor of the cold room. The *opus signinum* rendering of the walls was carried up for a distance of 0·40 m., where it turned vertically for another 0·50 m. where it was probably smoothed over to join the re-turned vertically for another 0·50 m. where it was probably smoother over to join the re-levelled floor of the cold room. The outflow was constructed of tiles, rectangular in section, at a point in the south wall 0·61 m. from the east side of the bath. There was no exterior drain or specially made sump—the water poured out directly upon the alluvium to spread out and be absorbed in it. No relics were found beneath this outflow.

The cold room with its cold plunge bath became disused and continued so for much of the third century, in common with the rest of the house. Reconstruction took place, however, late in that century, and not only was the floor of the cold room levelled, but the northern part of that floor was packed with rubble to conform with the rest of the floor, and what appears to have been a wooden floor was placed, perhaps temporarily, upon this *c.* A.D. 300. This later floor contained a number of conical post-holes averaging 7·5 cm. at the top and 0·15 m. in depth, all clearly having held pointed stakes; and although at least two lines of such post-holes could be recognized, the shape and purpose of the temporary structure cannot be gauged. However, in the carbonized level beside one of these post-holes was found a worn *antoninianus* of Claudius II (A.D. 268–270), while in the charcoal contained in another post-hole was found an *antoninianus* in good condition of Allectus (A.D. 293–296). Both these coins were securely sealed by the mid-fourth-century concrete floor, and together with the post-holes and the wooden floor are transitional between the late third-century reconstruction and the further reconstruction in the fourth century. The first use of the cold room and the cold plunge bath lies between the late-Antonine construction of the baths and the early years of the third century; the late third-century use perhaps extended into the fourth century, when the further and last reconstruction took place.

This last reconstruction was ushered in by the laying directly upon the carbonized remains of the wooden structure, which appears to have been destroyed by fire, of a heavy floor of pink concrete, incorporating small stones and pebbles and with its surface smoothed to a fine finish. This floor averaged 7·5 cm. in thickness and was furnished with a very large quarter-round moulding throughout, the walls being rendered with a fresh facing, this time of plain pink plaster. Part of this floor was removed by the excavators and a coin of Constantine II as *Augustus* (A.D. 337–340) was recovered from the mortar, having been mixed in with it when the floor was laid. Fragments of late colour-coated wares and of late Castor vessels were also recovered from the body of this floor.

With this last reconstruction came a radical alteration to the cold plunge bath, with the construction beside it on the south of a small additional cold bath. The floor of the large cold bath was raised 0·35 m., attaining now a height of approximately 0·61 m. above the earliest floor. The reason for this heightening of the floor may have been due to a climatic change or a land-tilt which might have obliged the builders to construct a higher outflow involving a shallower bath. At any rate, from a bath in which one could swim in its early period, and easily immerse oneself even after the first reconstruction, the depth of the bath in the last period was reduced to 0·61 m., the successive depths being:

Original building	1·06 m.
First reconstruction	0·83 m.
Second reconstruction	0·61 m.

As the cold room was doubtless used for undressing and dressing, it is unlikely that the floor was awash, the bath being therefore inconveniently shallow, swimming for an adult being difficult.

This new floor of the bath was laid upon a base of puddled chalk which in turn rested upon three successive layers of chalk blocks placed upon the remaining tiles of the middle floor. This new floor was made of *opus signinum,* 0·12 m. thick beneath the step and sloping very gradually to a thickness of a little under 7·5 cm. at the east, where the outflow was made above the previous outflow. This floor was then fitted overall with square red tiles with a quarter-round moulding of *opus signinum* throughout. Up to this final reconstruction the bath had been rectangular, but now 0·61 m. were removed from the west–east dimension, resulting in a square bath, and these 0·61 m. were packed with coursed flints in cement, thus providing with the original east wall a new wall 1·42 m. in thickness which might have been considered suitable to buttress this part of the bath building where it projected out into the soft alluvium of the flood-plain.

The step up to the floor of the cold room, constructed in the late third century, was not retained. It was packed with flints, and a face of *opus signinum* rose vertically from the quarter-round moulding for a height of 0·30 m. where it was smoothed over horizontally to form a new step, higher than the previous step which it now concealed, and extending back horizontally for 0·20 m., whence it turned vertically again, rising against the original face for a height of 0·35 m. and joining the latest floor of the cold room which was extended eastwards to meet it. The angle was probably rounded over as with the previous step.

The new small cold bath was built on the east exterior of the hot room and abutted on to the south side of the large cold bath. A foundation of flints was spread upon the alluvium at this point and consolidated with cement, and upon this was laid a fine pink *opus signinum* floor edged all round with a small quarter-round moulding. 1·83 m. from north to south, and 1·22 m. from west to east, the little bath possessed a curious re-entrant at its north-west corner, lessening the capacity of the bath. At this point the original wall appeared to remain truncated, and its existence may have conditioned the re-entrant. The sides of the bath were rendered in smooth pink cement; the outflow in the middle of the east side was well constructed in the cement, the water draining away upon the exterior alluvium as in the case of the large cold bath. The necessity for an additional cold bath, and so small a one at that, is not apparent, unless it was intended for the children, the large bath being retained for the adult members of the family; both baths were in use together. The soak-away area of each outflow contained at the top Roman level a few fragments of late fourth-century pottery and two coins, an imitation Constantinopolis (A.D. 330–335) and a radiate minim, which may perhaps be assigned to the late fourth-century series of such coins. The floors of both cold plunge baths were found to have been damaged by medieval robber-pits, probably of the fourteenth century and presumably dug in search of tiles for building material.

The cold plunge baths continued in use until *c.* A.D. 385. The whole baths were then dismantled, the floors of the cold room, tepid room, hot room and hot bath were totally removed with their supporting *pilae,* and the establishment thus ruined was filled up with tips of earth and rubble. Occupation of the villa continued, however, into the early fifth century, and it is indeed possible that this dismantling may have taken place when Christianity was adopted by the inhabitants; but the rapidly deteriorating economic situation that supervened towards the end of the fourth century may have rendered the upkeep of so extensive a series of rooms too costly, especially when coupled with the probable cessation of cheap household labour. The Valentinian use of the baths and the later overspread is supported by the coin evidence from the back-fillings after all necessary building materials had been removed. A coin of Gratian (A.D. 367–383) lay upon the latest tessellated floor at the bottom of the stairs, sealed by successive rubbish tips, which also contained a coin of Valens (A.D. 364–378); and a coin of Valentinian II (A.D. 383–392) lay beneath six successive tips in the hot bath. The majority of the succeeding coins of the House of Theodosius were found in the northern part of the villa in association with the Christian rooms. A large quantity of broken roof-tiles and hypocaust-tiles lay over the floor of the cold room, the hypocaust-tiles showing a large number of different varieties of roller-patterns.[26] These tiles may have been used in the construction and reconstruction of the baths; one box-flue tile with diamond pattern still remains *in situ* in the hot bath, where it forms part of the rising flue in the south-west corner.

The following investigations into other parts of the baths have confirmed the general dating picture.

The Furnace 16

A study of the fillings of the furnace and of the two sections leading to it from the north and from the west (Figs. 20a and b) was most informative. The furnace had been cut out of the natural chalk in the shape of a rectangle, the sides sloping down to a shallow channel in the centre leading to the main flue. The furnace had been cleaned out at the last reconstruction, but fragments of metallic-glazed Rhenish ware remained in the earliest trodden level, suggesting the late second century for first use. Later rake-back deposits had not been removed except towards the mouth of the flue and, forming together a mass of laminated levels of charcoal and thin clay seals rising to a height at the west end of the furnace of 1·06 m. showed a latest trodden surface of thick carbonized material sloping up from the flue-mouth at a steep angle. This top level contained fragments of fourth-century flanged pie-dishes and red colour-coated rosetted ware. Evidence of wall and roof destruction lay over this and over the west end of the furnace, sealing a truncated wall, and over the deposits inside was a clay seal averaging 0·35 m. in thickness. The surface of this clay seal had a semi-circular pattern of seven small post-holes upon it, but their significance is unknown. The radius of this semi-circle was approximately 0·61 m., and the arc covered was approximately 1·37 m., the post-holes being equidistant.

The entrance to the main flue lies 4·27m. from the back wall of the furnace and is 0·61 m. wide, its sides built of large, roughly squared blocks of Kentish ragstone, all embedded in

[26] *op. cit.* in n. 13.

clay; the packing on either side between these blocks and the outer walls consists of chalk blocks fitted in irregularly (Pl. XXb). Between the furnace and the flue entrance into the hot room projected heavy flint and mortar offsets which were probably intended to support an iron water-tank to supply steam for the hot room, an intense heat being generated at this point. The whole flue area was reddened by burning, the blocks of ragstone tending to disintegrate in flakes. In the floor of natural chalk within the flue entrance is a semi-circle of five circular post-holes, tapering as they descend into the natural chalk to an average depth of 0·22 m. (Pl. XXc). Here was provided an iron grille to prevent débris from being sucked along the flue from the furnace. The shallow channel in the floor of the furnace is probably the result of scraping back over a long time with the stoker's iron shovel. The flue was 2·13 m. long, then debouching eastwards beneath the long floor of the hot room. The latter originally consisted of thick *opus signinum* bearing tiles, and was supported on two rows of rectangular *pilae* of red bricks. Vertical flues occupied the east end of the room, but these had been destroyed by the insertion of the modern valley sewer; but a small construction existed here of flint and tiles embedded in clay, which may have been a small starting-point to draw forward the initial draught from the furnace. The tiles forming this construction were found to be heavily vitrified by intense heat, and the clay reddened by contact with flame.

The Hot Room 21

As has been said, the treading-floor of this room was originally very thick and floored with tiles, supported upon rectangular brick *pilae*. Slabs from this floor were found to have been re-used for the coigning of the west wall of the nearby Church of Lullingstane, and suggest the thickness of the floor of about 0·17 m. Clay slopes had been inserted along the bases of both north and south walls of the room for protection of the walls from flame, and these slopes narrowed down to the central hypocaust channel, which itself received a floor of very tough cement containing tile fragments and small pebbles. The bases of the rectangular supporting *pilae* jutted out from these clay slopes at right-angles to the walls, the central channel being 0·91 m. wide (Pl. XXd). A parallel to this arrangement is seen in the similar room in the villa at Darenth, where such slopes are again in evidence.[27] The level of the treading-floor of the room coincided with the single brick course visible in the walls almost throughout the baths. The hot room was probably entered through a doorway, curtained, from the tepid room 20, but no evidence of this remained. Judging from some large fragments of tufa found in it, the hot room may have been roofed with a long arched roof of tufa blocks, but this remains uncertain. The roof may equally have been of wood and tiles, and based upon this latter type of roof a tentative estimation of the fuel consumption was worked out upon an estimated thermal storage, taking into account internal capacity, number of flues, and heat loss. On an estimated tepid room temperature of 80° F., and hot room temperature of 120° F., with an exterior temperature of 40° F., the fuel consumption, based on dry fuel, worked out at approximately 117 lb. per hour. This calculation is of course very tentative, but it may provide a guide to fuel consumption.

[27] *Archaeologia Cantiana*, xxii (1897), 60–1, and Plate G.

The hot Bath 22

This small bath projected south of the hot room. Its floor also consisted of heavy, thick *opus signinum,* with fillets round the walls; it was supported centrally by a small *pila* of tiles set in clay, the two low channels beneath the floor leading each to flues set upwards in the corners of the west wall. Each flue was constructed of three complete box-flue tiles, which were not, however, set vertically one above another; they were positioned so that the opening on the exterior occurred only some 0·91 m. above the exterior ground level (Fig. 20c). The lowest box-flue was placed vertical, the second upon it at an outward angle of 22 degrees, the third upon the second at an outward angle of 44 degrees, passing thence through the west wall to the exterior. The flue in the east corner had largely disappeared, but that in the west corner survives for its whole height and shows on the lowest box-flue a simple roller-pattern of diamond design. It is interesting to note that at some time these flues proved too powerful, the exterior orifice of the western one having been blocked by the mortaring-in of a large selected flint to reduce the draught. As in the hot room, of which it formed a part, clay was built up along the sides beneath the floor to protect the lowest courses of the walls and to canalise the heat to the flues. The hot bath was re-floored late in the third century, and two successive wall-renderings were present. When in use, the floor was probably shaped like a shallow, square bath into which the bather stepped direct from the floor of the hot room. There were two successive exterior drains, one above another in the middle of the south wall, corresponding to the two floors (Fig. 22a). Each drain was constructed of upper and lower *imbrices* set in mortar and *opus signinum.* The earlier probably contained a lead pipe; it had been extensively damaged for the extraction of the lead, and fragments of the metal were found on the exterior, with a complete lead pipe-outlet nearby. When the floor of the hot bath was raised at the late third-century reconstruction, the upper *imbrex* was removed to get at the lead pipe, and the damaged drain was filled up with clay. The earlier drain had been horizontal, but the later, higher drain sloped slightly downwards towards the exterior.

Gullies led out from these drains, curving round towards the east and emptying beside the large cold plunge bath upon the alluvium of the valley. The earlier and lower of the two gullies contained a bronze brooch of dolphin type, dating from the turn of the first and second centuries; it is a survival. The gully leading from the upper drain followed the same course as the lower gully, but slightly to the south of it, and contained coins of the House of Constantine and the House of Valentinian, and continued in use until the closing down of the baths. Both gullies had remained open during their successive use.

The tepid Room 20

This room lies immediately south of the stairs and west of the cold room. Its floor, the original character of which is not known, rested upon *pilae* built of square bricks, impressions of which were observed in the under-floor surface, with one rectangular tile remaining *in situ.* The floor had originally coincided with the stairway corridor along the north side, but at the reconstruction late in the third century it had been heightened and carried over the bottom step of the stairs, and surfaced with red-brick *tesserae,* part of which remained in the internal corner on the south-east of the room. The heat was diverted at right-angles from the furnace flue through an aperture of brick, and was drawn under the floor to a pair of vertical box-flues set in the east wall. These had been robbed out at the destruction of the baths, but some brick remained mortared into the wall. A third flue was constructed at the north of the room. Unlike the vertical pair, this flue was horizontal and led beneath the site of the stair corridor floor to the north wall of the latter, in which it turned up at a right-angle within the wall. At the reconstruction late in the third century, the original wooden door-frame at the bottom of the stairs was removed, the recess in the north wall that had contained one of its uprights receiving a flint and mortar block. The entrance from the stairs into the tepid room may have been curtained, no evidence remaining of a door-frame. As with the hot room, the level of the floor coincided with the single brick course in the walls of the bath suite. A small, shallow drainage-gully had been cut into the natural subsoil beneath the floor of the room. It extended from south to north beside the foundation of the west wall and ended in a soakaway. This gully and soakaway may have been associated with a urinal or similar contrivance upon the floor of the room in its north-west corner.

General Comments

The thick clay seal over the furnace denoted its final disuse, and was in its turn sealed by a thick level of black silt containing late fourth-century pottery fragments. This last deposit stretched northwards from the furnace, sealing all previous deposits for 9·76 m. in a northerly direction (Fig. 20b), and contained six coins of Valentinian I and Valens with nine Constantinian coins and two third-century survivals of Postumus and Tetricus. It is clear, therefore, that the baths were closed down *c.* A.D. 385, which agrees with the latest date for the use of the later drainage gully leading away from the hot bath, which also contained in its upper fillings coins of the House of Valentinian. The red colour-coated rossetted ware preserved in the rake-back of the furnace would thus appear to be of pre-Valentinian dating.

A section was excavated into the hillside behind the furnace, and was carried westwards for 9·45 m., the Roman ground level being found to have been cut down in two rising levels towards the west (Fig. 20a). Immediately behind the furnace wall was a drainage gully 0·61 m. wide, containing Antonine pottery; this gully curved round the south-west corner of the furnace and continued to the Well 24, into which storm water could be diverted. This gully was succeeded by the first horizontal level, 0·45 m. above the base of the gully and 1·67 m. long. This then rose abruptly another 0·45 m. to the second level, which proceeded horizontally for 6·1 m. turned vertically for 0·61 m., and then disappeared beneath the hillside. This second level, like the first one, was cut in the native chalk with its surface puddled, and is part of the floor of a building situated west of the furnace. The width of this building, its character and purpose, are not known, but its date is suggested by a fragment of Antonine pie-dish trodden into its surface. It is a further part of the Lullingstone complex that is known to exist but which, owing to the immense deposits over it, could not be excavated. A sloping deposit of silt had formed over it and over the shorter level eastwards, and on this had been built a rough heap of dry flints running from north to south which at a later time had probably diverted storm-water from the hillside. These dry flints had in their turn been silted over, and against them, and stretching westwards for 2·13 m. was a deposit of charcoal. These silts contained Rhenish ware and late-Antonine sherds. This whole level was eventually covered by a mass of clay-with-flint hillwash, and over this the black

Velentinian deposit lay sloping westwards up the hillside. This suggests some late activity further still to the west at this point, but this has not been traced. Some 0·45 m. above the dry flints, now hidden by the Valentinian level, was a shallow gully cut into this later level, again probably for diverting storm-water, and this gully contained three coins—a Constantius II *Augustus*, a Valentinian II, and one of the House of Theodosius. The medieval surface lay over this Roman gully and stretched almost horizontally eastwards.

In regard to the Valentinian level proceeding northwards from the furnace, this lay over a well-laid cement floor, narrow and rectangular, stretching to the north behind the bounding wall of the house, with post-holes along the long sides; its total length was 3·50 m. (Pl. XXIc). It was interrupted by a wide medieval pit at its south end, and thence a thin spread of cement continued to the north wall of the furnace. This sealed more rake-back from the furnace, consisting of laminated charcoal and clay, the lowest level containing Antonine sherds with much broken tile towards the north. At the lowest level and 3·96 m. from the furnace wall was a small semi-circular trough 0·30 m. wide and 0·30 m. deep, with a diameter of 0·91 m. This trough contained very fine, clean sand of a pale, slightly yellowish colour, a sample of which was submitted to Dr I. W. Cornwall, who very kindly analysed it, suggesting that the feature may have been for moulding—a few small fragments of lead were found on removing the sand from the trough, but it is not possible to suggest what objects may have been manufactured here (Pl. XXIa).

The flint and earth packing under the stairs leading down to the baths was sectioned (Fig. 22a). This involved the destruction of much of the already severely damaged stairway surface, which had lost its tiled treads in antiquity. The successive steps were preserved down the south side to allow any future reconstruction of the stairs. The packing beneath the stairs contained little material, none of it providing close dating for their construction. It consisted of a fragment of early first-century native-type store-jar, with some fragments of a poppy-head beaker. The latter is difficult to date with precision, but it would seem to have been of the type usually allocated to the middle of the second century or a little later. If this tentative dating is correct, a late second-century date for the original construction of the baths may be further confirmed.

The Well 24 (Pl. XXIb, Fig. 23)

The problem of water-supply to the baths was of paramount importance, and a close examination of the Roman level southwards revealed a well, 4·27 m. from the exterior wall of the furnace and 1·83 m. from the south-west corner of the hot bath. This well was carefully excavated with a view to confirming if possible the date of construction of the baths. It was found to have been constructed as follows:

(1) A circular shaft 1·83 m. in diameter was excavated through the natural clay-with-flint hillwash to a depth of 2·74 m., until the underlying chalk was reached.
(2) A circular basin was cut in the chalk approximately 0·61 m. in depth in the centre.
(3) A framework of four interlocking oak planks was bedded down on edge so that the four corners rested firmly on the chalk, leaving the circular basin exposed. This framework was 1·22 m. square, the north and south planks being tenoned, the west and east planks being mortised. The former pair averaged 5–7·5 cm. in thickness,

while the latter pair were less than half as thick. This had caused weakness in the framework, and it was found that the latter pair of planks had largely perished and could not be saved. The thicker pair were successfully removed, but it was found that they had been cut in such a way as to be useless for tree-ring analysis; all that could be said was that the tree from which they had been cut had grown on a very wet site.

(4) A lining of flints, mortared directly on to the circular shaft of clay and flint, was built upon this framework. It continued upwards for just under 0·91 m., but for some reason had not been continued to the surface. All these flints were found to have come away from the shaft wall, and in many cases individual flints showed mortar on one side and blackening from contact with water on the other.

(5) The top 1·22 m. of the shaft showed no sign of any lining, and it may have been covered when in use by a wooden floor with a trap in the centre to prevent the destruction by weathering of the clay and flint side. No sign of this appeared, however, either by impressions on the surface or in the well filling.

A study of the well fillings (Fig. 23) indicates a gradual silting during use, and a subsequent deposit of brown sandy clay, probably the result of storm-water. The primary silting contained a fragment of samian, Form 33 (*c.* A.D. 90–100), and the brown sandy clay contained a *mortarium* rim which Professor Eric Birley suggested may be attributed to the late second or early third century. A zone of grey sludge separated the primary silting from the brown sandy clay deposit, and this again was succeeded by grey sludge. This latter deposit appears to indicate the beginning of disuse, as it contained broken pieces from the wooden framework, and many fragments of pine-cone. These fragments appear to belong to *Pinus Pinea,* the stone pine, and may have come from imported cones, bearing in mind the essential pagan religious aspect of the villa during the last two decades of the second century. The objects recovered from the grey sludge consisted of two bead-rims of first-century native ware; two coins, one burnt and indeterminate, the other also indeterminate and much worn, though with a radiate head, the features of which recall those of Hadrian; and an iron hoop from a bucket, of diameters 0·33 m. and 0·36 m., and width 4 cm. A further fragment of one of the bead-rim vessels found in the grey sludge was also found in the primary silting, suggesting that the use of the well was not a lengthy one.

Immediately above the upper zone of grey sludge rested the mass of flints from the lining of the shaft, and among them was the mouth and handle of a globular *amphora,* a type which persisted into the late-Antonine period. Much clay-with-flint accompanied the fallen flints, and the whole was sealed down by a thick, blackish level of surface scrapings containing pottery of late-Antonine date, together with a few sherds of third-century pottery. Among the late-Antonine pottery were two examples of samian, Form 31, from the same vessel whose fragments were found in the late-Antonine level in the Northern Complex.

This blackish level, predominately Antonine, was sealed down in its turn by a filling of dry flints with brown clay and flint, indicating a levelling-up; and above this had been constructed a rough basin of yellow mortar. This contained a complete side of an Antonine pie-dish. The purpose of this basin is not clear, but it may have been associated with the repairs to the baths which were carried out late in the third century. This in turn was levelled-up, the surface becoming part of the fourth-century treading level outside the baths.

The well thus went out of use after the second-century occupation, and the subsequent source of water-supply is not known, though the baths continued in use until *c*. A.D. 385. On excavation of the well, water was found to enter quickly from all sides, at the junction of the chalk with the clay-with-flint. It was clear, pure spring water. The well had been dug to the approximate level of the bed of the nearby river which flows some 61 m. to the east, and the water-level in it still rises and falls seasonally.

It remains to consider the method adopted to conduct the water from the well to the adjacent rooms of the baths. When first constructed, the cold plunge bath alone would have contained some 1800 gallons, which would have needed frequent change. The water for the hot room and the hot bath would have been changed frequently in addition, thus adding to the amount needed. Such a copious supply of water could scarcely have been carried in buckets from the well-head to its destination; some arrangement for conveying it to the various rooms would have been both convenient and necessary. This may have taken the form of a small wooden aqueduct system, small shutes upon bedded trestles diverging from the well-head and entering through small apertures in the walls. Evidence for such a construction was sought immediately south of the walls, between them and the well, and a series of post-holes was found. They averaged from 0·11–0·26 m. in diameter, and showed packings of tile and flint. Their distribution, however, was irregular and could not provide a definite plan of any structure; but their existence tends to confirm the likely proposition of a small adueduct system.

The following table records the successive reconstructions and dating of the baths:

Dating	*Action*
c. A.D. 180	Stairs and all rooms completed, except small cold plunge bath Tessellated corridor to large cold plunge bath. The well dug and completed.
c. A.D. 280	Corridor to large cold plunge bath disused and tessellated floor of cold room extended over it. Tessellated floor of tepid room carried over the lowest step of the stairs and a horizontal flue constructed beneath the floor. Large cold plunge bath re-floored. Well already disused, silted up, and not cleared out.
c. A.D. 300	Further alteration to the cold room.
c. A.D. 340	Cold room provided with a thick concrete floor. Large cold plunge bath re-floored and shortened. Small cold plunge bath added. Hot bath re-floored and second outflow provided. Furnace repaired.
c. A.D. 380–390	Entire baths dismantled and filled-in. Valentinian and Theodosian deposits formed over its site.

The Kitchen Area (Fig. 24)

This section treats of the kitchens during the second-century occupation. It does not include that of the fourth century, which was established within the residence itself after the former had become disused and covered with the downward creep of hill-wash, and when, by *c*. A.D. 300, that slope had become the way up to the newly built temple-mausoleum on the terrace above. This fall of hill-wash occurred during the third century, when the villa was not occupied and while it was falling into ruin.

The improvements at the second-century reconstruction of the villa involved extensive cutting back of the hillside to obtain a level area upon which to site the kitchens and to provide room at the back of the house for light and yard-space. Everywhere, this area was cut into the natural chalk, the inconsistencies in level being smoothed out by rendering with flints and puddled chalk rammed down. The kitchen site was chosen behind the mid-point of the residence and well towards the artificial cliff at the west, an unoccupied space 3·05 m. wide being left between the back wall of the house and the edge of the kitchen platform. This platform, 9·15 m. west–east, and 6·10 m. north–south, was raised very slightly above the surrounding excavated level and was rammed down hard, consisting of chalk, flint and mortar. Ten very large and deep post-holes bounded it, one at each corner, one midway along the west and east sides, and two equally spaced along the north and south sides, the spaces between the post-holes being each 3·05 m. long. All the post-holes were uniformly 0·61 m. in diameter and 1·22 m. deep from Roman ground-level, their depths equating to within 5 cm., except the three westerly ones, which averaged 7·5 cm. deeper than the others.

The great size and depth of these post-holes suggest that they were designed to hold planed tree-trunks intended to support a heavy superstructure of large timbers, providing a strong attic storey, the roof being of thatch—the total absence of tiles confirms this. These prepared tree-trunks were inserted in the following manner. A hole between 0·91 m. and 1·22 m. in diameter having first been excavated into the natural chalk to the required depth, the tree-trunk was lowered into it and held firmly in a vertical position. A mixture of puddled chalk, flints and mortar was then poured in and rammed down, and when set hard, it thus enclosed the tree-trunk in a sheath of rubble-concrete. The surfaces that had been in contact with the tree-trunks were found to be uniformly round and smooth, and showed the areas of planing which had rendered the large posts circular.

It is difficult to suggest the method of walling the building. There was, however, a skin of raw clay, averaging 0·22 m. in width, along both the north and west sides of the floor, and it is therefore possible that the walls were of wattle and daub, which would agree with this primitive type of building. Such clay walls also appear in the temple, with its Palm-and-Panel wall-decoration, at the northern end of the second-century house, and abundant examples occur at the neighbouring Farningham II villa, where they are securely dated to the Flavian period. Such wall construction would therefore not be a departure from normal practice. Traces of wide, shallow gullies on the north, west and south sides indicate the disposal of rain-water from the roof, whose ridge ran west to east.

With regard to the internal arrangement of the building, a number of small holes cut in the surface of the hard platform, some of which are sharply rectangular, suggest wattle partitions; but the largely haphazard plan of these small holes provides no suggestions of the size or purpose of such partitions—the holes may not have been cut at the same time.

A pair of ovens, of equal size, occupied the western part of the floor (Pl. XXIIa). Depressions had been cut in the floor to provide the firing chambers, the remainder of the constructions being built up above floor level with carefully selected flints and tiles, embedded in clay; and judging from the great amount of burnt clay that sealed down the ovens, the latter had been walled and roofed of that material, strengthened by judiciously placed tiles. The cruciform plan, however, of the northern of these two ovens suggests perhaps an open, circular hearth with foundations on either side for the uprights of a cross-bar from which to hang vessels over the flames. This open hearth was soon reconstructed to conform with the oven on the south side; a long, rectangular oven was bedded upon its remains, similarly built of flints, tiles and clay. But again, upon either side of this were found shallow post-holes, which may have contained a second pair of uprights, while in the narrow entrance to the firing-chamber was a circular seating of hard clay which suggests the vertical pintle of a draught-director of "butterfly" type. The oven on the south, having the heating apparatus of the subsequent tannary superimposed upon it, could only be partially excavated; but its shape conforms with that of its neighbour, though the lateral post-holes are absent.

In its original form, therefore, this kitchen, with its heavy timbering, clay walls and thatched roof, contained two ovens, with partitioning of wattle here and there. It continued to function as a kitchen for some long period, for the second oven which had replaced the first one on the north side had clearly been in full use for a considerable time—the clay was burnt hard right through and the firing-chamber was encrusted with hard, grey ash. Some long time elapsed before the kitchen fell into disuse, to be replaced by the subsequent tannary early in the third century.

An infant inhumation burial was found occupying the inside corner at the north-west (Pl. XXIIc). The method of deposit adopted was of especial interest. The floor at this point was modelled into a shallow basin, roughly smoothed inside and oval in shape, some 0·37 m. long and 0·25 m. across. Its depth was sufficient to allow the body of the infant to lie snugly and not to obtrude above floor level. The baby was laid in this prepared "cradle" in a crouched position, on its left side and with its head to the south. No grave-goods accompanied it, and it was securely sealed over with clay, chalk and small flints. That this was a foundation-burial rather than a casual infant inhumation is undoubted. The bones appear to represent an individual in the first month or two of infancy; the sex cannot be ascertained, and no evidence appeared suggestive of the cause of death, whether natural or otherwise; all that can be said is that an infant of tender age died at a suitable moment for its use as a foundation-burial.[28] A complete pie-dish of late-Antonine date was found positioned immediately above the site of the burial; this may bear a relationship to the burial, or it may be fortuitous—its date is some years later than that of the building, which is obtained from the following evidence.

The floor of the building had upon its surface an intermittent, hard-trodden level of grey ash, which contained small quantities of broken bird bones, together with fragments, small and burnt, of bead-rim pots, and pie-dish rims showing traces of acute lattice decoration on the exteriors. The latter are suggestive of a Hadrianic-early-Antonine period, and the romanized fabric of the bead-rims conforms with this; this material does not show Flavian or Trajanic characteristics. The ovens contained no datable pottery, except in the reconstructed oven, where a typical fragment of pie-dish with over-hanging rim and lattice decoration suggests a Hadrianic-early-Antonine date. A study of the contents of the large post-holes, shovelled in with the surrounding débris after the timber posts had eventually

[28] This burial was removed complete and is on permanent exhibition in Dartford Museum.

been withdrawn, provided almost exclusively material not later than about the middle of the second century in date, though some fragments of Castor ware and Rhenish ware found high in some of the fillings, point to a final disuse of the kitchens late in the second century. The contents of the ten large post-holes consisted of pottery sherds representative of four vessels of first-century survival; seventeen vessels of Hadrianic-late-Antonine date; with one samian base and one sherd of samian Form 37. These suggest the occupation period, while six vessels of late-second to early-third-century date suggest the post-occupation period. Among the latter were two cooking-pots with obtuse-angle lattice in a broad band round the girth, as is common in the fourth century; but the rims in these two cases remain of second-century form. There is no fourth century material from the contents of these post-holes. It is clear that the obtuse-angle lattice decoration is not exclusively confined to the fourth century, but occasionally, if rarely, appears in the late-second and early-third centuries. It would seem, therefore, that any attempt to date by lattice-form must depend upon whether the rim oversails the girth or not.

Summing up, it seems clear that the heavy timbered building was first constructed sometime in the first half of the second century, but that it continued in use almost to the close of the century, when, in common with the rest of the house, its function as a kitchen ceased.

The Tannery

At the end of the second century, or possibly early in the third century, the kitchen area was radically modified. The ovens were covered over, and the apparatus necessary for a small tannery was erected. The materials used for this consisted of clay, flints, fragments of brick and tile, and wood; the durability of the constructions was therefore inconsiderable, unlike the earlier kitchen, which had been a very stoutly built building. Before describing in detail these new arrangements, it is necessary to list the main elements of tanning, so that the new series of constructions may be intelligible and may be seen to conform closely to the established process.

Briefly, six stages are involved in tanning, as follows:

(1) *Washing and soaking*. The skins are immersed for a short time in water for the removal of blood, the extraction of albumens, the removal of nitrogenous matter, and for the cleaning of the outer surfaces.

(2) *Unhairing by the liming process*. This loosens the hair sheath and renders easy removal of the hair. The skin is immersed in a mixture of lime and water, periodically being withdrawn and allowed to drain, until the epidermis is sufficiently loosened for unhairing.

(3) *Fleshing*. This is effected by hand over a wooden plank or beam, the fat being scraped with a knife from the underside of the skin.

(4) *Washing and de-liming*. This is preferably done in soft running water for the removal of the necessary proportion of lime.

(5) *Tanning*. Laying of the skins in a vat or pit containing vegetable liquor of varying strength, for varying periods, with solid tanning material between each skin.

(6) *Drying*. The skins are hung in a current of air, having first received a thin coat of oil.

On referring to the plan (Fig. 24), it will be seen that at this later reconstruction of the kitchen area, provision was made under the aforesaid headings in the following manner:

(1) *Washing and soaking*. Pit 1 may have been used for this, though the clean condition of its base and sides, and the fact that part of the baulk (see (3) below) seems to have been constructed partly upon its filling, renders this uncertain. Had the pit possessed a wooden lining, however, it and the baulk could have been in contemporary use.

(2) *Unhairing by the liming process*. The oven, and the deep tank-seating beside it, which no doubt originally was furnished with a wooden lining, make provision both for making lime and its transfer to the tank with addition of water, in which the hides would be steeped (Pl. XXIIb).

(3) *Fleshing*. The long and very substantial baulk, constructed mainly of clay over a flint core and placed along the west side of the complex, between the pits and the oven-and-tank, was supplied with a long wooden board firmly seated upon its eastern slope. This board lay longitudinally along the baulk and was tilted at a steep angle immediately above a narrow drainage gully—the whole arrangement is exactly suited for the fleshing process (Fig. 25).

(4) *Washing and de-liming*. There is no recognizable receptacle for this, but the gully running east had remarkably straight sides, and a wooden trough may have been seated here; a length of sheet-lead, 0·75 m. long by 0·12 m. wide, with small staple-holes along each edge, suggests part of the sealing of such a wooden trough, somewhat like that found at Caerleon, though on a much smaller scale.[29]

(5) *Tanning*. Pit 2 provided strong evidence of this process. It had been entirely lined with clay, and contained not only a remarkable quantity of leather, but a concentrated deposit of seeds, pips, and fruit-stones. The leather took the form of a large number of sandals pressed vertically into the clay lining and horizontally over the clay base of the pit, whereon was also laid a large sheet of leather. The vegetable liquor derived from the fruit and other organic material was thus in contact with a large area of leather, and into this liquor would have been placed the hides for tanning (Pl. XXIId, Fig. 26a).

(6) *Drying*. No construction remained for this purpose, but a simple arrangement for suspending the tanned hides in a suitable current of cold air was no doubt used.

The Tannage Pit (Fig. 26a)

This pit was carefully dug into the natural chalk to a depth of 1·37 m., and was approximately 1·52 m. square, with vertical sides. The bottom was flat and curved slightly up to the bases of the sides. Over the bottom, the chalk was levelled and puddled, making a neat, well-constructed, and serviceable container below ground level. Before final preparation of the pit for tannage, a small amount of rubbish and silt collected in it. This consisted of the complete skull of a lamb, with broken pottery, including the neck and handle of a globular *amphora* of second-century date. Castor and Rhenish sherds were also present, with Antonine pie-dish rims, the rim and side of a coarse folded beaker, and some

[29] V. E. Nash-Williams, *The Roman Legionary Fortress at Caerleon in Monmouthshire*, Cardiff, 1930, 13 and Fig. 11.

typical late second-century cooking-pot rims. This deposit was not cleared out when the pit was prepared for tannage. For this, a lining of clay was carried all round the sides up to the top, and over the bottom, a seal impervious to drainage and capable of holding liquid almost indefinitely. On excavation, this clay was found to be entirely deflocculated, having turned a moss-green in colour in the process.

The clay lining having been prepared, a large sheet of leather was spread over the bottom, stretching across most of the northern portion, and a large number of leather sandals was pressed into the clay, most of them firmly placed round the sides, the uppermost still retaining their vertical position (Pl. XXIId). The sheet of leather had the appearance of an apron such as is used by shoeing-smiths, and the sandals retained their iron studs, toe-caps and heel-tips, with cleats and bronze rings for securing the straps. They were in a very delicate condition, which worsened the higher up they were, and no sandal could be removed in complete condition; but an assessment of the material involved suggests that some thirty-four sandals were present. Traces of wicker-work support for the clay was also observed.

The pit, thus prepared to hold liquid, and with the leather present in abundance on the bottom and sides to promote the tanning process, was filled with a strong solution of water and acid juices from fruit that had possibly been pulped for the purpose. Large quantities of seeds, pips, and fruit-stones, with short fragments of innumerable stalks, occupied the pit in considerable volume. Specimens were submitted to the Director of the Royal Botanic Gardens at Kew, who very kindly reported upon them; several different species of *Prunus* were present, such as the sloe, the bird-cherry, and the cherry-plum. The multitudes of smaller pips could not be identified.

During the course of its use, this upper part of the pit became contaminated by a few animal bones, including a complete skeleton of a sucking-pig, a typical late second-century cooking-pot with a graffito SΛS upon it, a fine Rhenish-ware vessel, with fragments of Castor Hunt-cup, and other sherds of late second-century cooking-pots. It will be seen that little difference exists between the pottery in this higher level above the sandals and clay, and that sealed beneath them in the bottom of the pit. It seems clear that both deposits are contemporary in date, which suggests that little time elapsed between the original digging of the pit and its use for tannage. The continued presence of the skeleton of the sucking-pig and the large fragments of pottery is easily explained; such objects, having found their way in, would immediately have disappeared from sight in the deeply coloured and turgid liquid. There was no evidence that any lid covered the pit. After its use came to an end, it was filled up with red clay and flints.

Dating of the Tannery

Material for dating the layout shows a consistent second-century period throughout all the constructions; most of it is of a date late in the century and of survival significance; though the paucity of recognizable third-century material suggests a short survival time only in that century. This material is best examined from the filling of the tannage pit and from the make-up of the fleshing-baulk.

In regard to the tannage pit, the presence of Castor Hunt-cup, fine Rhenish ware, late-Antonine pie-dish sherds, and typical second-century cooking-pots, suggests the last decade or so of that century. Castor probably begins in southern Britain *c*. A.D. 170, and Rhenish perhaps *c*. A.D. 180–190, and as this late material was sealed down before the pit was finally prepared for tannage, the very end of the century or the beginning of the third century is indicated. Typical third-century pottery, as far as this can be recognized in southern Britain at present, finds no place; and while a tanning industry is to modern ideas unlikely to have been operated while the house was occupied as a private residence, this is not impossible.

The material from the fleshing-baulk make-up confirms a late second-century date for its construction. While a small amount of Hadrianic–Antonine pottery is present, with a little late first-century survival material, the general dating from the interior of the baulk runs from *c*. A.D. 160–190, the samian, especially a finely decorated sherd from a Form 30, corroborating this. The southern end of the baulk, where it tended to override Pit 1, sealed portions of Castor Hunt-cup, while the primary silting of the gully immediately east of it contained late second-century material. No appreciable difference in date between the tannage pit and baulk is apparent; both point to the turn of the century for their construction.

The oven-and-tank complex does not provide much information as it was allowed on excavation to remain complete, not being dismantled; but the burnt clay levels associated with the collapse and spread of the construction were sectioned, and again the material found in it, sparse though it was, suggests the same dating. Also, the large "apron" of rammed chalk on the northern side leading steeply up from the whole complex sealed pottery dated *c*. A.D. 170–200, with samian sherds of the same period, which provides further confirming evidence.

Taken all together, the evidence points to a date very close to the turn of the century. On general evidence, the whole residence became abandoned *c*. A.D. 200, so the question whether the tannery came into being before or after abandonment can hardly be definitely answered. In any event it did not continue long into the third century.

Subsequent History of the Tannery Site

As has been stated above, the tannery does not seem to have continued in use long after A.D. 200. The fleshing-baulk received a further slight clay make-up, and the area immediately north of the oven-and-tank complex was also made-up to a higher level with raw clay, and chalk blocks were placed upon this to provide some further construction; but of this so little remained that it is not possible to determine its purpose after the disuse of the tannery. The gullies on the west and north sides also became quickly filled up, and hill-slip, containing late-second and early-third-century pottery, with coins of Tetricus I and Carausius, quickly spread down over the whole area, indicating that abandonment had been complete for some time. Further falls descended over this hill-slip, with a thick black level containing much material dating from second to fourth centuries, clearly referable to a heavy deposit lying upon the higher ground to the west, ground upon which was subsequently found the temple-mausoleum. The succession of levels can be clearly seen in the large section (Fig. 25). It was upon this slope of hill-wash and débris that access to the temple-mausoleum from the house below was made *c*. A.D. 300.

Drainage from the Tannery (Figs. 24 and 26b)

The narrow gully immediately east of the fleshing-baulk turns along the edge of the original rectangular kitchen area and thence north-eastwards towards the back wall of the house, where a pit already existed, the original purpose of which is not known. This pit had been dug down to the natural chalk which here was subsequently found to be punctuated by a series of natural solifluxion pipes of cylindrical shape, two of which were discovered in the base of the pit. This pit had originally been cut in a sub-rectangular shape, 1·98 m. in length north–south and 1·52 m. east–west, with rounded corners. The sides originally were vertical. The gully referred to debouched into this pit at its south-western edge and the pit thereafter served as a soak-away for the effluvient from the tannery. On reoccupation of the site in the late years of the third century, the tannery having long gone out of use and having been concealed by the downward creep of hill-wash from the west, its gully and pit no longer served their original purpose.

The pit was situated 1·06 m. outside a doorway in the wall of the back corridor of the house at its northern end, and had originally been cut down to a depth of 1·37 m. In the early fourth century the end of the corridor to which the doorway belonged became a kitchen, and the pit, proving convenient by its position was used as an exterior refuse-pit for that kitchen. It was, however, radically altered. The sides and bottom were now lined with clay and it assumed a circular shape with the clay on either side thickening as it approached the bottom to approximately 0·45 m. and lying over the bottom in a thickness of 0·30 m. In the clay on the side nearest the house was a coin of the House of Constantine; but the most interesting and important objects found in the clay on the west and south-west sides were first, the fragmentary skeletons of two ducks lying nearest and parallel with the original wall of the pit, and over them, secondly, still packed in the clay, two geese. Both geese lay with their wings extended, the lower one facing south, the upper one facing north. It is clear that these birds were deposited in an extended position, as if in flight, when the clay lining was inserted. The uppermost of the two geese was found to be in such perfect preservation that the fibrous rings of its gullet still survived, and it is without doubt the most complete example of a goose that has survived in Britain from the fourth century. The dating of the deposit of these birds is attested by the coin, but more particularly by the associated pottery which is all of the fourth century.

The interpretation of the deposit is difficult, but is likely to be referable to a pagan ritual cult which demanded the burial of these birds with their wings extended within the new lining of an older pit. The skeletons, with particular reference to the goose nearest the surface of the clay, were in so complete a state that no disarticulation had taken place; the birds had been immured as complete entities and have no reference whatever to food remains. It will be remembered that in Roman times the goose possessed a certain aura of pagan religiosity.

The pit thus formed was used only during the first half of the fourth century, when a second pit was dug inside the kitchen, and the door leading out to the west exterior blocked. This change took place sometime during the period A.D. 337–345. The outside pit rapidly silted up, and the higher level was found to contain builders' rubble associated with the blocking of the doorway; and above that, further rubble associated with the reconstruction of this part of the house *c*. A.D. 385, when the kitchen inside became in its turn transformed into the vestibule of the Christian establishment.

An additional find of especial interest was made in the bottom of the pit, in the clay lining. This consisted of two large portions of querns, both of identical grit-stone, one from the upper stone, the other from the lower stone. Their dimensions are as follows:

Upper Stone	Diameter *c*. 0·75 m.
	Diameter of central hole *c*. 7·5 cm.
	Thickness *c*. 7·5 cm.
Lower Stone	Diameter *c*. 0·85 m.
	Thickness *c*. 7·5 cm.

The size of this quern when complete was likely to have been too large for human activation, and suggests animal power. At this time the granary was in full use, and the grinding of corn on a large scale at the villa is indicated.

PART IV

EXTERIOR BUILDINGS

1. The Granary
2. The Circular Shrine
3. The Temple-Mausoleum
4. The South Outbuilding

The Granary (Pl. XXIIIa)

The area between the residence and the river was partly bounded on the north side by the granary, whose long axis was at right-angles to that of the residence, the south-west corner lying 21·35 m. from the north-east corner of the residence, in a north-easterly direction (Fig. 2). The granary stood entirely detached, its east end approximately 16·47 m. from the present river-bank; and there is nothing to suggest that at this point the river has in any way radically changed its course since Roman times. The proximity, therefore, of the granary to the waterway may be significant, suggesting export of surplus grain from the villa by water. The size of the building may also suggest collection and storage of grain as tax from neighbouring farms in addition to its own contribution; and this is reinforced by the fact that no other example of any similar granary has yet come to light among the other Romano-British establishments so far excavated in the valley, except at Horton Kirby, near Farningham and possibly at the Darenth Roman villa. Lullingstone is also centrally placed along the river, a fact that might have facilitated collection.

The building is rectangular, its exterior dimensions being 24·40 m. by 10·06 m., excluding the buttresses on the north side (Fig. 27). It was possible to conduct a virtually total excavation, except at one point on the north side where the roots of a large elm prevented work, and on the exterior of the north wall towards the river, where the modern road begins to overlie the wall. The subsoil consists of a thick deposit of alluvial clay lying upon the flood-plain gravel, and it was into this alluvial clay that the original foundation-trenches were dug. The site selected probably appeared as a grass field, gently sloping to the river bank.

This alluvial clay contained (1) flint flakes, (2) fragments of bead-rim pottery of native fabric, which may be dated in the first century A.D., (3) fragments of Patch Grove ware vessels, (4) sherds of carinated and rouletted vessels of hard, grey fabric and of Belgic derivation, probably imported, and (5) a little samian, both plain and decorated, mainly of Trajanic date, but including some Hadrianic sherds. Of these five categories, the flakes and native bead-rims tended to occupy the lower half of the clay, the Patch Grove ware, the carinated wares, and the samian, the upper half, the latter coming mainly from the top

7·5–10 cm. Large numbers of calcined flints and roughly globular "pot-boilers" also occurred towards the bottom of the clay, and in one place a concentration of them in a thick zone of black earth upon the flood-plain gravel indicated a hearth. No pottery came from the lowest few cms. of the clay. This material in the alluvial clay supplies a latest dating of *c*. A.D. 130–140 for the rubbish-scatter over the field, which had gradually descended from the surface. There was no Antonine or later material in the clay.

A ditch had been dug into the flood-plain gravel at the north-west corner of the granary, but long preceded it in time, the masonry corner having been constructed over the curved end of the ditch. The latter contained pottery dating from *c*. A.D. 55–100, and it was noticed that the native pottery fragments scattered over the area became more concentrated towards this ditch. This perhaps indicates the direction in which the earliest occupation site may have existed before the villa was constructed in masonry late in the first century. This ditch will be discussed in detail later.

Construction. The flint and mortar foundations were trenched into the alluvial clay to an average depth of 0·30 m., and are uniformly 0·61 m. in thickness. Above this build-line, which is level throughout the site, the walls were free-standing and were found remaining to an average height of 0·61 m., consisting of carefully laid and level courses of mortared flints. Both exterior corners at the west end were strengthened by well-laid columns of flat bricks rising from the lowest free-standing flint course. It was not possible to ascertain if this was the case at the north-east corner which was over-laid by the modern road, and the south-east corner had collapsed in antiquity and had been roughly re-built with lightly mortared flints without any tile coigning. The interior was divided into two longitudinal areas, of internal widths 6·10 m. and 2·75 m. respectively, hereinafter described as the north and south compartments, the latter being subdivided into west and east sub-compartments, with the southern entrance between them. The northern entrance was sited in the north wall opposite the southern entrance.

An arrangement, unusual with civilian granaries in Britain, for aeration beneath the wooden floors within, was provided by low arches, fully turned with bricks, at ground level. One was provided at each end of the central axis of the north compartment; and a third on the axis of the west portion of the south compartment. The east part of the latter does not seem to have been thus provided, though a wooden floor with underlying air-space was inserted here, as with the remainder of the granary.

The rectangular supports for the wooden floors, again of flint and mortar construction, were next positioned inside the building (Pl. XXIVb). They were not trenched, but stood free upon the building surface; and their finish with smooth mortar on the tops and chamfered round the edges provides evidence of careful construction. In the north compartment twelve piers, in two rows of six each, occupied both the western and eastern parts, making a total of twenty-four piers, while in the centre of this north compartment was placed a pair of "boxes", their wall-tops rendered smooth like the tops of the piers (Pl. XXIVa). The purpose of these two "boxes" is obscure. They were separated, however, by a channel 0·76 m. wide, and everywhere the mortar rendering upon their surfaces was covered with the impressions of dogs' paws and the hobnail impressions from the soles of boots and sandals. Along either side of the wall-tops bounding the channel were three evenly-sapced small rectangular impressions of wooden plates, and it is possible that at this point a narrow wooden stairway led up to the roof-space, the plate impressions at the west end being strongly suggestive of a diagonal downward thrust which might well be related to the sides of such a stairway.

The "boxes" contained a lightly packed mass of small flint and gravel which must have lain beneath the overlying wooden floor, if such existed at these two points. However, this packing suggests a strong foundation in each "box" for some kind of container or bin; the wooden plank floor of the north compartment may therefore have been interrupted at the central point, and a narrow walking-way may have been provided over the central channel and between the wooden walls of such bins, though the narrow stairway, if such was the construction, would have made any passage inconvenient, though not impossible; the point remains uncertain.

The northern entrance opened directly upon one of these "boxes", but whether there was direct access to the southern entrance is problematical; the wall that divided the north and south compartments may easily have risen to rafter level though with probably a doorway through it from north to south.

The piers in the north compartment were rectangular, 0·25 m. in height, 0·76 m. long, and 0·61 m. wide, their long sides west-east. They were supplemented at both extremities by another pair, somewhat smaller, butting on to the walls beside the brick arches at either end. No ledges were provided along the inside of the walls of the north compartment, nor any slots in them for rafters. The central "nave" between the two rows of piers is not quite 1·83 m. in width, and the piers average a mere 0·76 to 0·91 m. between each. Such dimensions are quite unlike those of other recorded granaries, which almost certainly carried upright posts to support their roofs; and had these particular piers served this purpose, the congestion of wooden posts would have proved quite unsuitable for storage space and unnecessary for roof support. It seems clear that these piers carried wooden plates and longitudinal sleeper-beams, which in turn carried lateral rafters at each pair of piers; and upon these was fitted an overall floor of planks. The walls were carried up in flint and mortar, the roof being supported by a series of substantial beams crossing from north to south and with a span of some 7 m. A continuous air-space was thus provided beneath the floor, with a narrow channel centrally placed to induce forced draught, and with an open brick arch at either end for admission of cold air in accordance with either easterly or westerly winds. The remains of a flint and mortar wall with some tiles incorporated in it lay outside the western arch, lying at an angle of 13 degrees to it, and this may have acted as a draught-director. The absence on the inside walls of ledges or holes for supporting the ends of rafters does not preclude a wooden floor of the type suggested; the sides of such a floor would scarcely have been free-standing, but wooden brackets at the ends of each rafter, fitted against the walls, would have provided the necessary stability along the edges of the floor, to provide a sufficiently stout platform upon which a considerable weight of grain could be safely stored.

The arrangement within the south compartment of the granary was different from that on the north, and it differed again between its east and west sub-compartments. The eastern of the latter was provided with a central row only of six piers, 0·61 m. square, that abutting on the south entrance wall being 0·15 m. longer than the others. Three small piers remained along the north wall of this sub-compartment towards the west, but the internal flooring here could not be assessed as the exterior walls and south-east corner were in bad condition and had been roughly repaired after below-floor aeration had ceased altogether throughout the whole building.

The west sub-compartment, however, was remarkably well preserved. It was furnished with eighteen small piers averaging 0·40 m. square and 0·25 m. high, arranged in three rows of six each, the centre row free-standing, the side rows butting against the walls. There was slight evidence from mortar-skim "ghosts" of some previous piers of similar size; but these had certainly stood for a very short time, being possibly a try-out in design; there appeared to have been two centre rows of these instead of the final single centre row. The eighteen piers referred to above were not trenched but stood free upon the building surface. The north-west internal pier showed a mere trace, and the two small piers north of the brick arch were evidenced merely by mortar spreads, though the two south of it were intact, butting against the wall beside it. This arch, like its fellow in the north compartment, was centrally placed, and a group of small piers at the opposite, east, end of the sub-compartment probably formed the lowest part of the original draught-vent at this point. The eighteen main piers were carefully rendered with smooth cement on their surfaces, as with those in the north compartment, and they too originally supported a wooden floor.

Sometime before the final dismantling of the granary, the wooden floor of the north compartment was completely removed, no doubt for use elsewhere—there was an almost complete absence of iron nails here. In the west sub-compartment, however, an area only only 9·76 m. by 2·74 m., no less than 500 iron nails were found:

Lengths	1·25 cm. to 5 cm.	425
	5 cm. to 7·5 cm.	70
	10 cm. to 12·5 cm.	5

Of these, only 36 had been "hooked" at their ends, and the distribution was evenly spread over the area. It is likely, therefore, that the floor here was never removed but rotted *in situ*.

The entire north compartment of the granary was roofed in some material such as thatch, the wooden framework, supported on transverse beams, 7 m. long, resting upon the wall-tops. There were no fallen roof-tiles anywhere over this whole area, except in the west sub-compartment of the south range, where they lay so thickly as to demonstrate with certainty that this part was so roofed. Tiles were not so numerous in the east sub-compartment of this southern range, but it is likely that a pentice-roof of tiles stretched the whole length of the granary on its south side, beginning at the end of the thatched roof of the north compartment and sloping down at a less steep angle. A row of small rectangular slots in the highest remaining course of the south wall, three of which slots remained intact, each 0·30 m. long and 0·22 m. wide, provided the seating for the timber uprights (Pl. XXIVb). This indicates a wall of no great height incorporating timbers 1·22 m. apart to support the lower edge of the tiled pentice-roof, the flint wall being carried up in the spaces between the timbers. These slots are situated too high up to have been either vents beneath the interior wooden floor or seatings for joists for such a floor. They are exactly the same in principle as those discovered in the exterior walls of the Flavian barn-house at Farningham (Villa II), where timbers had been similarly placed, slotted into the flint foundation-walls but with clay as in-filling between them.[30]

As has been said, the entrances to the granary occupied central positions opposite each other in the north and south walls. That on the north, being 2·44 m. wide, would have needed stout timber uprights to take the thrust of the roof. A very large, squared flint, securely mortared down, was provided as a base for the western upright, but the existence of its fellow can only be surmised on the east side, as excavation here could not be carried out. A prepared slope of flints, gravel and chalk led up from the exterior to this entrance. The opposite entrance, on the south side, showed a packing of flint and gravel on the exterior, between much damaged flint and mortar bases of short, narrow walls jutting out, indicating here an entrance width of 3·05 m.; the lighter type of roof here would not have needed such stout foundations. A porch of wood, slightly projecting, may have stood over this entrance, and there was slight evidence of widening at a later date.

Phases of Construction

(1) In no instance was there any under-floor heating; no external furnaces appear, and the aeration was entirely of cold air. No charcoal was found upon the building level between the piers, except in the west sub-compartment of the south range. Here, a thin scatter of charcoal, including small pieces of carbonized twigs, fanned out inside the brick arch. This scatter was also found beneath the piers, and represents a very small fire just outside the arch before the wooden floor was constructed. The draught through the arch had produced this fan-shaped area of thin charcoal, and may have been a try-out for the aeration.

Immediately upon this thin charcoal scatter lay a concentration of small mosaic *tesserae,* some of which were found beneath the piers. The sub-compartment seems therefore to have been used as a sorting-floor for these *tesserae* during the short time elapsing between the completion of the walls and arch and the insertion of the wooden floor and of the piers which supported it. These mosaic *tesserae* consisted of:

81 from samian vessels (including 7 from rims, 3 from bases, and 1 from a decorated vessel).
755 from hard white chalk.
289 from grey stone.
72 from deep-purple Greensand rock.
59 from yellow brick.
54 from red brick.
35 from brown stone.

Total 1345

It is not possible to date the samian vessels from which the *tesserae* were cut, though the dull glaze suggests a later rather than an earlier date for them. Their surfaces were badly abraided by wear, and, together with the great majority of the other *tesserae,* they bore traces of cement, clearly indicating previous use in a mosaic floor. Such a floor has been found in the villa, the lowest and first level of the cold room in the baths having been shown to

[30] *Archaeologia Cantiana,* lxxxviii (1973), 5.

contain broken-up samian bowls with samian mosaic cubes and *tesserae* of other colours. This first floor had once been decorated with a mosaic panel towards its southern end; but this had been much broken when the next floor was superimposed late in the third century, when the baths received new floors. It may therefore have been from here that these *tesserae* came which were found in this sub-compartment of the granary. For what purpose they were collected is unknown; no single example of samian *tessera* is incorporated in the surviving fourth-century floors in the villa. It is clear that these *tesserae* are not the remains of a small mosaic floor inserted in the sub-compartment; they are single cubes, only in one or two cases are a pair cemented together. Also present were a small number of coarse *tesserae* consisting of:

	16	from red brick.
	4	from yellow brick.
	113	from chalk, double-cube form.
	79	from chalk, single-cube form.
Total	212	

This thin carbonized level contained in it a sherd of Rhenish ware, while four similar sherds and one of Castor "Hunt-cup" were found upon its surface. An equally thin level of rammed chalk sealed down this level.

(2) The piers were next inserted and the wooden floors laid, this following on with little delay.

In the rubbish level between the piers but below their tops, a level only a few cms. thick, were found three coins, of Postumus (A.D. 259–67) and the two Tetrici (A.D. 270–73), together with sherds of Rhenish ware and late-Antonine pie-dishes. The occupation make-up on the south exterior contained a coin of Allectus (A.D. 293–96) in new condition, and a small circular, enamelled brooch of late-second to early-third century type. And on the building level in the north compartment was found a coin of Aurelian (A.D. 270–75). A *dupondius* of Vespasian (A.D. 69–79) in the post-build level on the north exterior is a survival of the extensive pre-build occupation nearby.

It would seem, therefore, that the building of the granary took place in the last quarter of the third century, and the coin of Allectus suggests the last decade. Five other coins of Allectus, all in good condition, and one of Gallienus (A.D. 253–68), found in and about the southern part of the granary, but not securely stratified in occupation levels, reinforce this suggestion. They are associated with destruction levels, but cannot so date them, as the granary continued in use through the reigns of Valentinian I (A.D. 364–75) and Gratian (A.D. 367–83), as will appear below.

(3) The granary was so used throughout the age of Constantine I and his sons, the occupation make-up on the north exterior, and the occupation levels in the south range, containing coins of Constantine I (A.D. 307–37) and Constans as *Augustus* (A.D. 337–50), with one Urbs Roma (*c.* A.D. 330) and one minim, all of which, together with sherds of red colour-coated ware, flanged pie-dishes, and horizontal-rilled cooking-pots, attest its continued use until *c.* A.D. 350 as a granary. To these stratified coins and potsherds can be

added, from the generally unstratified material associated directly with the granary, the following sherds:

Flanged Pie-dishes.	18 vessels represented.
Coarse Cooking-pots.	3 ,, ,,
Rilled Cooking-pots.	2 ,, ,,
Straight-sided fourth-century Pie-dishes.	14 ,, ,,
Red colour-coated wares.	13 ,, ,,
Beakers—fourth century.	1 ,, ,,
Grey vessels with white slip.	9 ,, ,,

together with unstratified coins as follows:

Constantine I.	(A.D. 307–37)	1
Constantinopolis.	(*c.* A.D. 330)	1
Urbs Roma.	(*c.* A.D. 330)	1
Constantius II as *Caesar*.	(A.D. 323–37)	1
Constans.	(A.D. 333–50)	1
Magnentius.	(A.D. 350–53)	2

The granary continued in use as such until the middle of the fourth century at least; some of the coarse wares, notably the red colour-coated vessels and the rilled pots, date from well into the second half of the century. The general occupation of the villa was intensive throughout the period from *c.* A.D. 280 to *c.* A.D. 385, at about which time the Christian house-church was established in it; and it may have been about this time that corn-raising ceased, involving a change in the use of the granary.

(4) The north wall received buttresses in the time of Gratian (A.D. 367–83), a worn coin of that emperor being found sealed in the thick mortar spread upon which they were built. This indicates that after nearly a century of use as a granary, the north wall no longer adequately supported the roof; and when the wall was buttressed, the east portion of the north compartment continued to be used. The wooden floor was removed throughout its length, and the piers in the east portion were truncated and covered completely with a rough level of earth and flint cobbles; this filling also covered a shallow gully some 0·61 m. wide that had previously been dug along the inside of the north-east corner, but the purpose of this gully remains unknown, except that it may have been designed for local drainage. This earth and cobble level spread throughout the east portion of the north compartment and contained two worn coins of Urbs Roma and Helena, a very worn *sestertius* of Faustina II, and one of either Valentinian I or Valens (A.D. 364–78) also in worn condition, with more sherds of red colour-coated ware, together with the major part of the skeleton of a large dog which had been buried here in Valentinian times. A small quantity of carbonized grain was recovered from this level, where it had survived, fortuitously covered by a large fragment of tile. At the same time as this level was put down, covering the truncated piers, a doorway 1·52 m. wide took the place of the east brick arch, the door-posts being founded upon the two interior adjacent piers which were heightened and remodelled for this purpose. The lowest bricks of the original arch were found to be heavily crushed and pounded, and it is likely that this east

portion was used for stabling and a standing for small carts. A rammed gravel slope on the exterior led up to this doorway.

It is not known to what purpose the western portion of the north compartment was put at this time; but the brick arch here was largely destroyed, the remaining aperture in the wall having the appearance of a narrow entrance very roughly made and only about 0·61 m. in width. The western portion of the south range, however, began to have a new use. The brick arch here was blocked with flint and mortar courses (Pl. XXIIIb), and the small rectangular space inside thus became completely enclosed without any egress to the exterior at the low level. A large number of broken egg-shells of poultry lay scattered in the top of the previous occupation filling between the piers, and in the angle formed by the south wall and the fifth pier from the west lay a complete straight-sided platter. It rested level upon its base and had clearly been placed in this position to contain perhaps water or food. The final use of this small sub-compartment seems to have been for small live-stock, perhaps functioning as a chicken-run. A hard, trodden area, with at one place the remains of a wooden plank embedded in it, ran along the north interior edge of this space.

(5) The final destruction of the granary took place before the close of the fourth century. It was systematically pulled down and levelled over, and was not destroyed by fire as was the main building containing the Christian house-church, an event which occurred early in the fifth century. As has been said, no tiles appeared anywhere in this destruction level, except over the "chicken-run" where they were abundant, mixed thickly with flints from the destroyed walls. A coin of Gratian lay upon the truncated top of the main wall dividing the north and south compartments, and fragments of hand-made cooking-pots, with heavy, coarse store-jars with rims of square section, were contained both in the wall levelling spread and among the fallen tiles. Coins ranging from Allectus to Gratian were found associated with this final levelling down.

Dating Summary

(1) The granary was constructed late in the third century, perhaps in the last decade.
(2) It continued in use as a granary until the last quarter of the fourth century, when its wooden floors were removed, except that in the south sub-compartment, which remained.
(3) The eastern portion of the north compartment became a covered area for stabling and a standing for small carts, while buttresses were added to the north wall, all *c.* A.D. 380. The small south sub-compartment became a pen for small animals, or a chicken-run.
(4) Its final destruction and levelling over took place not long afterwards, probably in the last decade of the fourth century.

This granary was never elaborated at a later date, or turned into any sort of dwelling for the villa farm-hands, as was the case in some other such buildings in Roman Britain—evidence of such occupation was entirely absent; and the building remained throughout its history a place for grain storage, and latterly for more mundane, and much shorter-lived uses. The uniqueness of the building lies in the design for under-floor circulation of cold air by small brick arches set low in the end walls, a feature that apparently does not appear in any granary or barn associated with a villa in the lowland zone of Roman Britain, except of course at military establishments.

The Ditch. Underlying the north-west corner of the granary was found the beginning of a ditch (Pls. XXVa and b, Fig. 28c), its curved end beneath the west wall and extending from a point 0·61 m. south of the corner for a total width of 1·83 m. onwards in that direction. The ditch extended westwards for 2·75 m., where a section was cut across it and annotated; but further west on the same line it became indeterminate, though fragments of native-type pottery of the first century lay in the area on its line.

This ditch may be connected with an occupation of the site prior to the building of the first villa *c.* A.D. 80–90, as it contained much native pottery, with a little Gallo-Belgic material, and a large samian platter dated A.D. 55–75 in the primary silting. The native pottery included part of a jar with triangular stabbing between horizontal incised lines and with traces of red coating; parts of two large jars with stabbing decoration; part of a lid in native fabric; part of a bowl of Belgic form also in native fabric; and numbers of native bead-rims. The Belgic material consisted of a shallow bowl, two carinated vessels in grey fabric, two fine, wheel-made and cordoned pots, and part of a lid with horizontal grooves in groups. All this pottery occupied three successive levels above the primary, a total depth in the middle of 0·83 m., suggesting a fairly speedy filling of the ditch. Above the primary silting lay a thickness of burnt daub, extending up the north side of the ditch, which was of shallow, non-Roman, profile, with a widely curving base.

The first century surface was sealed over by a thin deposit of clay, some of it reddened by flame, and upon this was the build-level of the granary. Above this again lay the fourth-century level, averaging 0·22 m. in thickness, with the Valentinian level at its top, covered by large flints and earth.

The Circular Shrine (P. XXVIa, Fig. 29)

This building was discovered situated upon a prepared terrace 24·40 m. north-west of the villa and 10·37 m. north of the temple-mausoleum. At this point the terrace had been levelled at about 2·44 m. above the lower Roman treading-level, the original hill-slope, consisting of clay and flint hill-wash overlying the descending natural chalk, being cut back to form a semi-circular area for 6·40 m. from east to west at its widest. The building was laid out so that its most westerly curve could be free-standing some 0·45 m. at its narrowest from the chalk slope at the west, much of the chalk being removed to accommodate the western part of the foundation. In a shallow foundation-trench was constructed a circular wall of flint and mortar whose width was consistently 0·35 m., without exterior buttresses, the internal diameter being 4·72 m. This wall was of excellent construction though not rendered smooth either upon the outside or the inside; four courses of selected flints were found free-standing, each course interleaved with a thick level of hard white mortar. That portion of the wall in which the entrance had originally been placed to the east was found to have collapsed with the eastern face of the terrace; but on excavating at this point, post-holes were discovered in the underlying and much weathered natural chalk, post-holes which had been part of the wooden stairway by which the shrine was originally approached from the lower level. The top surface of the curving wall was observed to be uniformly level, and two small post-holes, each approximately 7·5 cm. square and 1·67 m. apart, had been at some time cut in the centre of this surface. It was first thought, therefore, that a wooden superstructure may have been erected upon it. On careful reconsideration, however, this level surface appeared more likely to have been one of the mortar interpolations, and the wall of the shrine probably rose to a height of some 2·44 m., upon which rested a conical roof of wooden construction; it was not tiled, but was probably of thatch. It had no centre post, the wooden horizontal members tying into the top of the circular wall and easily spanning the building. While no evidence survived of the doorway or of the approach-stairway, these are likely to have been made of wood. No window-glass was found in association with the building; it may therefore have been lighted only through the doorway, the interior probably remaining dark. Only in the early morning would direct sunlight have penetrated through the doorway.

The floor of the building consisted of white pebble-concrete varying in thickness from 5–7·5 cm., and this concrete had received a surfacing of coarse *tesserae,* mainly of red brick but including a large proportion of yellow brick *tesserae* evenly distributed over the floor. An interesting phenomenon was observed. The circular concrete floor with its tessellated surface had been placed in position before the wall was built, and this resulted in an eccentricity in which the centres of the two circles were found to be nearly 0·30 m. apart. This had caused a gap of similar dimension at the north between the edge of the concrete and the beginning of the wall construction, and at the south where the *tesserae* and the underlying concrete were oversailed by the wall. There is no explanation for this eccentricity of layout, but only one period of building is concerned.

This concrete and tessellated floor did not completely fill the shrine. In the western part, opposite the entrance, a rectangular area had been left, 2·44 m. from the north to south and stretching nearly 1·83 m. back to the enclosing curve of the wall. A shallow slot of average width 0·22 m. ran along the eastern edge of this reserved area, which contained throughout large slabs of fallen plaster, some lying face up, others face down, the faces showing extensive areas of red and white paint but exhibiting no positive scheme of decoration except the possibility of red and white panels. Abundant wattle impressions appeared on the backs of the fallen slabs. In this area only was painted plaster found and a partition of wattle and daub probably stood in the slot with its painted side opposite the entrance. It is not known whether this partition returned north and south, but this reserved area may well have originally contained the *podium* for a cult object, though no trace of either remained. The dedication, therefore, of the shrine remains problematical, though it may have been associated with some woodland deity. There was, however, a small compact group of fragmentary tiles and bricks in the northwest part of this area, lying against the wall, and this may represent the remains of some structure or cist. Only here was any brick or tile found. A possible buried altar was sought without success within the building, and no deposits came to light immediately outside the wall.

On excavation it was found that much of this floor had been removed, the *tesserae* having been stripped from the underlying concrete, probably for use elsewhere; and in this connection it is of interest to note that the tessellated floor of the small projecting Room 3 at the north-east corner of the square ambulatory within the house, next to the *nymphaeum,* was composed of red and yellow brick *tesserae* distributed in the same way as in the circular shrine; and the quantity of *tesserae* on the floor of Room 3 roughly equals the quantity removed of the floor of the shrine. It is thus possible that the *tesserae* from the shrine was re-used here, and if this is the case then the shrine must have gone out of use by the end of the second century. A limited area immediately within the entrance of the shrine showed by the reddened and burnt clay that small fires had been lit at this point. Nowhere else within the shrine was such burning in evidence, and it may be that this limited area of reddened clay may represent the site of ritual fires which may from time to time have been lit.

Dating

It was decided not to interfere with the wall nor to remove any further portion of the tessellated floor or its underlying concrete, and a positive dating for the earliest foundation of the building is not closely assigned. It was considered that the pottery recovered from the silt over the floor and from the fallen plaster, with that from the exterior of the wall, sufficed to assess the earliest dating. This pottery contained a significant quantity, often in large fragments, of Patch Grove vessels together with a little early second-century grey ware with lattice decoration, and on the south exterior of the shrine, next to the wall, and at its base a complete flagon-rim which may be dated A.D. 100–130. The relative abundance of Patch Grove ware, dating as it does from the late first century well into the second century, combined with the small amount of late Trajanic-early Hadrianic wares, is strongly suggestive of construction in the early years of the second century. As the silt over the floor was very thin, these Patch Grove fragments may have been accidentally deposited during the occupation of the building, and certainly at its destruction; but as the destruction levels on the exterior contained Antonine pottery, the destruction date may be put towards the close of the second century. The shrine was dismantled down to the fourth flint course above the foundation, and not destroyed by fire, and a humus showing a clear turf-line developed over the interior silt. The remnants of the building were thus quickly concealed from view. Above this ancient turf-line was a thick deposit of yellow chalk mixed with mortar and building débris, containing fragments of tufa blocks and mortared flints, a deposit which represents a final destruction of the neighbouring temple-mausoleum. This thick deposit fanned out from the direction of the latter building, covering much of the site of the circular shrine, and containing some large fragments of rouletted ware which may be dated to the late fourth century. The hill-slip which carried away the eastern part of the circular wall together with the entrance probably occurred not long after the deposit of the yellow chalk and building débris. A west–east section was cut at this point and in it were plotted every fallen *tessera* and every wall-flint (Pl. XXVIb, Fig. 30), from which can be seen the profile of the slope shortly after the collapse. Above both the yellow chalk and this profile was a subsequent deposit of clay and flint hill-wash containing a little medieval pottery of the fourteenth century. This was surmounted by humus from which was recovered a coin of Valens which has, of course, no significance.

The following table represents the chronological sequence:

c. A.D. 100	Construction.
c. A.D. 180	Cessation of occupation. *Tesserae* removed and building dismantled.
c. A.D. 385	Fall of building material associated with the demolition of the temple-mausoleum.
c. A.D. 400–425	Collapse of eastern portion of the building, associated with the final destruction of the house below and the desertion of the site.

Interpretation and possible Parallels

Such circular buildings standing apart from other Romano-British buildings are uncommon, but are usually associated with religious cult-worship. The interior arrangement of this example, providing as it does a possible sanctuary reserved against the west wall, divided from the tessellated area by a low wattle-and-daub plastered partition which shows much red and white paint, suggests that here, too, is a building devoted to pagan cult-worship though of what nature there is no evidence. The rusticity of the building, roofed as it must have been in a somewhat flimsy manner, suggests that the cult was pursued by persons more in the Celtic than in any sophisticated Roman tradition; and the foundation of the building coincides in time with the period during which the owner of the first substantial house was experiencing romanization.[31]

Examples of such buildings may be adduced. As an example of exterior appearance, though completely built and roofed with stone, the structure known as Arthur's O'on in north Britain may be cited.[35] As with the Lullingstone example, Arthur's O'on has its entrance facing east, but with a small window above it, and its internal diameter is only 1·37 m. greater. Its construction in stone is applicable to the geology of its neighbourhood, whereas at Lullingstone a similar building would naturally be built of flint and mortar with a roof-framework of wood. The example at Brigstock 1, in Northamptonshire,[36] shows a circular shrine whose entrance was to the east, and which had evidently been the object of public pilgrimage, as many coins and other small votive objects were recovered from its interior. The total absence in the Lullingstone shrine of any coins or votive objects does not vitiate its identification. This shrine served a private family and therefore would not have received a multitude of small objects and coins which the Brigstock example exhibited. The circular shrine at Bowes 2 not only had an eastern entrance, but had an altar placed within against the curving wall opposite the entrance, an arrangement similar to that at Lullingstone. The shrine at Maiden Castle again had its entrance towards the east. Some comparative dimensions (interior) are as follows:

Arthur's O'on	6·1 m. diameter	Entrance E
Brigstock 1	9·45 m. ,,	,, E
Bowes 2	5·18 m. ,,	,, E
Maiden Castle	6·71 m. (average)	,, E
Lullingstone	4·72 m. diameter	,, E

The Temple-Mausoleum (Figs. 31–33)

During the investigation of the western exterior of the villa, the stub of a wall was observed protruding from the rising slope at a higher level, with an even slope of chalk some 6·10 m. north of it. An exploratory trench was dug between these two points and extended upwards towards the west, and further walls were discovered, indicating a building of some size. The area was thereupon gridded, and after five months work the complete building was revealed.

It consisted of a Romano-Celtic temple 12·20 m. square, containing a rectangular *cella*

[31] *op. cit.* in n. 11, 78–83, 187–8.

6·40 m. long and 5·18 m. wide (exterior dimensions), with its entrance placed midway in the longer side and facing south, opposite which, in the ambulatory wall, was the concrete slot that had once contained the treader of the wooden exterior entrance.[32]

Beneath the *cella* was a tomb chamber, 3·35 m. deep and 3·66 m. square. This chamber had originally contained two lead coffins laid parallel and orientated north–south, with an array of grave-goods disposed in a line beside them on the west. Of coffins and grave-goods, the coffin on the east side and the grave-goods had survived; the second coffin that had occupied the central space had been removed in antiquity. The building can therefore be described as a temple-mausoleum, constructed *c.* A.D. 300, for the burial of two persons only, and for the subsequent celebration of the rites connected with them.

Overlying the western part of the temple-mausoleum was the exterior west wall and the remains of the north and south walls of a later building. This was found to be the ancient church of the parish of Lullingstane, lost to sight since its ruins were noted in the eighteenth century by John Thorpe and described by him in his *Custumale Roffense,* published with a woodcut of the church in 1788. The church is first recorded in the Chrism Rent Roll of the diocese of Rochester in A.D. 1115, which may be an adaptation of an existing Roll; this is suggestive of a Saxon origin for the church. It is orientated in such a way that its sanctuary would have been sited over the *cella* of the temple-mausoleum, the two axes differing by only 2 degrees of arc, the orientation of the church being 30 degrees south of east. This orientation is suggestive of either the use of the Roman walls as foundations, or as an example of the early, Augustinian, practice of siting Christian churches upon buildings that had once been used for pagan worship, and purified for the purpose.[33] The graveyard was discovered a few feet south of the church, the inhumations lying in some cases over the south ambulatory of the temple-mausoleum. An inhumation was discovered within the area once occupied by the Christian sanctuary, and another is known to lie on the north side of the church just outside the north ambulatory wall of the temple-mausoleum. It was found that the downward creep of hill-wash during the centuries had completely carried away the east ambulatory, together with the easterly portion of the church above it.

The temple-mausoleum had continued in use as a memorial temple from its inception *c.* A.D. 300 into the last quarter of the fourth century, when the whole religious aspect changed with the adoption of Christianity by the villa owner and his family. Henceforth, the temple-mausoleum was allowed to decay, and by the end of the century sinkage of the *cella* floor encouraged investigation by tomb-robbers (Pls. XXVIIc and d). A pit was dug here and the coffin which occupied the central part of the floor below, that of the tomb chamber, was found and removed, some of the lead being left below and the bones of the occupant of the coffin being thrown back into the hole. The back-fill contained many chalk blocks from the walls of the *cella,* hundreds of large fragments of the painted *opus signinum* that had once decorated the interior of the *cella* walls, and many voussoirs of tufa, curved in two directions, and coated on both sides with pink cement, voussoirs that had formed part of a dome, or perhaps a vaulted roof, of the *cella.* This back-fill also contained fragments of late fourth-century pottery and coins of Valentinian I and Gratian, and was covered with a thick

[32] *Ibid.,* 19, 167.
[33] *op. cit.* in n. 2.

deposit of heavily carbonized wood and iron slag. The pit dug by the tomb-robbers was inexpertly excavated, the sloping sides giving it the shape of a wide funnel; in consequence, when the robbers reached the floor of the tomb chamber, the lead coffin on the east side, and the grave-goods on the west side, remained concealed from their view.

From this time onwards the temple-mausoleum was robbed of its wooden superstructure and roof, and most of the finely shaped chalk blocks of which the walls of its *cella* had been constructed; little, if anything, is likely to have remained above ground when the Christian church came to be built, though local memory of its previous existence and purpose may well have persisted, by which the siting of the church may have been afterwards conditioned.

Order of Building

(1) The first action taken by the villa inhabitants *c.* A.D. 300 was to excavate for the tomb chamber, having first levelled the hill slope. The original dimensions for the tomb chamber were 4·57 by 3·66 m., but having dug down 0·91 m., it was decided to shorten the chamber by 0·91 m., making it 3·66 m. square. Excavation continued until the natural chalk was reached 2·74 m. down, and 0·61 m. of this chalk was removed, possibly to obtain the chalk from which the blocks were fashioned for the *cella* walls. The total depth of the floor from the surface was therefore 3·35 m. A square room was thus obtained, though the chalk floor was left uneven with flints appearing here and there, especially towards the east side where a shallow depression running north–south continued the uneveness of the floor. The sides were probably revetted with timber before the burials took place, traces of this being noted, particularly at the north-west corner. Such revetting was necessary, as was found during excavation of the chamber, for the natural hill-slope over the chalk contains much sand and loose gravel, which tends to make the sides collapse.

The two coffins were then lowered down and disposed upon the floor of the chamber, parallel with each other, heads to the north, and the grave-goods were placed in a line on the west side parallel with the coffins. No other burials were contemplated. A heavy sarcophagus of wood, 7·5 cm. thick, was then positioned to cover and protect the coffins and grave-goods. This sarcophagus was probably pre-fabricated above ground and bolted together in place below, its stability being ensured by heavy angle-irons and 0·22 m. spikes of iron which secured it to the west face of the chamber. Its roof was strengthened by two transverse battens secured by iron bolts. All these angle-irons, spikes and bolts were found in position on the west face of the chamber and in lines upon the floor, upon which they had fallen when the sarcophagus eventually collapsed. The flat top of the sarcophagus stood 1·22 m. above the chalk floor, and in consequence a large air-space existed between the lids of the coffins and the underside of the sarcophagus. The whole construction, when bolted together and in place, was not stable owing to the uneveness of the floor upon which it stood, where there was still a space between the chalk surface and the south-east corner of the sarcophagus; this corner was wedged with a grid-iron, brought perhaps from the nearby kitchen in the house, two large flints, and a small iron cup (Fig. 32b). The sarcophagus was now immovable, and the spaces between it and the sides of the chamber were packed with brown gravel and earth, containing fragments of third- to fourth-century pie-dishes and other vessels.

Two objects remained, however, outside the south side of the sarcophagus and upon the floor. One of these objects was a wooden keg, standing originally in an upright position, bound with four iron bands, the topmost of which carried an iron handle folded down. These bands were found collapsed in succession upon each other, from which the height and shape of the keg could be established. 0·42 m. high, its girth at the middle 0·20 m., diminishing to 0·12 m. at both top and bottom, it was an elongated, slightly bulbous container. The reason for its deposit in the tomb chamber, yet outside the sarcophagus, is unknown, as also is the contents, if any. It was quickly covered by the gravel packing. The second object lay upon the floor, west of the keg, and also outside the sarcophagus. It appeared to be the remains, very much crushed and decayed, of a long tree-branch, lying east–west. It was just under 1·52 m. in length and was extremely fragile, flattened as it had been by subsequent pressure from above.

Traces of two shallow slots were observed, roughly parallel with each other and both outside the north and south sides of the sarcophagus. They showed traces of lead in them, but their significance is not known.

The final stage of the double burial was the deposit upon the sarcophagus of a heavy packing consisting of alternate layers of puddled chalk and gravel, six of each, laid one upon the other so that the highest gravel layer might form the floor of the intended *cella* to be built above (Fig. 32a). A dead weight thus lay directly upon the wooden top of the sarcophagus, which remained unsupported except at the corners, and by the gravel packing around it, and strengthened by the two wooden battens across the top. This proved of importance some decades later, when the wood began to rot and sag, subsidence beginning.

(2) The *cella* was then constructed. A rectangular foundation of immense strength, 1·06 m. thick, of puddled chalk and flint, was sunk to a depth of 1·52 m. all round the upper part of the tomb chamber, to support the massive walls of mortared chalk blocks. This foundation did not exactly conform to the sides of the tomb chamber, which was now hidden from view, the eccentricity being 4 degrees east–west and 8 degrees north–south; the *cella* was not therefore a perfect rectangle. The walls were then carried up, 0·76 m. thick, to a suitable height, perhaps some 3·66 m., to accommodate the pentice roof of the surrounding ambulatory, and a dome, or perhaps a quadripartite vault, completed it. This was constructed of tufa voussoirs, rendered on both interior and exterior with hard, pink cement, each voussoir being curved to shape and diminishing in size as the apex of the dome or vault was reached. There was no evidence of clerestory windows.

The entrance was sited on the south side. The doorway was provided with a heavy wooden treader, and a narrow porch projected 0·91 m. into what was to be the south ambulatory. A pair of oolitic lime-stone pillars were positioned each in a thick spread of pink mortar, giving a small pseudo-classical portico to the *cella,* the architrave being possibly of stone to conform with the pillars. Connecting each pillar to the main wall of the *cella* was a thin partition, probably of masonry. This portico was exceedingly narrow, only 0·76 m. wide inside, and as the surviving lead coffin was 0·53 m. in width, and 2 m. long, and was packed with gypsum, to manoeuvre such an awkward and heavy burden through so narrow an entrance would have been an operation of great difficulty. In addition, the puddling of the chalk layers and the deposition of the gravel layers above the sarcophagus would have been much more easily effected before the erection of the *cella*. The eccentricity in plan of the two constructions is again strong confirmation of the erection of the *cella* after the burials and the attendant work had been completed.

The interior walls of the *cella* were decorated. A layer of mortar 2·5 cm. thick was applied to the chalk blocks forming the walls, and a further 2·5 cm. of *opus signinum* was applied to this mortar, with a very thin layer of plaster applied to the *opus signinum*. This plaster received the painted decoration. A red dado some 0·61 m. high was divided horizontally by a narrow yellow band from the main colour of the walls, which was green; and against this green background were portrayed human figures engaged possibly in some cult dance or ritual. From the dimensions of one pair of naked feet and lower legs that has been assembled from the fragments these figures were about two-thirds life-size. Many fragments of this decoration were recovered, but the weathering suffered by the walls after the temple-mausoleum had gone out of use makes the piecing together of them extremely difficult. The painted decoration was carried round the inside door-posts, showing green on one face and yellow on the turn outwards; several fragments of this were recovered from inside the doorway where they had fallen.

(3) The *cella* stood for a time by itself before work began on the ambulatory. A drip-gully was found immediately outside the walls at their bases on all four sides, interrupted only where the portico stood. Included in the gully silting were fragments of third- and early-fourth-century pottery, with some second-century survival sherds. Some months must have elapsed, therefore, before the ambulatory was begun. Its wall, unlike that of the *cella,* was constructed of finely dressed flints set in hard mortar; and while north and south it had partially shared in the collapse downhill of the eastern section, on the west, north, and south it remained in places at its original height, 0·83 m. from the ground level, beneath which its foundations descended for a further 0·53 m. Its width was 0·61 m., and the exterior was rendered with pinkish-red cement like the tufa roof of the *cella*. This coloured cement was carried up over the exterior edge of the horizontal wooden sleepers which lay along the top surface of the wall, much of this chamfered cement being recovered along the base of the wall, while some small portions of it still remained adhering to the wall top in its original position. According to the usual practice with Romano-Celtic temples, the uprights of the wooden arcade were no doubt mortised into the horizontal sleepers, in turn supporting the horizontal members which took the thrust of the pentice roof. Of this roof there was no trace, and the absence of tiles suggests that it may have been of wood. One large fragment of masonry, consisting of three tile courses set in pink mortar, was found lying on the surface of the north ambulatory and may have come from the upper part of the *cella*. Nearby was a large sarsen-stone, shaped into a rectangular block and showing traces of *opus signinum*; it certainly had formed part of the Christian church, but the *opus signinum* is suggestive of some previous use in Roman times. Fragments of a second sarsen lay a few feet away. These sarsens probably underlay the north-east and south-east corners of the later church.

The ambulatory (Pl. XXVIIa) was floored with pink *opus signinum,* thickening upwards towards the exterior walls, as evidenced in the north ambulatory, where much of the original flooring was still present. This floor is carried over the shallow drip-gullies beneath the walls of the *cella,* passing over their filling right up to the walls. The width of the ambulatory varies; on the north it is 2·13 m. wide, on the west 1·67 m., and on the south 3·20 m., all interior dimensions. The width of the east ambulatory is of course unknown. The south ambulatory was of some importance (Pl. XXVIIb). Not only were the entrances situated here, both on the same axis, but just inside the ambulatory entrance, on the west side, and set back 0·45 m., was a small structure 0·15 m. square built of flint, mortar and clay, which may have been the base of a plinth supporting a cult statue or altar. The ambulatory entrance beside it showed a beautifully made slot of white cement which once provided the seating for the treader of the wooden door-frame. The grain of the wood was plainly visible on the surface of the cement, and the slot was curved and chamfered at its eastern end. It would seem that the builders had used a thick plank sawn from the bottom portion of a tree-trunk which had been undercut to facilitate felling, and the plank had not been trimmed square before being embedded in the seating of wet cement.

The pathway leading southwards from the ambulatory entrance was approximately 1·83 m. wide and was composed of rammed clay and gravel. It continued for 7 m. before ending in steps which turned through a right-angle downwards to the house below, the side of the pathway towards the house being revetted with wooden posts and timber. The steps had originally been provided with wooden risers and treaders, but those had been removed at a later time, probably when the temple-mausoleum went out of use. Below the point where the steps turned, the site of the second-century kitchen and the subsequent tannery had already become covered by the downward creep of hill-wash which had occurred during most of the third century, when the villa was uninhabitated; and this slope was made use of for the steep path leading down from the steps to the level of the villa. There was no sign of post-holes on either side of the steps or pathway leading down which might have suggested a covered way, unlike the pathway which was discovered leading upwards on the north exterior of the temple-mausoleum between it and the circular shrine (Fig. 2). This latter pathway was of gravel and was 3·81 m. wide, bounded on the south by a solid flint and mortar wall-base 0·50 m. thick, and on the north by a row of small post-holes suggesting a hand-rail, a necessary adjunct to the steep gradient. This flint and mortar wall-base had been partially cut into when the hillside was levelled to receive the temple-mausoleum, and the surface of the path contained a few sherds of second-century pottery trodden into it. This pathway leads upwards to a possible terrace higher still than that occupied by the temple-mausoleum and the circular shrine, and its significance is as yet unknown.

The Burials. No details are available in regard to the coffin that was removed late in the fourth century by the grave robbers, except that, like its fellow, it was of lead, and that it, too, had once contained a body. But of the coffin that remained, crushed though it was, the dimensions are easily obtained, as follows:

	Head	*Foot*
Length	2 m.	
Width	0·52 m.	0·37 m.
Height	0·45 m.	0·37 m.

The coffin was thus sub-rectangular, slightly tapering both in width and height from head to foot. The lid fitted closely over the sides and ends, with a fold-down averaging 7·5 cm.; it was not soldered or riveted in any way and contained no nail-holes. Both coffin and lid exhibited an embossed cable motif, at the ends of the former and upon the latter. A group of three embossed scallop shells decorated the head end of the coffin, with one embossed scallop shell upon the foot end; the lid showed a group of three similar shells at the head, and one at the foot. The lead was in places between 83 mm. and 1·25 cm. thick (Pl. XXVIIIa).

The body had been packed in gypsum, the whole mass completely filling the coffin; but the permanent dampness of the environment, below the level of the natural chalk, had never allowed the gypsum to set hard, and therefore no cast of the body and its cerements was preserved, as with examples at York. The gypsum remained in a damp, slightly powdery condition, its surface stained brown through prolonged contact with the lead of the coffin, and continually affected by vegetable juices percolating down from above, and with the chemical substances related to the decomposition of the body.

The skeleton (Pl. XXVIIIb) was that of a young man aged about twenty-four years, some 1·77 m. in height. It lay extended full length upon its back, the arms stretched straight on either side and close to the body, the head turned to its left. The bones were deep brown in colour, sticky to the touch, and the whole emitted a noxious smell; indeed, it was at first thought possible that complete decay had never taken place. The odour was not, however, caused by any lack of decay; it was found to have been produced by the chemical reaction over a great period of time of vegetable acids upon body fluids, lead, and gypsum.

The coffin was raised, with the skeleton inside it, and taken to the workshop, where it was examined by Professor Keith Simpson, of Guy's Hospital, and then excavated from the coffin by Mr R. F. Jessup, F.S.A. and the author. On close examination, evidence came to light showing that the corpse had been buried in a shroud of coarse linen, beneath a species of short jerkin of what appeared to have been leather. The type of neither garment is known; the leather had greatly decayed to a few large black patches, while of the shroud only a small area remained over the breast. No metalwork such as buttons, pins of buckles were present. Also, no grave-goods had been placed in the coffin, except for a small pebble, pierced longitudinally, which lay among the bones of the left hand, and which may once have been strung round the wrist, perhaps as an amulet.

The grave-goods (Pl. XXIXa, Fig. 32b) associated with the double burial had been carefully disposed in a row on the west side of the tomb chamber, parallel with the coffins. Here, the floor of the tomb chamber was slightly higher than elsewhere, forming a very low and narrow platform along which the objects were placed.

Two flagons, one of bronze, the other of pottery, lay close together in the centre. Equidistant from the flagons, both to north and south, lay groups consisting each of two glass bottles accompanied with a knife and a spoon, with two glass bowls near the flagons towards the southern group. A small stone of rectangular shape for sharpening the knives lay nearby. A date for the bronze flagon is uncertain, but the pottery flagon can be closely dated to *c.* A.D. 280–330. Three of the glass bottles, all of which are cylindrical, were ornamented each with two pierced vestigial handles in the shape of a dolphin's head, while the bodies of the bottles are encircled at intervals with pairs of thin horizontal lines buffed on the wheel. The character of the fourth bottle could not be ascertained owing to its complete disintegration. These dolphin-handle bottles can also be closely dated to *c.* A.D. 275–325, agreeing in date with the pottery flagon; and from these objects the approximate date of the burials may be determined. Of them all, only the bronze flagon was stoppered; it presumably held some liquid for the sustenance after death of the two persons encoffined nearby.

The duality of these grave-goods bears striking relationship to the two individuals for whose use they were intended—the fragmentary bones from the absent coffin, most of which had been thrown back by the tomb robbers, were found to be those of a young woman about 1·67 m. in height, and some two or three years younger than her companion. The objects found lying upon the lid of the coffin of the young man, placed above his head, confirm this duality. These objects consisted of the remains of a wooden games-board with other objects upon it. The dimensions of the board could be determined, in spite of the almost complete disintegration of the wood; three of the bronze angle-pieces still lay *in situ,* giving a board 0·47 m. square, and a little over 2·5 cm. thick. Two bronze split-pins were also present, but their purpose is obscure, unless the board was a folding one and they had formed the hinges. The grain of the wood was clear, but nothing remained of incised or painted decoration upon what had once been its surface, to indicate the type of game that was played upon it. In the centre of the board had been carefully placed a roundel of bone incised with a human face, of grim visage with staring eyes and turned-down mouth, its tresses long and curling with what may have been intended for a parting in the middle. The head (Pl. XXIXb) was originally part of a larger incised figure, and the chin had been slightly cut away when the roundel was cut from the original object. As now cut, the disc with its face was clearly intended to form an important part of the grave furniture, and while snakes are missing from the hair, it would seem to have been intended by the mourners to represent the aspect of Medusa, and to lie upon the head of the coffin as a protection against evil influences. The head of Medusa appears embossed in medallions upon the lid of a lead coffin of the Romano-British period from Milton-next-Sittingbourne in Kent, where the head is slightly larger than the Lullingstone example, and again upon the end of another coffin from the same place.[34] The Lullingstone roundel would appear, therefore, to be intended to represent a Medusa; the parallel is too expressive to be ignored.

On either side of the bone roundel was a group of small objects, also resting upon the remains of the games-board. A few centimetres to the east was a compact group of thirty glass gaming-pieces, and a similar distance west of the roundel was an equally compact group of small bone pieces, incised with simple decoration, seventeen in all.

The thirty glass gaming-pieces consist of fifteen white and fifteen red-brown, forming a complete set. This is the only example known in Britain of a complete set of such pieces, and it is therefore of unique importance. The pieces are all of the same simple form, domed above and flat beneath. The glass is opaque and is inlaid with dots of the same material, coloured purple-blue on the red-brown pieces, red on the white pieces, and with some that vary through shades of pale-blue to iridescent green on both the red-brown and the white pieces. It might be thought that the dots, either by their number, arrangement or colour, might have been intended to distinguish either the numerical value of the pieces or their types. But for this to be so, the dots would have to match up systematically with those on pieces either on their own side or on the other, or both. An exhaustive analysis shows that in fact they do not; neither number, arrangement nor colour remotely suggests any systematic ordering of the pieces. There is a certain technique in the positioning of the dots upon the pieces; for instance, in the case of twenty of them groups of dots gyrate about a central dot. But this is undoubtedly due to an arrangement of the dots natural to the craftsman. This conclusion is

[34] G. Payne, "Roman Coffins of Lead, from Bex Hill, Milton-next-Sittingbourne", *Archaeologia Cantiana,* ix (1874), 164–73; *Antiquities of Roman Britain,* British Museum, London, 1951, 66 and Fig. 32.

important. In many museum displays of only two or three such glass pieces they are often said to have numerical value by the number of dots appearing on them. This complete set shows that the dots are in fact only decorative.

It is not possible to say what sort of game was played with these pieces. They are so formed that the game probably involved pushing the pieces over the board rather than picking them up in the fingers and transferring them to different parts of the board. Neither is it possible to balance them one upon another, as when in draughts a piece becomes a "king". A third point is the absence of dice. A fourth, that fifteen pieces constitute a side. The two most likely games are the *ludus duodecim scriptorum,* a game similar to our backgammon, and the *ludus latruncularum,* a game akin to chess or draughts. The latter apparently was not played with dice, and each game involved fifteen pieces a side. It is therefore possible that the *ludus latruncularum* might have been the game in this case. It is also interesting to observe that both man and woman enjoyed such contests of skill, and the presence of a game for two persons further reinforces the duality of the grave furniture.

The group of small bone pieces, cut to shape and decorated, may have ornamented a small wooden box which had completely decayed. In some cases, on close examination of the edges of these pieces, the line of discoloration due to the adhesive is observable. The pattern of insertion upon such a box cannot be known, and it may be that not all the pieces were used for such a purpose; some may have been used in the board-game. It is tempting to think that such a little box may have been the container in which the thirty gaming pieces were normally kept.

Erected *c.* A.D. 300, the temple-mausoleum was not used for any further burials, and by the last quarter of the fourth century it was falling into ruin. This can be understood when it is remembered that about this time the inhabitants of the villa had embraced Christianity, doubtless giving no further attention to the preservation of this pagan building, enshrining, as it did, persons who had been dead for some three generations. It had been founded in pagan times as a resting-place for two young people of obvious importance in their day, perhaps the villa owner himself and his wife. The temple erected above their tomb shows that pagan beliefs still obtained in the villa when they were living, and the absence of any subsequent burials, or evidence of rituals to keep their memory alive, clearly rendered the building unimportant to later generations. Eventually, it may well have been demolished. The floor of the *cella* had certainly sunk with the sagging and break-up of the wooden sarcophagus below, and the back-fill of the robber-pit contained, as has been said, numerous voussoirs from the fallen roof, chalk blocks from the *cella* walls, slabs of weathered plaster from the inside walls of the *cella,* and much charcoal, wood-ash, and iron slag, in addition to the dating material which has been mentioned. The iron slag suggests some activity nearby, and the pottery associated with this activity is already losing its Roman form and fabric when compared with the late Romano-British residual fragments with which it is found. It is likely that the position, at any rate, of the building was still remembered when the church of Lullingstane came to be built over it many centuries later. But when the villa was finally destroyed by fire early in the fifth century, the temple-mausoleum had for some decades ceased to dominate the site.

Interpretation. Always provided that the east side of the ambulatory, having fallen away in antiquity, did once complete the plan, the latter is normal for the Romano-Celtic temple-plan of north-west Europe, of which numerous examples occur in Britain. The presence of the small pillared portico at the entrance to the *cella* does add a slight classicising influence; but in general the plan remains Romano-Celtic. The reconstructions of such temples provide an excellent idea of their probable appearance.[35] Slight differences occur, however. The Lullingstone example is not built upon a low *podium,* and the small classical-type portico projects from the *cella* and not from the ambulatory. But these are minor differences; the essential plan remains the same.

The temple quarter at Trier[36] shows a remarkable concentration of such temples, together with some of circular plan and others exhibiting the classical aspect. The Romano-Celtic type is also remarkable in its adherence in many cases to a certain exterior size, often measuring about 12·20 m. square, to which the Lullingstone example conforms.

The proposition that we are dealing with a mausoleum is undoubtedly true, but the building above the tomb-chamber too closely conforms to the temple lay-out for its purpose to have been other than one intended for temple ritual connected with the cult of the dead. Here is not an object of pilgrimage or public worship; the absence of small votive articles or coins excludes the possibility of this. It was constructed solely for the private burial of two persons, and for the private devotions of their family to their memory.

The decoration of the internal walls of the *cella* has been briefly noticed. The pair of lower legs and feet disclosed on re-assembly of some of the painted plaster shows a stance which appears frequently upon frescoes of the Roman world. The figure is striding, or perhaps dancing, to the spectator's right, the knee probably bent and taking the weight of forward movement, the other leg lightly balanced on the toes of the foot stretched out behind. Some activity of mythological or ritualistic significance is suggested, and reinforces the proposition that the building had a religious use associated probably with the cult of the dead.

The only example in Britain that is at all reminiscent of the one under discussion was discovered in 1952 at Arbury Road, Cambridge.[37] Here, a stone coffin, lined with lead and containing a man's skeleton, had been buried about 0·91 m. beneath the Roman ground level, and a rectangular structure of chalk blocks, 5·03 by 4·19 m., was raised over it. The floor of this structure was made of rammed chalk, and the roof had been tiled. The floor ran right over the burial, but there was no subterranean tomb-chamber as at Lullingstone, though the building above ground may have served a similar purpose. The dating of the Cambridge building is slender, but the fourth century is suggested.

Closer parallels to the Lullingstone arrangement of subterranean tomb-chamber with above-ground cult-room are provided by Tombs 31 and 33 in the Minusio cemetery about 1 km. east of Locarno on Lake Maggiore. In both these cases, the burials were deposited in properly constructed masonry chambers below ground, the sarcophagi protected by ridge-roofs to take the weight of the earth and rubble back-fill. The burials were accompanied by abundant grave-goods, which, in the case of Tomb 31, occupied a small masonry annexe to the tomb-chamber. The superstructure of both tombs appears in reconstruction to have taken the form less of a recognizable temple as of a classical cult-room (Tomb 31), and an

[35] *op. cit.* in n. 11, 47–8.
[36] *Ibid.,* Fig. 110.
[37] *Proceedings of the Cambridge Antiquarian Society,* xlix (1956), 13–23.

altar upon steps (Tomb 33); a structure of Romano-Celtic temple plan is scarcely to be expected as far south as the Minusio cemetery.

A further possible parallel may be cited in the subterranean family vault at Weyden-bei-Köln, where there is evidence suggestive of an upper chamber. This vault measured 3·50 by 4·57 m. and was 4·11 m. high, the dimensions not differing greatly from the Lullingstone tomb-chamber (3·66 m. by 3·66 m. by 3·35 m. high). The Weyden example was constructed of tufa, with a red standstone entrance, and its internal arrangements and contents were most interesting. The carved marble sarcophagus that now stands in the midst has been put together, having been found in fragments; no doubt it had fallen from an upper chamber into the vault. Some structural fragments were also found, and these could have belonged to such an upper room whose design is, however, unknown. The sarcophagus is flanked by two stone chairs, carved to represent basket-work, and each of the three walls within was supplied with a large niche, in each of which stood a marble portrait-bust. Other wall recesses may have contained urns and grave-goods. The busts date from the second century, but the series of accompanying coins is dated from *c.* A.D. 260–340.

Some burials below ground, in coffins protected by brick and tile "roofs" are known from York, but there is no evidence of structures above ground in relation to them. One burial vault, however, is recorded from that city.[38] Rectangular in plan, about 2·44 by 1·52 m., it had a barrel-vault of tiles and mortar protecting the stone coffin, the crown of the vault perhaps protruding slightly above Roman ground level. Again, there was no evidence of any superstructure. These York examples were probably just what they seem, protected graves; and the same no doubt applies to those from Kent, at Langley, Southfleet, and Sutton Valence, though any superstructures that these burials may have had were probably cenotaphs and not above-ground cult-rooms. The structures at Keston in Kent, and at West Mersea in Essex, the latter with radiating "spokes", may have been mausolea with circular cult-rooms above; but there is little in these examples that can provide parallels with Lullingstone.

It will be seen that no truly close parallels exist in buildings so far discovered; the Lullingstone temple-mausoleum stands alone. It exhibits in plan a large and prominent above-ground building whose purpose can scarcely have been other than for temple ritual. Perhaps chambers await discovery deep beneath the *cellae* of other Romano-Celtic temples in this country.

The South Outbuilding (Fig. 34)

This building was encountered during mechanical excavation south of the baths for the reception of the protective building designed to cover the main part of the villa. A long section (Fig. 35), running east–west for 17 m., was cut from the modern road up into the steep hill-slope, and this exposed both the floor and one wall foundation of the Roman building, with two successive medieval levels from 0·61–0·91 m. apart, the upper disclosing a medieval building, whose wall footing ran north–south like the Roman wall, which lay 1·52 m. beneath it. It is likely that the medieval buildings are disposed from this point southwards, perhaps on both sides of the existing hollow way, now wooded, that runs up the

[38] *op. cit* in n. 6, Fig. 72.

hill westwards from here. The remains of the church of Lullingstane lie over the temple-mausoleum, and the record exists, dated A.D. 1412, when the then bishop of Rochester ordained that this parish be joined to that of Lullingstone, and that at that time only two families remained resident at Lullingstane. Medieval buildings later than this date are therefore unlikely to occur in the neighbourhood of the Roman villa.

It is of the Roman building, however, and its associated levels with which this report is concerned. The long east–west section was cut 8·23 m. south of the baths. The west wall of the Roman outbuilding came to light at this distance, but it had been destroyed further north. This north limit of the building was indicated by two post-holes. The wall lay 5·79 m. west of the modern road; the western post-hole, 0·25 m. in diameter and 0·40 m. deep, packed round with flints, lay in prolongation of the wall and 2·74 m. north of the section, forming the north-west corner of the building. The eastern post-hole lay 2·74 m. from the first post-hole and 2·44 m. north of the section. It was again 0·25 m. in diameter, but only 0·22 m. deep, and lacked the flint packing, having been dug in the northern edge of the floor of the building, a floor of consolidated gravel, flint and clay. At this northern end, a sleeper trench, 0·35 m. wide and 0·22 m. deep, was found cut into the same floor almost directly east of the western post-hole; but the eastern post-hole lay 0·22 m. south of this line, which formed the north end of the building. This small error can be accepted in the case of a somewhat flimsily constructed outbuilding, which this is likely to have been, and the north end was probably formed of wooden sleepers with, perhaps, three posts. Taking the eastern post-hole as central along this north side, a total width of some 5·79 m. west to east would be indicated for the building.

A parallel excavation was made 0·91 m. south of the east–west section, this excavation being 1·42 m. wide and extending for 5·49 m. westwards from the modern road. The Roman wall footing was again met with at 5·18 m. west of the modern road, which here curves slightly southwestwards, the line of the Roman wall footing stretching from the post-hole at the north-west corner southwards for 5 m. It was not possible to excavate further south, so the length of the building could not be obtained; but 5 m. of its west wall having been revealed, with an estimated width of 5·79 m., its total length may have been some 16·47 m., taking the estimated width at one-third of its length, and supposing that its long axis lay north–south.

The building was of simple construction. The floor was cobbled with selected flints of small size, tightly packed in clay and gravel; no large flints were encountered included in it. It sloped up gently westwards at a gradient of about 1 in 15, where it met the flint foundation of its west wall. The clay covering this cobbled floor was consistent and averaged 5 cm. in thickness, extending throughout the interior and serving as a treading surface. As has been mentioned, the north limit of the building was defined by two post-holes and part of a sleeper-trench, with no trace of a flint wall foundation, though such a foundation formed the west limit. Here, the flint foundation had never been carried up as a wall, but had supported a clay wall, possibly strengthened with wattles, much of which was found to have collapsed inwards, or perhaps purposely thrown down when the building went out of use and became ruined. This clay from the walls, for the east wall may have been similarly constructed, was found overlying the floor of the building, but separated from it in large areas by an occupation level and a thin level of rubble, which is associated with the destruction. This clay from the walls was found still lying at a thickness of 0·30 m. in places, and it incorporated towards the middle a number of small slabs of painted wall-plaster. This does not suggest, however, that the walls were rendered with such painted decoration; the fragments of plaster may have already been contained in the clay when it was brought from elsewhere for construction of the walls. No fallen roof-tiles were in evidence, suggesting a roof of slight construction, possibly of thatch, the ridge-pole running north–south, though, as has been said, the orientation of the building is not certainly known.

An important feature near the north-west corner of the interior was a pit, dug through the fallen clay walls and the clay floor and underlying cobbles. This pit was exactly circular, with a curving side and slightly rounded base, carefully lined with clay and resembling a very large basin. With the exception of a primary silting of clay, 0·10 m. thick in the centre, the pit had been empty when it subsequently became filled with black silt, with a little clay and specks of *opus signinum,* all of which came cleanly away from the side on excavation. Its dimensions were 0·35 m. in diameter at the base, 0·67 m. at 0·30 m. above the base, the side curving thence outwards and upwards to an approximate height of 0·47 m. to the line of the original level of the clay floor. These dimensions, with the circular shape of the pit and its even side-curve, may be significant, as they point to an object to contain which the pit may have been dug.

This object may have been a very large storage-jar, many fragments of which were found scattered over the site in the latest Roman levels, and which is dated to the second half of the fourth century. These large storage-jars were being made in the Alice Holt potteries near Farnham in Surrey at this time, and examples of at least three of them have been found during the excavation of the villa. They are decorated on the exterior with bands of combing in running scrolls and curving patterns, and are grey in colour. This particular example has been partially reconstructed, and its dimensions accord closely with those of the pit. The vessel has a diameter of 0·35 m. at the base, 0·70 m. at the girth, which is 0·30 m. above the base, and 0·61 m. in height. Its aperture has a diameter of 0·30 m. A comparison is as follows:

	Diameter at base	Diameter 0·30 m. above base	Height above base
Pit	0·35 m.	0·67 m.	0·47 m. (to floor level)
Storage-jar	0·35 m.	0·70 m.	0·61 m. (to aperture at top)

This large storage-jar may therefore have occupied the pit, late in the fourth century, which so closely fits it.

Dating of the Building. No precise dating material was obtained from the cobbles or the clay floor; but the method of building closely resembled that of the square cult-room at the north end of the villa, which is well dated towards the close of the second century. From the levels of the fallen clay of the walls, however, came fragments of samian Forms 33 and 18/31, dated to the mid- or late-second century, with a coin each of Valerian, Gallienus, Tetricus I, Diocletian and Carausius, spanning the years A.D. 253–305. These coins did not come from the body of the clay walls, but entered the levels after the fall of the walls. This suggest destruction towards the end of the second century, or at the beginning of the third century, which would agree with the known abandonment of the villa at that time, and its resulting dilapidation. These five coins were dropped over the already fallen building, and are associated with the late third-century re-occupation of the site, when the neighbouring baths was being rebuilt.

The level above the fallen clay walls was deposited over a considerable period, and consisted of black silt with chalk fragments and flints, with a varying thickness of up to 0·30 m. Eight coins occurred towards the top of this level—1 Constantine II *Caesar,* 2 Urbs Roma, 1 Constantine II *Augustus,* 2 Constans *Augustus.,* and 2 imitation *Fel. Temp. Rep.,* spanning the years A.D. 317–*c.* 355. These represent the earlier fourth-century occupation of the site.

Above this level again, in the clay-with-flint beneath the lower medieval level, were three coins—1 Constantinopolis, 1 Valentinian I, and an early first-century British coin depicting a galloping horse, a coin which had descended with the hill-wash from the higher ground to the west.

Two samian potter's stamps were recovered. One, SABIN·M, dated Hadrian/Antonine, was in the fourth-century level covering the filling of the pit, and therefore does not provide dating evidence; the other, CAMPINI·O, in a black level 6·25 m. west of the wall footing, an exterior level relating to the building when in use. This potter is not dated, but the complete base bearing the stamp is of Antonine date. The upper filling of the pit contained fragments of a samian dish, Form Lu. Tq, dated Hadrian/Antonine; but like the potter's stamp SABIN·M, it is a survival in a fourth-century level.

From this sparse evidence, it is probable that the building was erected late in the second century, was disused soon afterwards, and had become levelled shortly before the third-century re-occupation. The fourth-century coins attest the fourth-century occupation which succeeded this; but the building was never rebuilt. The floor was devoid of anything that might point to the use of the building; it does not seem to have been in human occupation, and was probably an outbuilding for general storage, or perhaps as stables. The pit having been dug later in what had been the north-west corner of the building, and possibly containing the storage-jar referred to, might suggest that hereabouts may have been, in the fourth century, something like a horse-standing. The jar has a capacity of approximately 26 gallons of water. This is, however, a conjectural use. No later Roman building was found in the area excavated.

The exterior level to the west of the building and contemporary with it, extended for 7·32 m. in that direction; and at 4·27 m. from the building it contained a thick deposit of green clay, 2·44 m. in length, with a shallow basin formed in it centrally, a basin 1·52 m. long and 0·38 m. deep in the centre. This feature contained approximately centrally again a cluster of six small post-holes, each 7·5 cm. in diameter, five sloping north at 30 degrees from the vertical, and one vertical. The cluster covered an area 0·61 m. from west to east, and 0·38 m. from north to south. A seventh post-hole of similar size lay 0·86 m. east of the centre of the cluster, and sloped west at 30 degrees from the vertical. This basin in the green clay was filled with reddish clay and charcoal, with tile fragments along the bottom, the charcoal deposit being about 0·40 m. thick, in the top of which was found the CAMPINI·O stamp. A considerable spread of burning had occurred here; but the significance of the green clay, and the basin contained in it, and the cluster of small post-holes, is not known. A level of pure red clay extended further westwards for an additional 4·27 m., rising with increasing steepness to the limit of excavation. It was noticeable that no protection had been accorded the building from flood-water from the high ground on the west, no trace of a gully exterior to the wall footing being found. The building was a construction ancillary to the villa, and was in use from the late second century to approximately the middle of the third century.

THE IMPORTANCE AND SIGNIFICANCE OF THE VILLA

The villa conforms generally in its chronology to that of many other such residential establishments in Roman Britain. Founded towards the end of the first century A.D., it continued in occupation until the last decade of the second century A.D. At that time its owner, who may have been an official of importance in the imperial service, relinquished it with some precipitancy during the political upheaval in the province caused by the withdrawal of the legions to Gaul by Clodius Albinus, which resulted in a military vacuum with its inevitable loss of confidence. The villa stood tenantless until the arrival of a new owner late in the third century, who brought it back to intensive farming, and remained in occupation, unlike many other villas, well into the fifth century A.D.

Religion, both pagan and Christian, played an essential part in the history of the villa, giving it significance for our better understanding of pagan cults and of early Christianity in Britain. The Deep Room was selected as the site for a *nymphaeum,* with an attached temple of Romano-Celtic plan closely connected with it, as the similarity of wall decoration of each makes clear. The painting depicting the three Water Spirits, though damaged, is a very rare example of a late second-century wall-painting of classical type still preserved in its niche in the *nymphaeum.*

Then, after a long period of disuse, the *nymphaeum* was transformed into a place where the ritual connected with the marble busts, deposited within it, could be followed. And finally, the room above, its walls decorated with large Chi Rho monograms and richly robed worshippers standing in prayer beneath a portico, became a Christian house-church, the only example for private domestic worship to have been identified so far in Roman Britain. This of itself is important, but the fact that the well-to-do owners of a country villa had embraced Christianity throws a new light upon what may have been a widespread religious practice in country districts towards the end of the Roman occupation.

The discovery of the marble busts was unique and important; it suggests that country villas in Britain may have been adorned with such family portraits among their domestic decorations, though perhaps only where the owners were of Roman rather than native stock. Marble sculpture, classical in character, was found in the Cotswolds villa at Woodchester; but the Lullingstone life-size portraits in marble, perhaps part of a family portrait gallery, are the first to have been recorded from a villa in Britain.

Again, the mosaic floors in the villa are unusual in their design and remarkable in the state of their preservation, while the Latin elegiac couplet included in the Europa panel is the longest and most complete mosaic inscription still *in situ* anywhere in the land.

These features of the Lullingstone villa are individually most striking and rare, but when taken together they demonstrate its paramount importance and significance among all the Roman villas hitherto excavated in Britain.

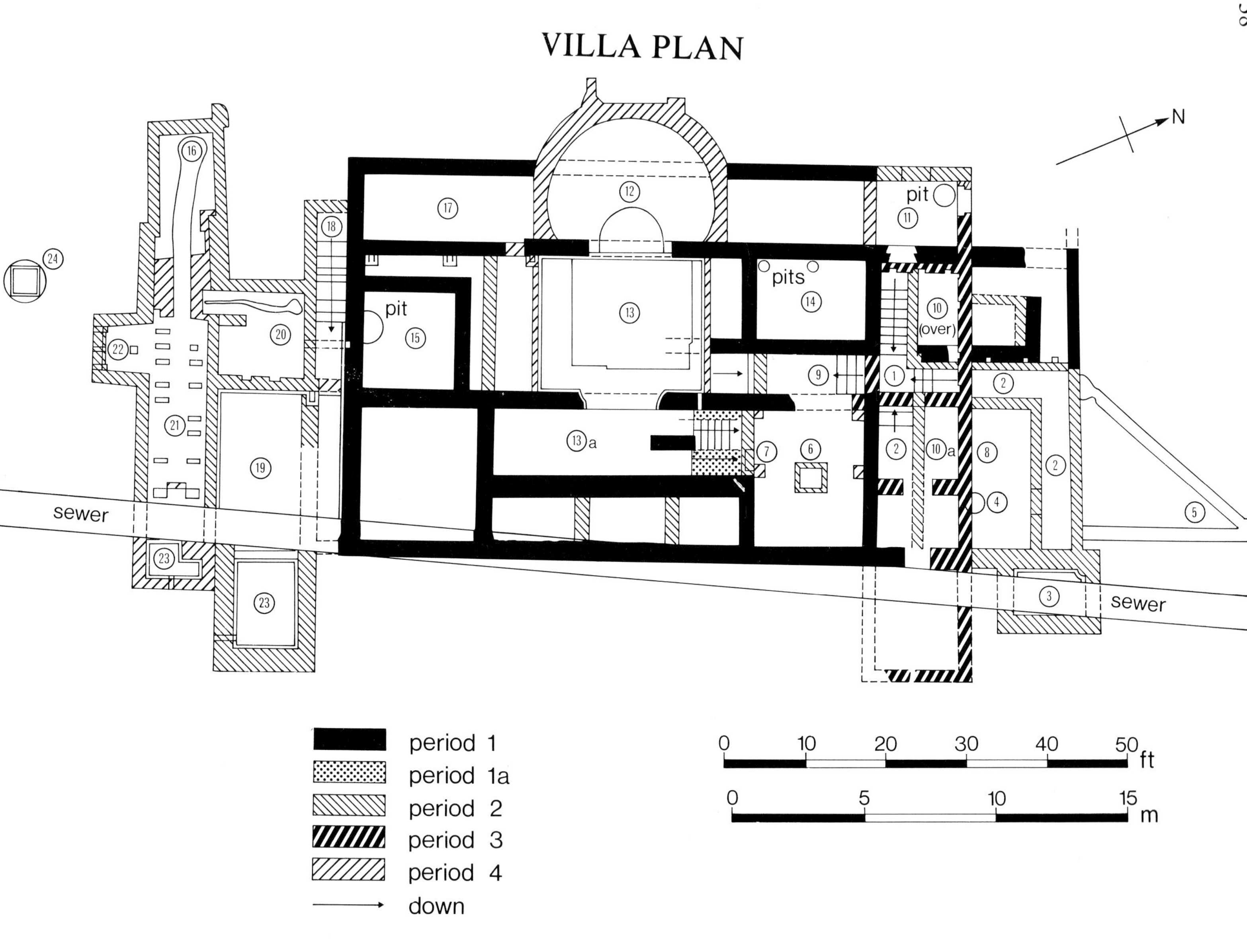

VILLA PLAN
N
pit
pits
pit
(over)
sewer
sewer
period 1
period 1a
period 2
period 3
period 4
down
0 10 20 30 40 50 ft
0 5 10 15 m

Fig. 6

DEEP ROOM destruction level on floor

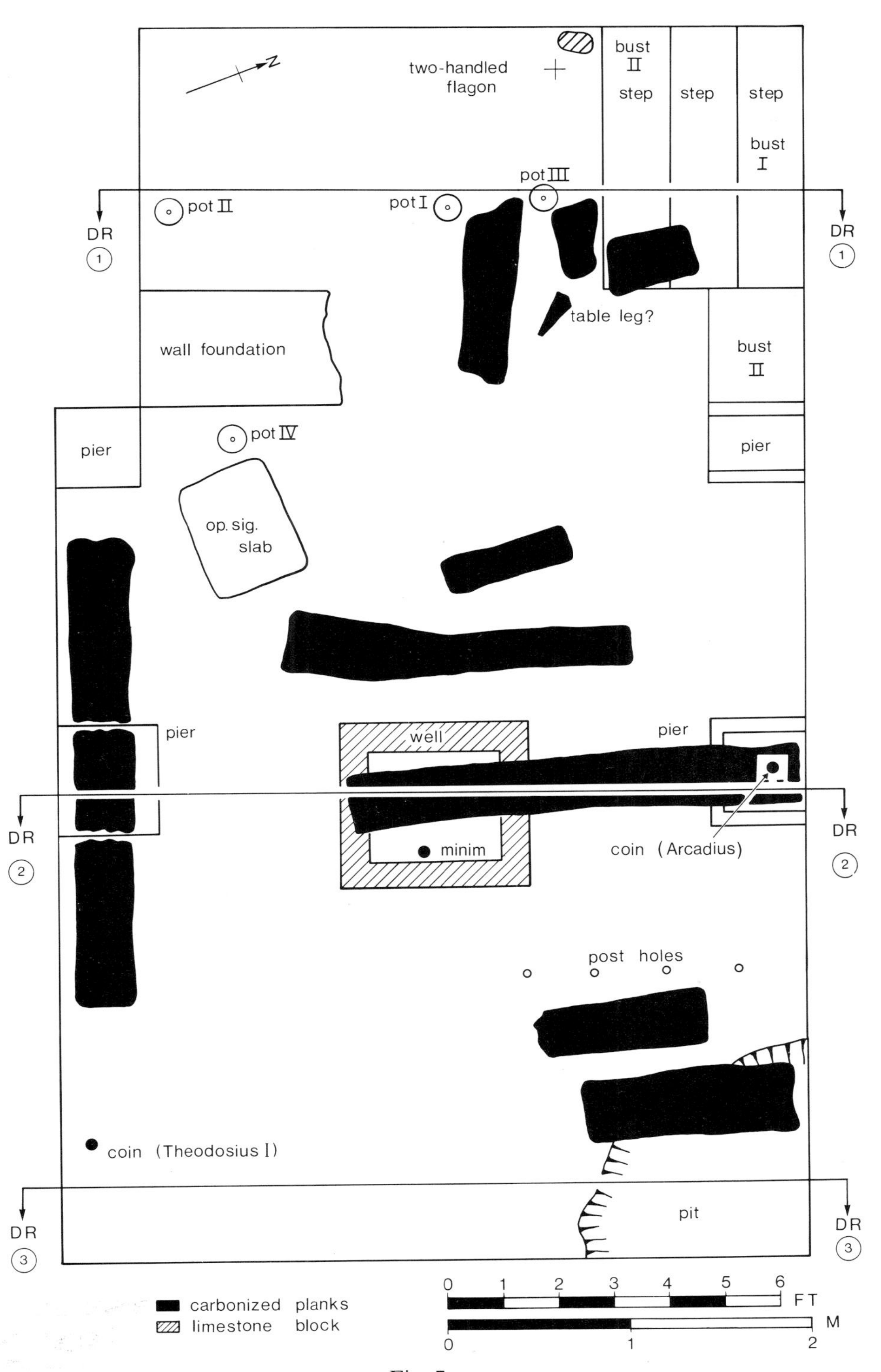

Fig. 7

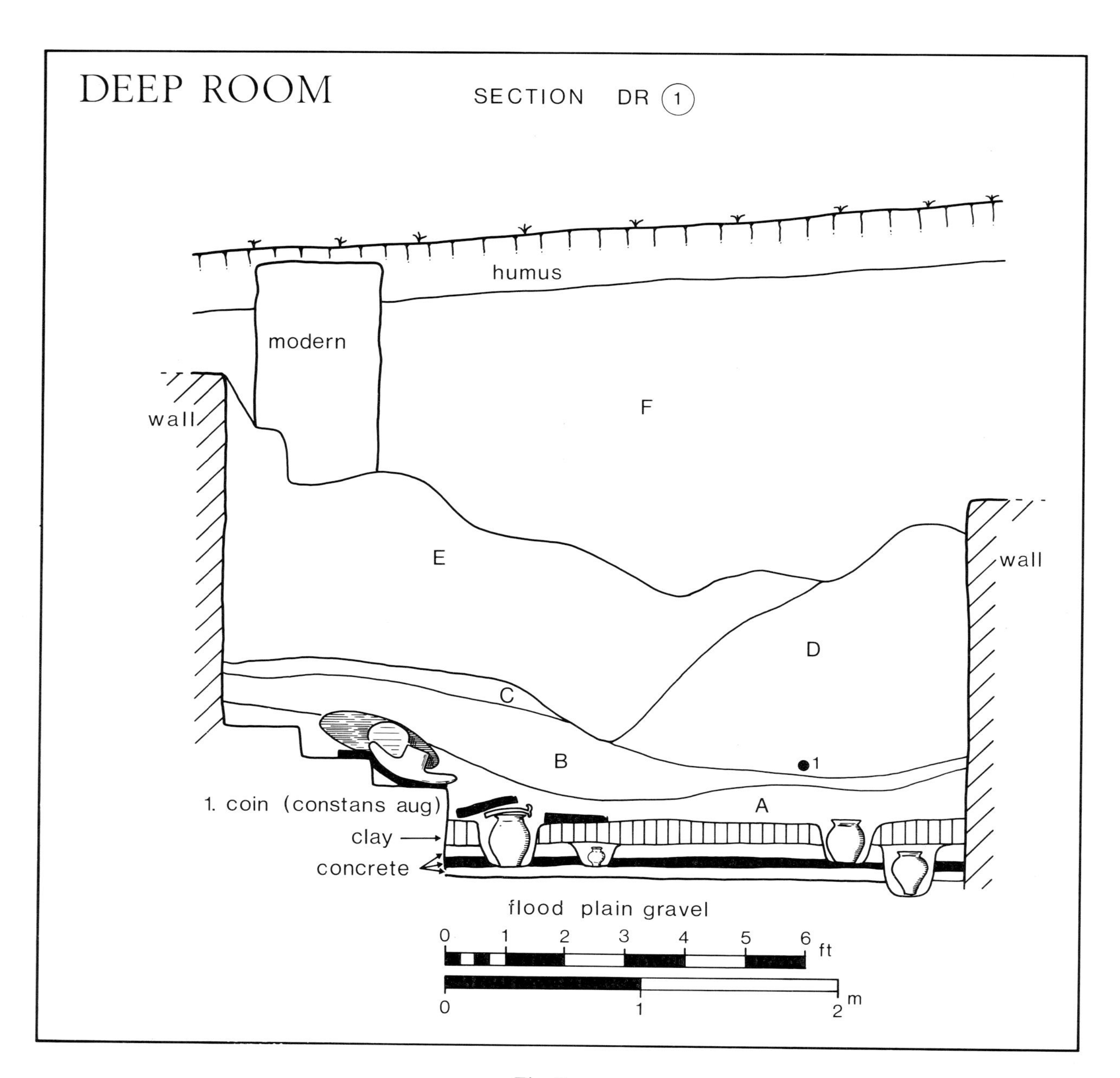
DEEP ROOM
SECTION DR 1
humus
modern
F
wall
E
wall
D
C
B
1
1. coin (constans aug)
A
clay
concrete
flood plain gravel
0 1 2 3 4 5 6 ft
0 1 2 m

Fig. 8a.

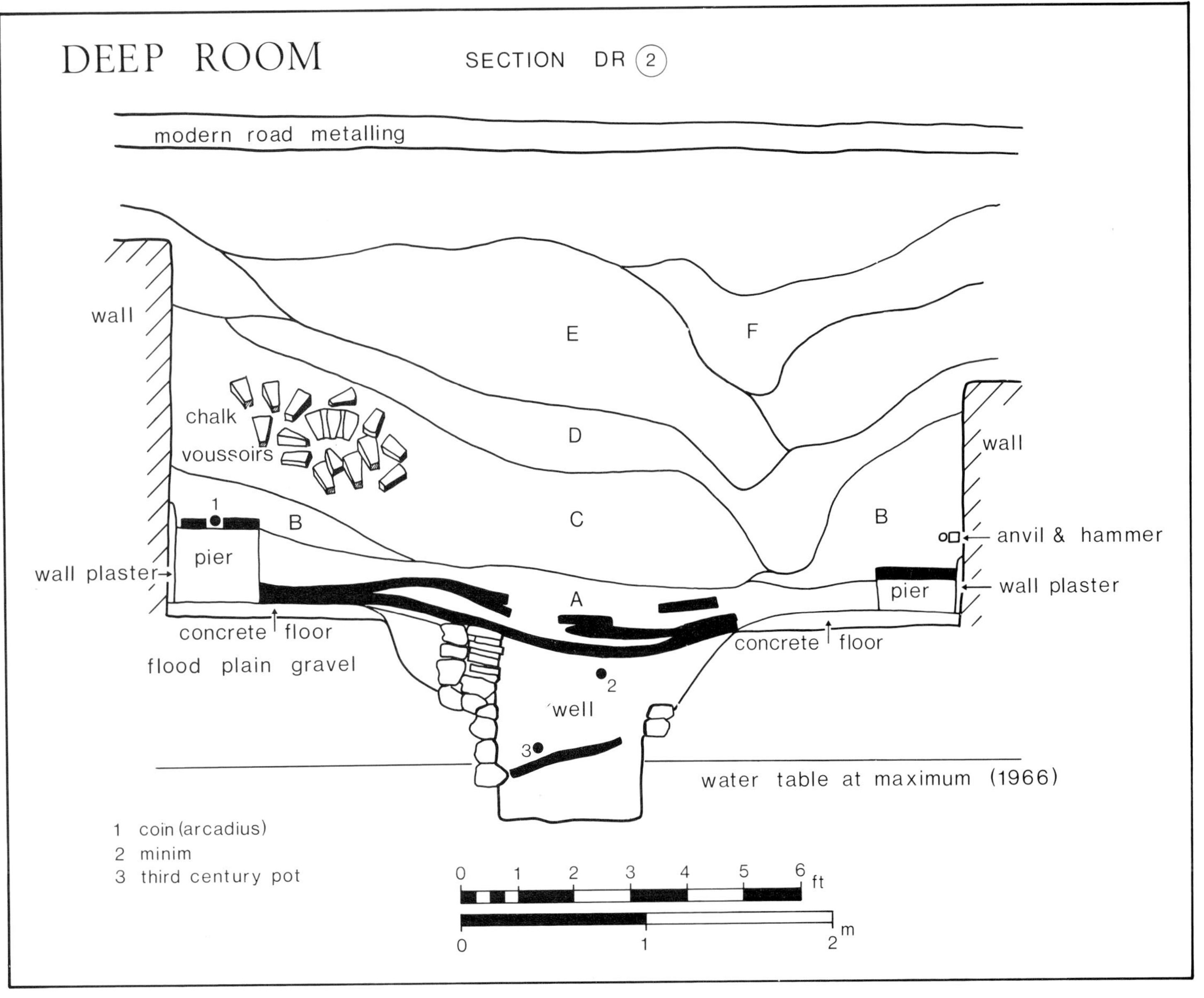
DEEP ROOM
SECTION DR 2
modern road metalling
wall
chalk
voussoirs
1
B
pier
wall plaster
concrete floor
flood plain gravel
E
F
D
C
A
B
wall
anvil & hammer
pier
wall plaster
concrete floor
2
well
3
water table at maximum (1966)
1 coin (arcadius)
2 minim
3 third century pot
0 1 2 3 4 5 6 ft
0 1 2 m

Fig. 8b.

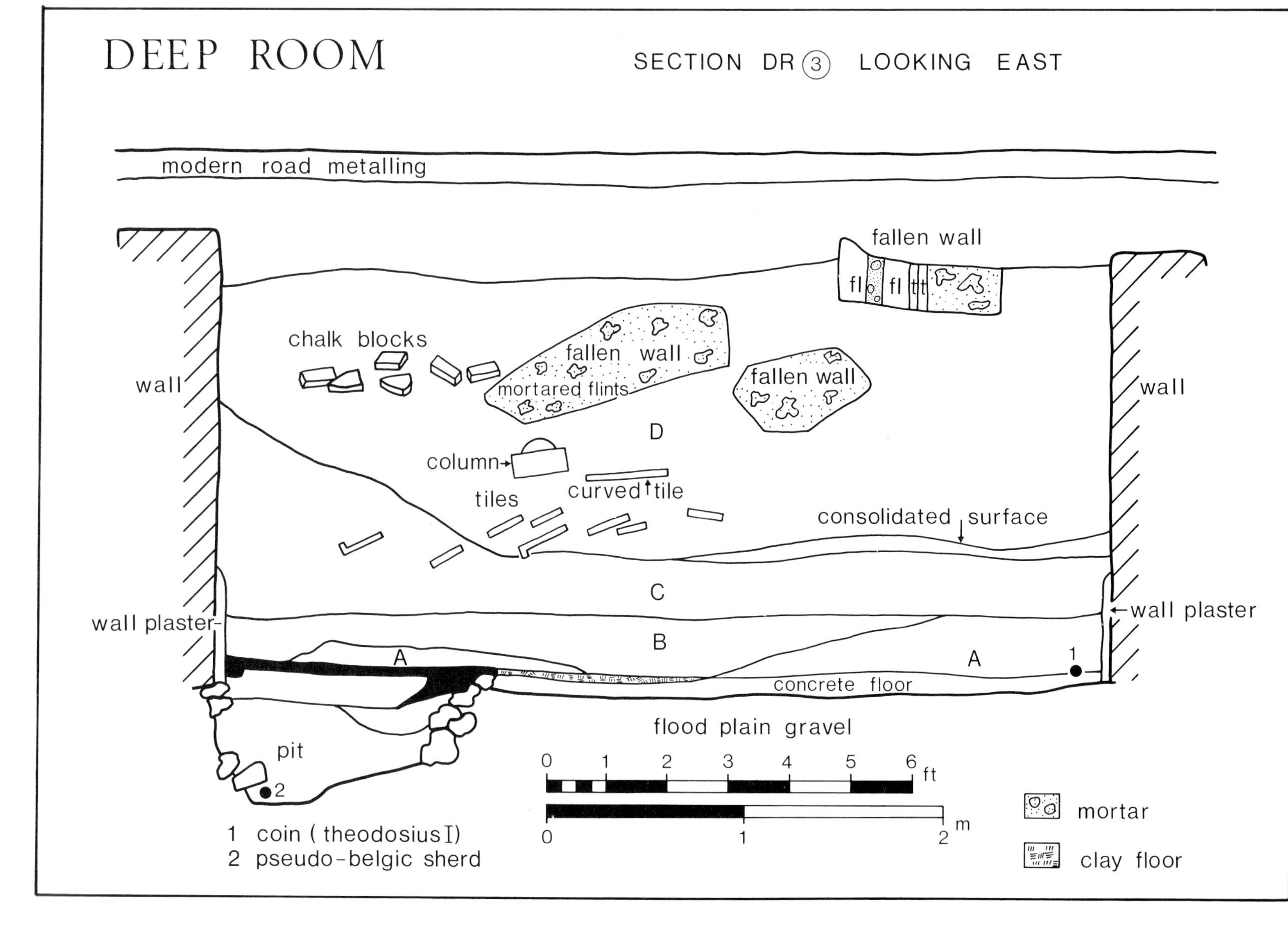
DEEP ROOM
SECTION DR (3) LOOKING EAST
modern road metalling
fallen wall
fl
fl
tt
chalk blocks
fallen wall
mortared flints
fallen wall
wall
wall
D
column
curved tile
tiles
consolidated surface
C
wall plaster
wall plaster
B
A
A
1
concrete floor
flood plain gravel
pit
2
0 1 2 3 4 5 6 ft
0 1 2 m
mortar
clay floor
1 coin (theodosius I)
2 pseudo-belgic sherd

Fig. 8c.

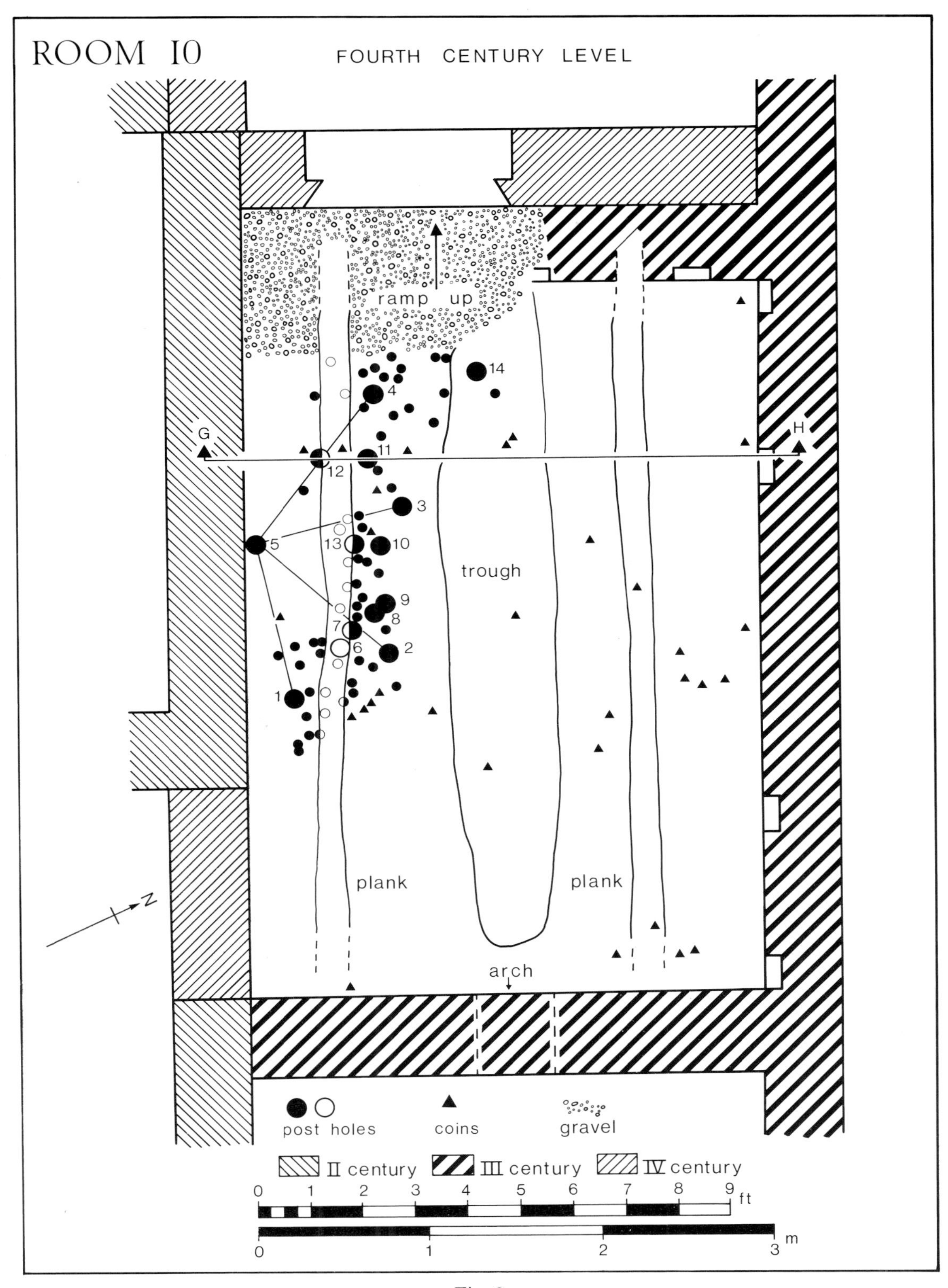
ROOM 10
FOURTH CENTURY LEVEL
ramp up
14
4
G
H
11
12
3
5
13
10
trough
9
8
7
2
6
1
plank
plank
N
arch
post holes
coins
gravel
II century
III century
IV century
0 1 2 3 4 5 6 7 8 9 ft
0 1 2 3 m

Fig. 9.

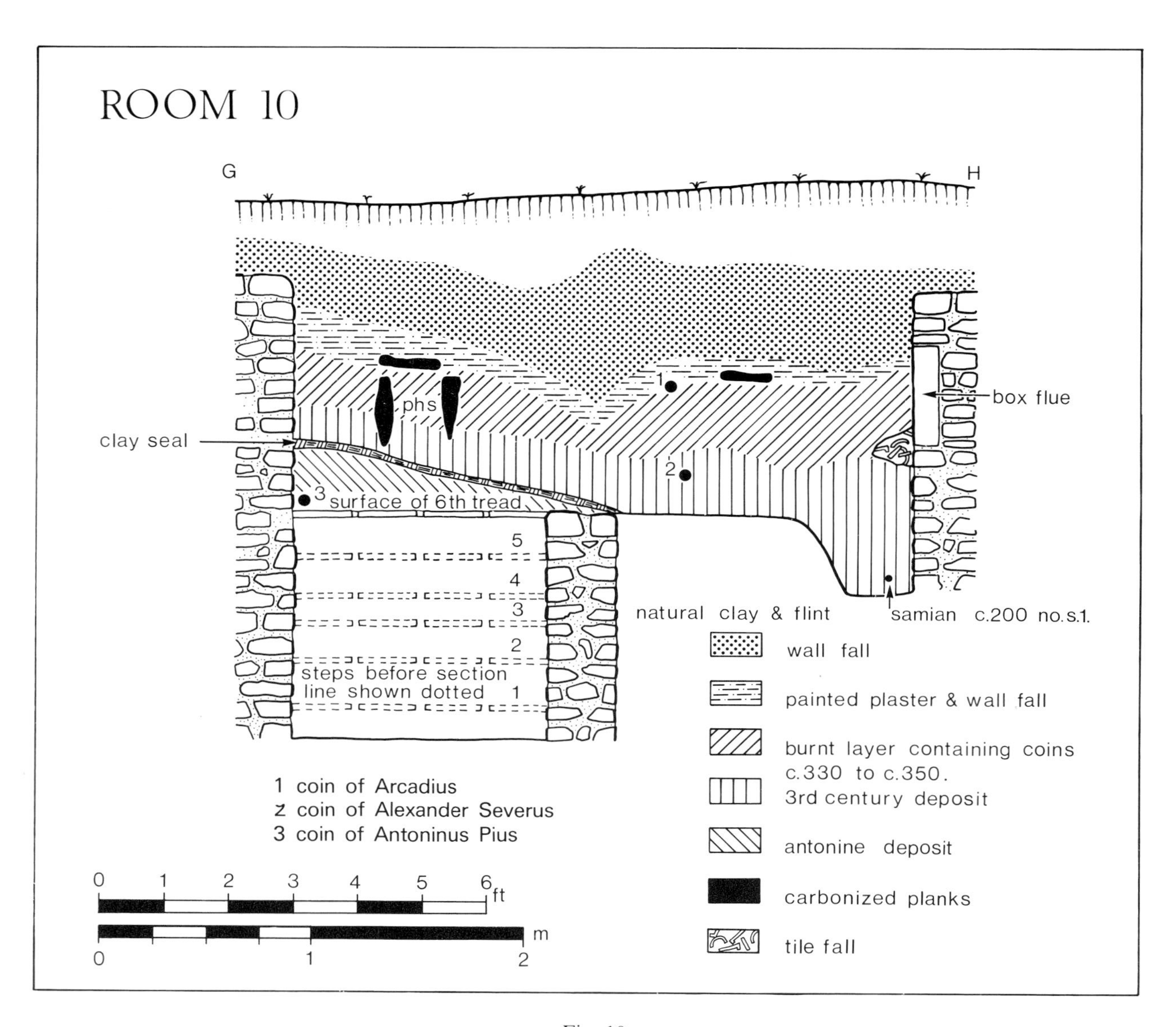
ROOM 10
G
H
box flue
clay seal
phs
1
2
3
surface of 6th tread
5
4
3
2
steps before section
line shown dotted
1
natural clay & flint
samian c.200 no.s.1.
wall fall
painted plaster & wall fall
burnt layer containing coins
c.330 to c.350.
3rd century deposit
antonine deposit
carbonized planks
tile fall
1 coin of Arcadius
z coin of Alexander Severus
3 coin of Antoninus Pius
0 1 2 3 4 5 6 ft
0 1 2 m

Fig. 10.

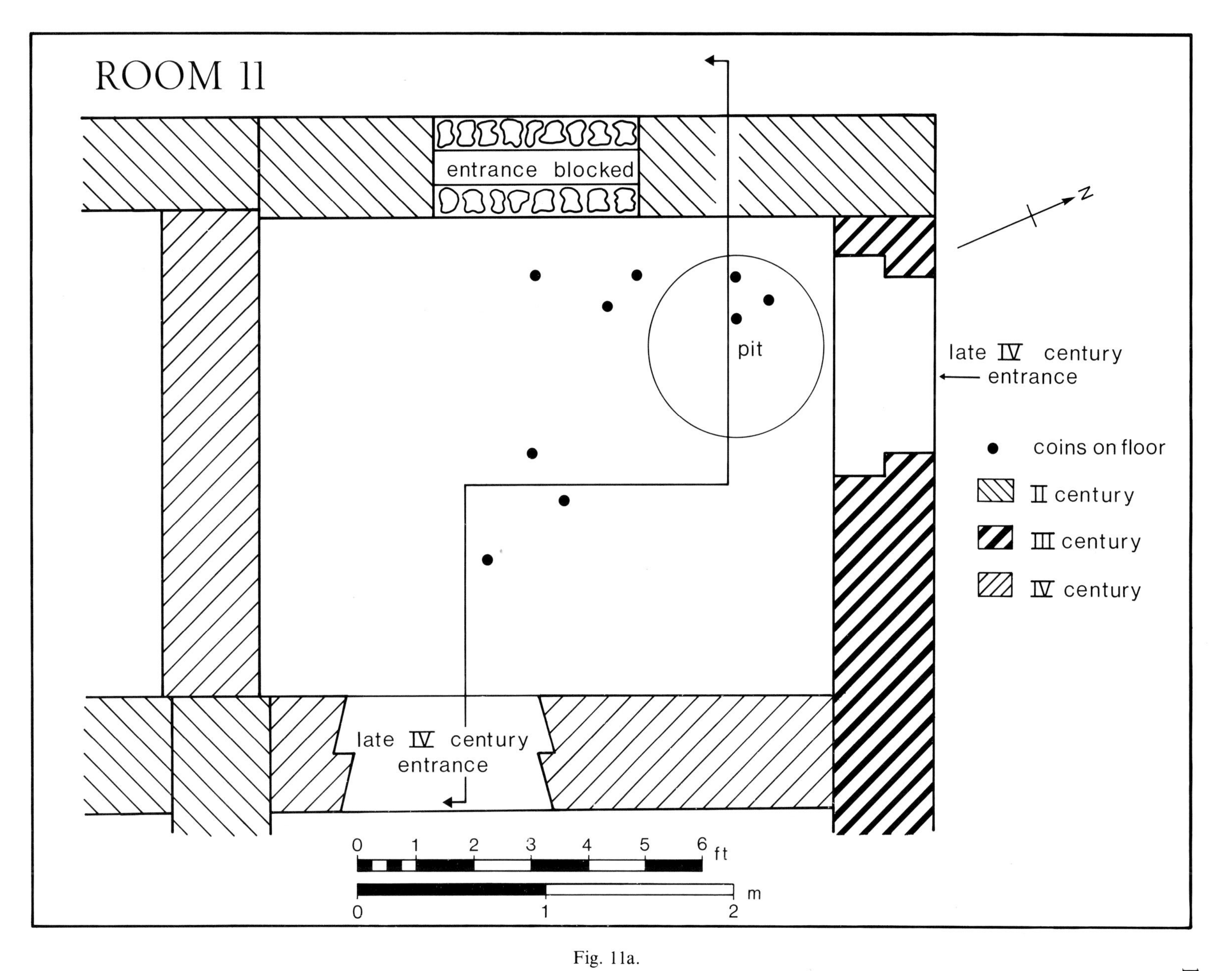
ROOM 11
entrance blocked
N
pit
late IV century
entrance
coins on floor
II century
III century
IV century
late IV century
entrance
0 1 2 3 4 5 6 ft
0 1 2 m

Fig. 11a.

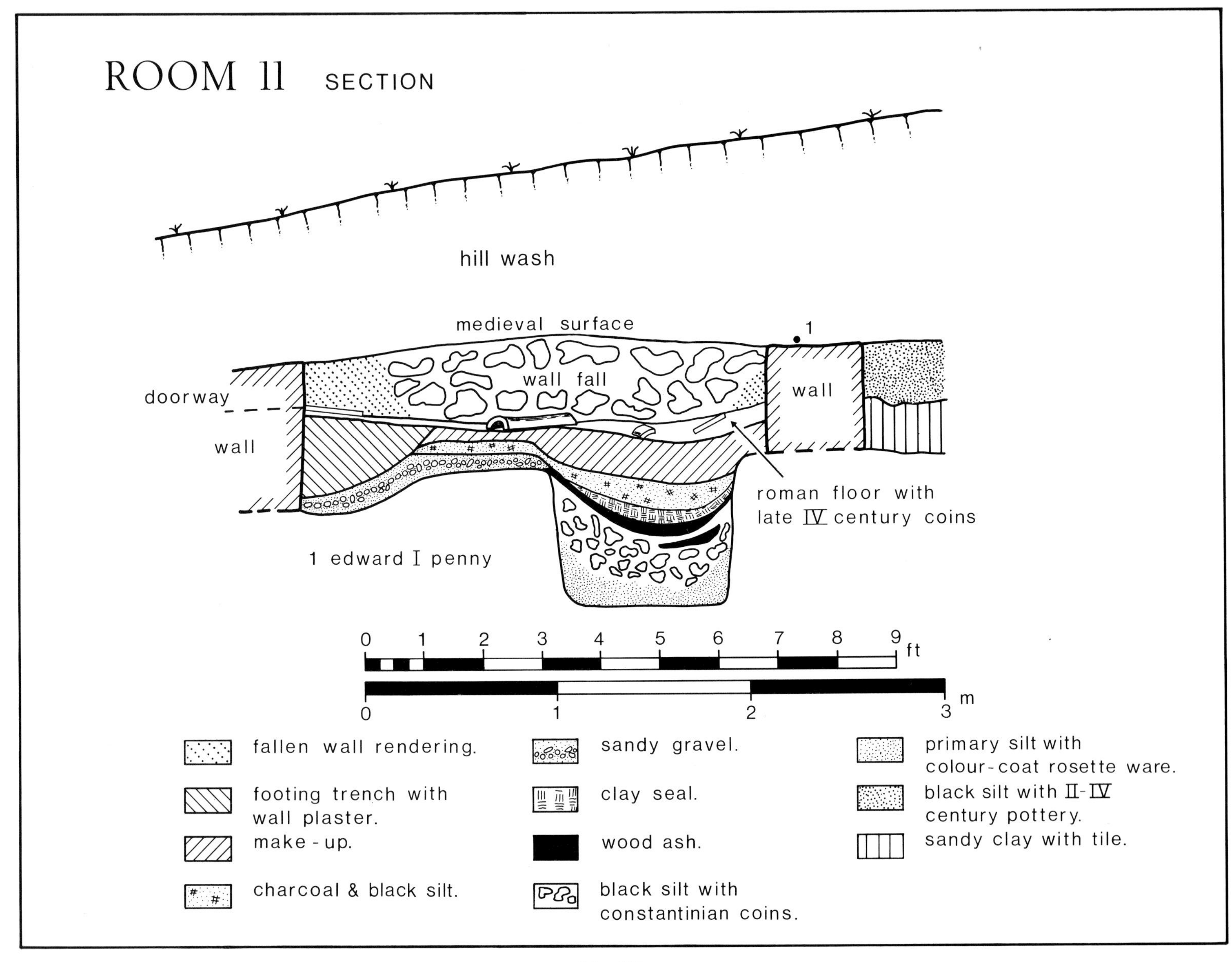
ROOM 11 SECTION
hill wash
medieval surface
1
wall fall
doorway
wall
wall
roman floor with
late IV century coins
1 edward I penny
0 1 2 3 4 5 6 7 8 9 ft
0 1 2 3 m
fallen wall rendering.
footing trench with
wall plaster.
make - up.
charcoal & black silt.
sandy gravel.
clay seal.
wood ash.
black silt with
constantinian coins.
primary silt with
colour-coat rosette ware.
black silt with II-IV
century pottery.
sandy clay with tile.

Fig. 11b.

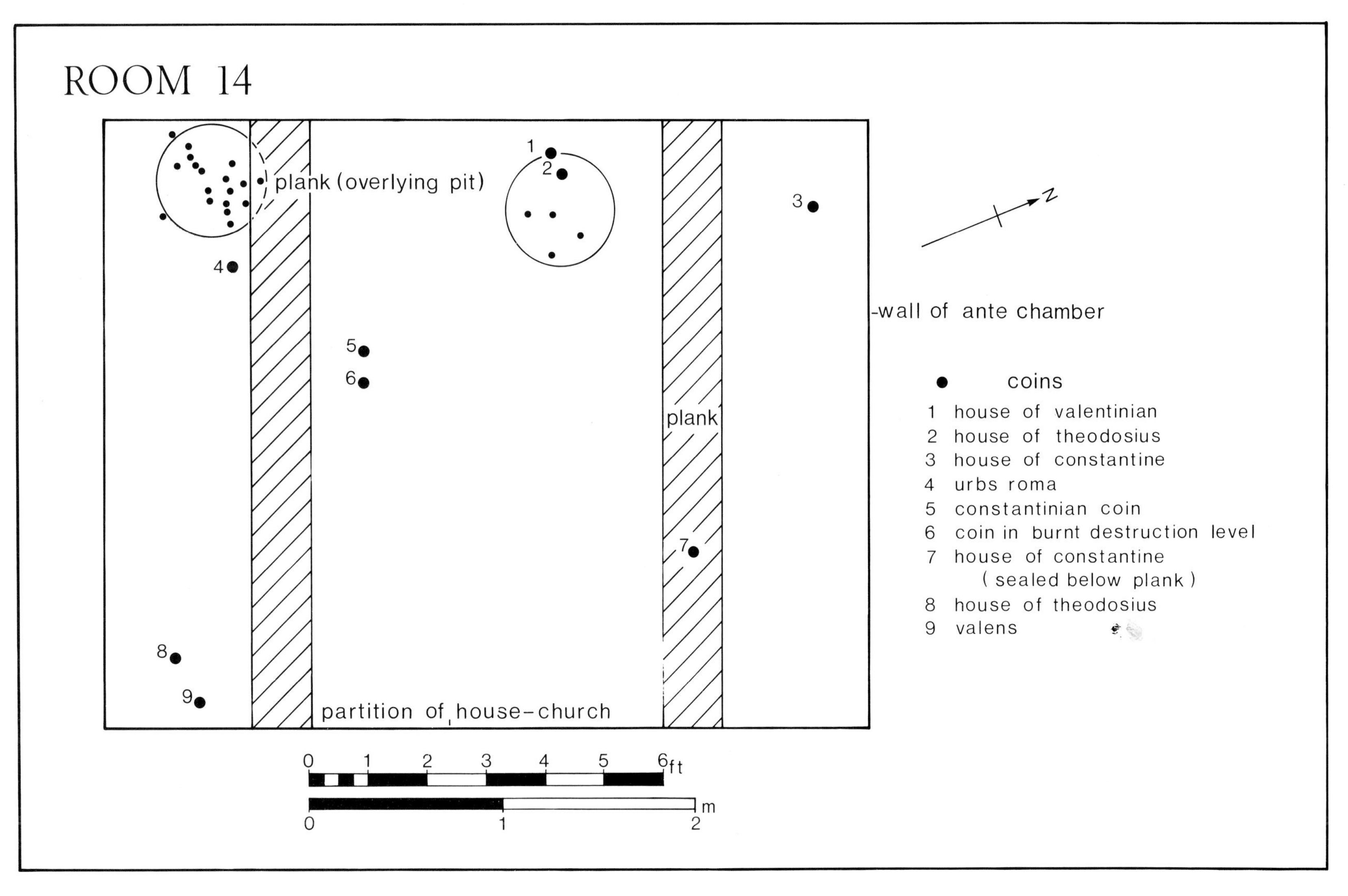

ROOM 14
plank (overlying pit)
partition of house-church
plank
wall of ante chamber
N
coins
1 house of valentinian
2 house of theodosius
3 house of constantine
4 urbs roma
5 constantinian coin
6 coin in burnt destruction level
7 house of constantine
(sealed below plank)
8 house of theodosius
9 valens
0 1 2 3 4 5 6 ft
0 1 2 m

Fig. 12.

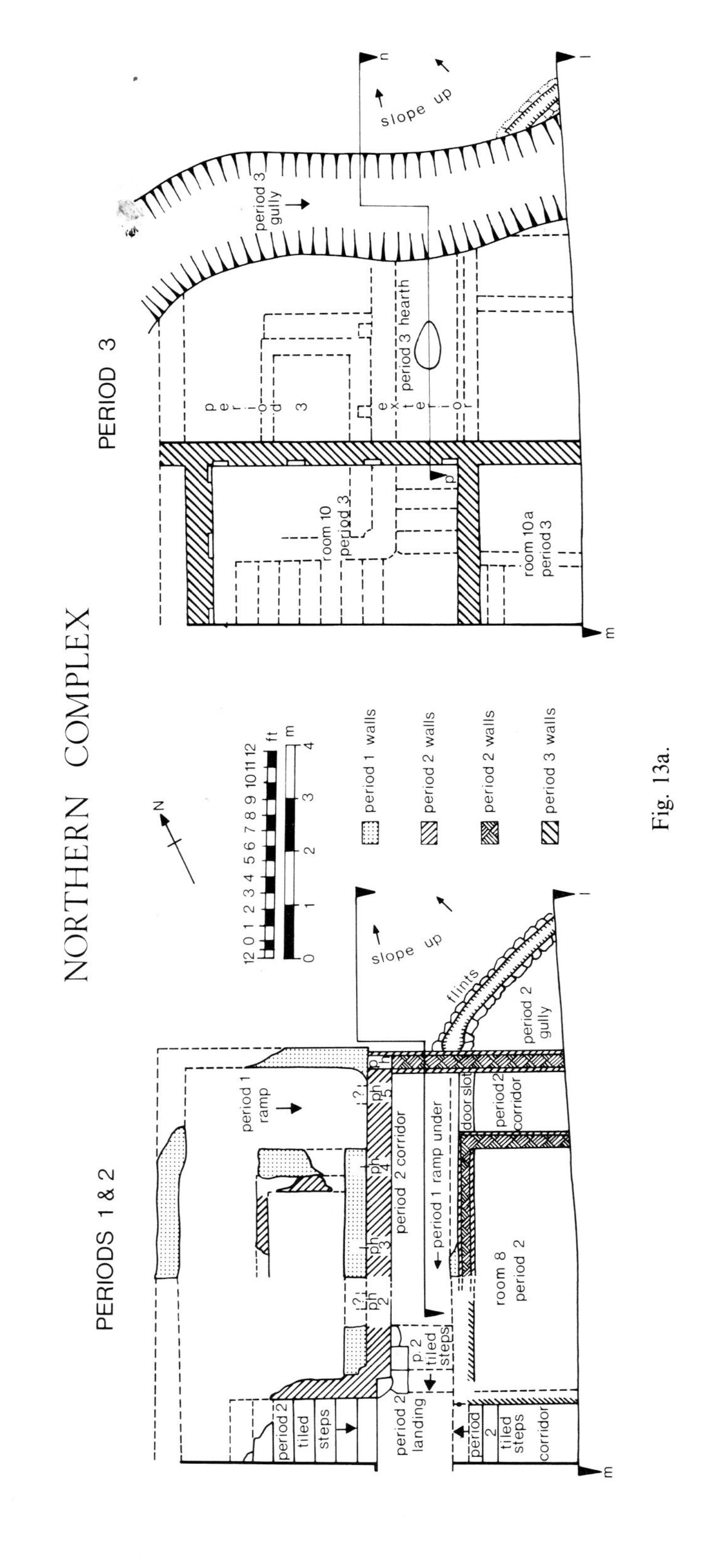
NORTHERN COMPLEX
PERIODS 1 & 2
PERIOD 3
period 1 walls
period 2 walls
period 2 walls
period 3 walls
ft
m
N
slope up
period 3 gully
period 3 hearth
room 10 period 3
room 10a period 3
period 1 ramp
period 2 corridor
period 1 ramp under
room 8 period 2
period 2 gully
flints
period 2 corridor
period 2 tiled steps
period 2 landing
p. 2 tiled steps
period 2 tiled steps corridor

Fig. 13a.

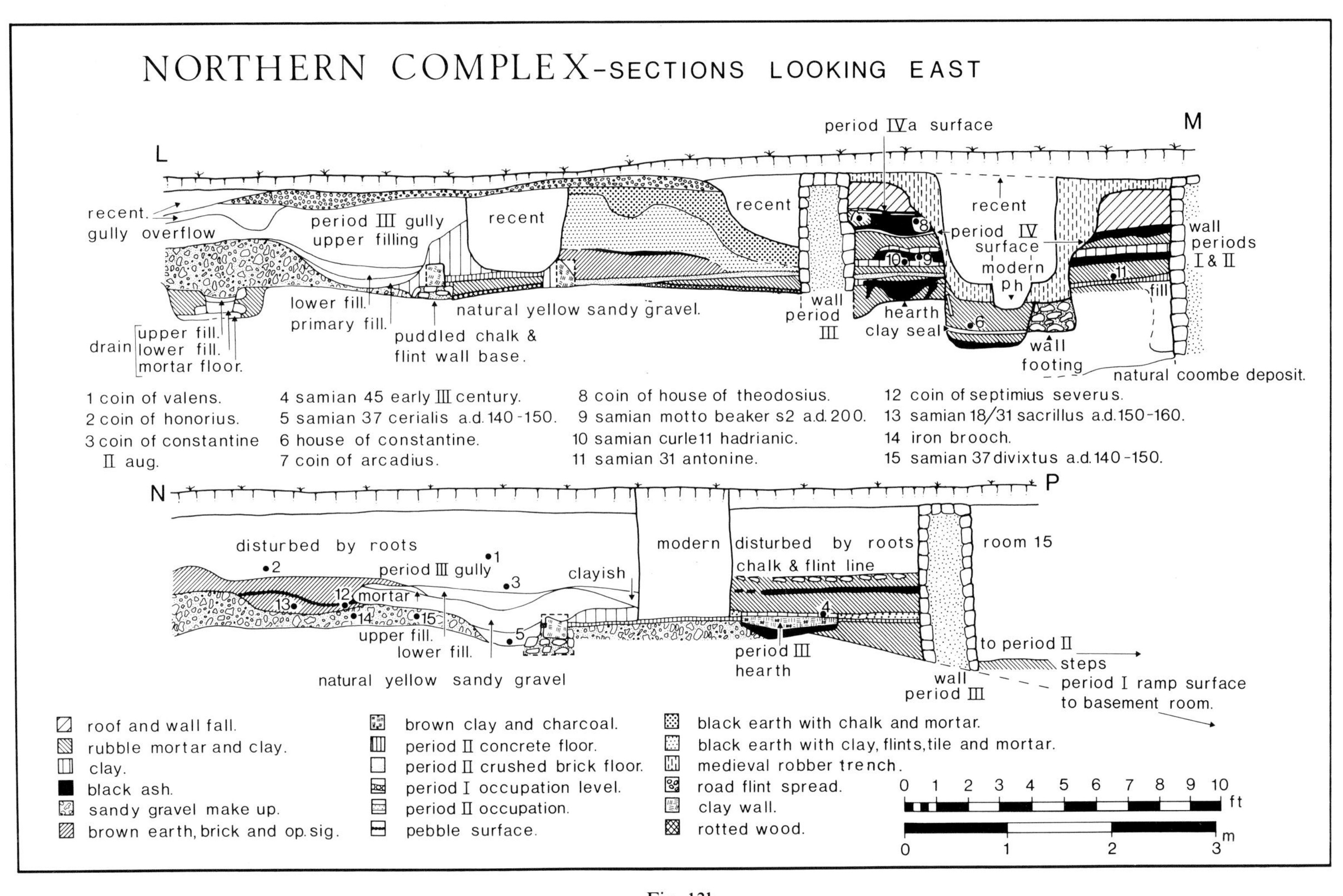
NORTHERN COMPLEX-SECTIONS LOOKING EAST
L
M
recent.
gully overflow
period III gully
upper filling
recent
recent
period IVa surface
recent
period IV
surface
modern
ph
wall
periods
I & II
fill
lower fill.
primary fill.
natural yellow sandy gravel.
puddled chalk &
flint wall base.
wall
period
III
hearth
clay seal
wall
footing
natural coombe deposit.
drain
upper fill.
lower fill.
mortar floor.
1 coin of valens.
2 coin of honorius.
3 coin of constantine II aug.
4 samian 45 early III century.
5 samian 37 cerialis a.d. 140-150.
6 house of constantine.
7 coin of arcadius.
8 coin of house of theodosius.
9 samian motto beaker s2 a.d. 200.
10 samian curle11 hadrianic.
11 samian 31 antonine.
12 coin of septimius severus.
13 samian 18/31 sacrillus a.d. 150-160.
14 iron brooch.
15 samian 37 divixtus a.d. 140-150.
N
P
disturbed by roots
period III gully
mortar
clayish
upper fill.
lower fill.
natural yellow sandy gravel
modern
disturbed by roots
chalk & flint line
period III
hearth
room 15
to period II
steps
period I ramp surface
to basement room.
wall
period III
roof and wall fall.
rubble mortar and clay.
clay.
black ash.
sandy gravel make up.
brown earth, brick and op. sig.
brown clay and charcoal.
period II concrete floor.
period II crushed brick floor.
period I occupation level.
period II occupation.
pebble surface.
black earth with chalk and mortar.
black earth with clay, flints, tile and mortar.
medieval robber trench.
road flint spread.
clay wall.
rotted wood.
0 1 2 3 4 5 6 7 8 9 10 ft
0 1 2 3 m

Fig. 13b.

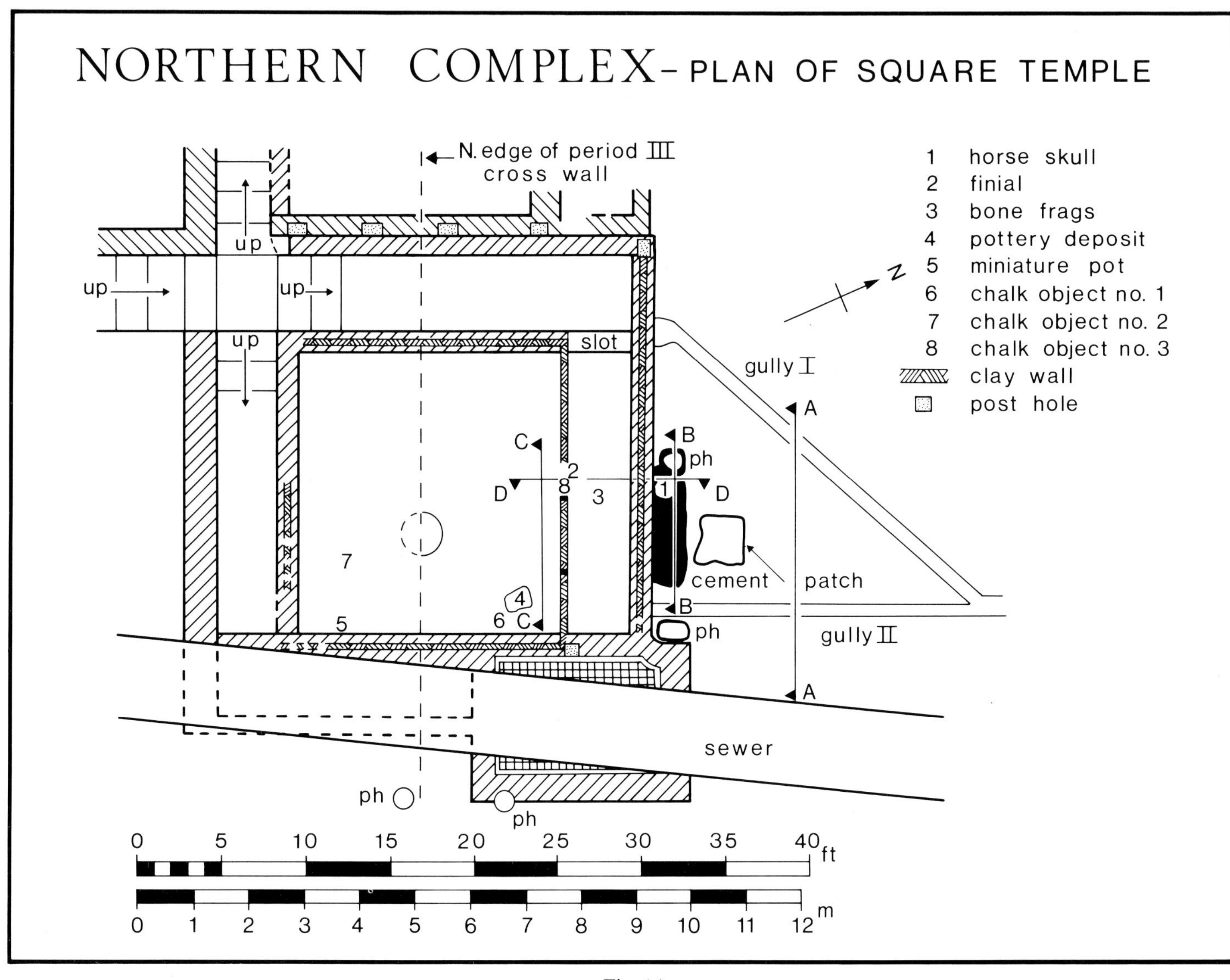
NORTHERN COMPLEX - PLAN OF SQUARE TEMPLE
1 horse skull
2 finial
3 bone frags
4 pottery deposit
5 miniature pot
6 chalk object no. 1
7 chalk object no. 2
8 chalk object no. 3
clay wall
post hole
N
N. edge of period III cross wall
up
slot
gully I
gully II
cement
patch
sewer
ph
A
B
C
D
0 5 10 15 20 25 30 35 40 ft
0 1 2 3 4 5 6 7 8 9 10 11 12 m

Fig. 14.

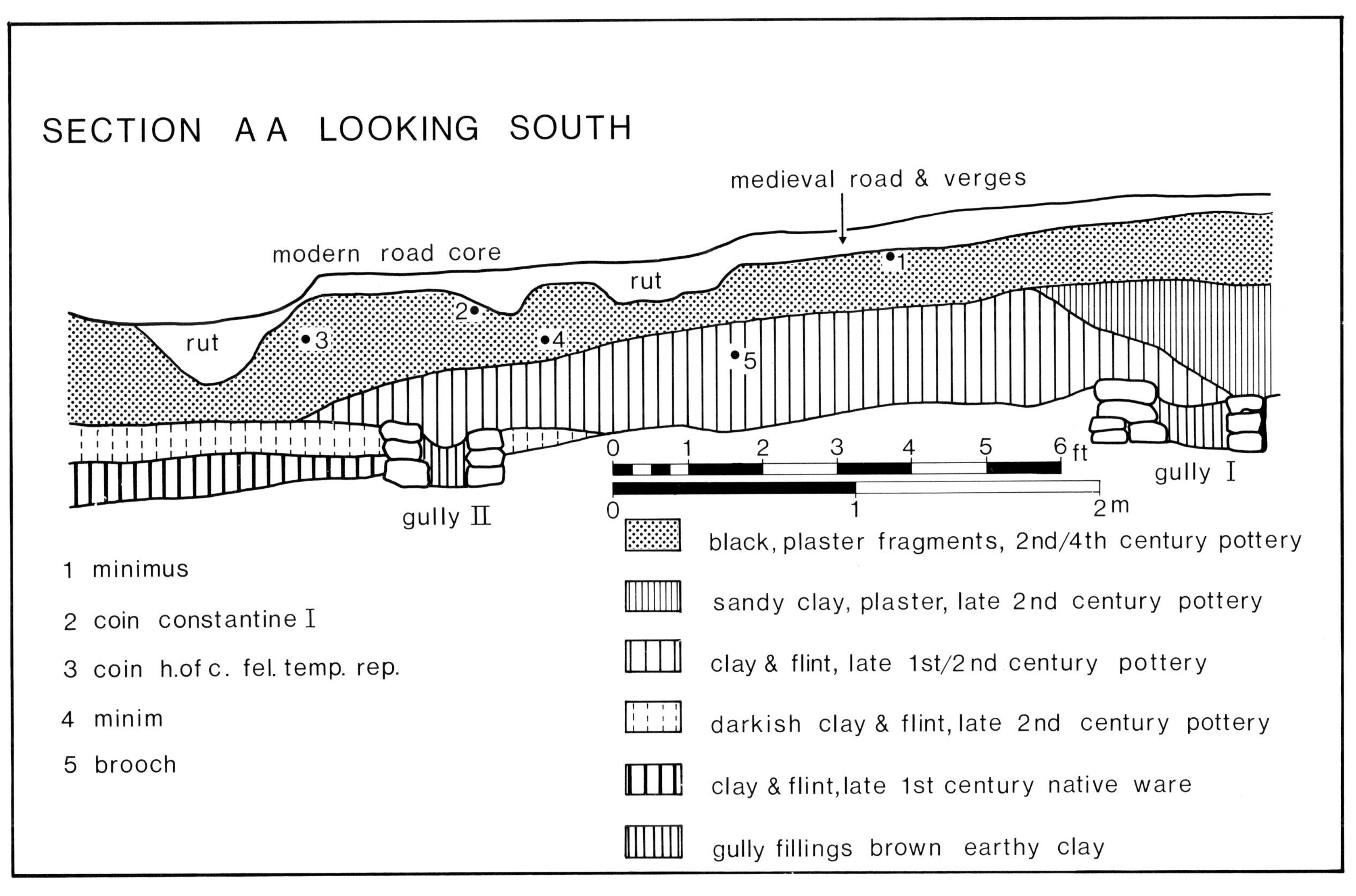
SECTION AA LOOKING SOUTH
medieval road & verges
modern road core
rut
rut
1
2
3
4
5
gully II
gully I
0 1 2 3 4 5 6 ft
0 1 2 m
black, plaster fragments, 2nd/4th century pottery
sandy clay, plaster, late 2nd century pottery
clay & flint, late 1st/2nd century pottery
darkish clay & flint, late 2nd century pottery
clay & flint, late 1st century native ware
gully fillings brown earthy clay
1 minimus
2 coin constantine I
3 coin h.of c. fel. temp. rep.
4 minim
5 brooch

Fig. 15a.

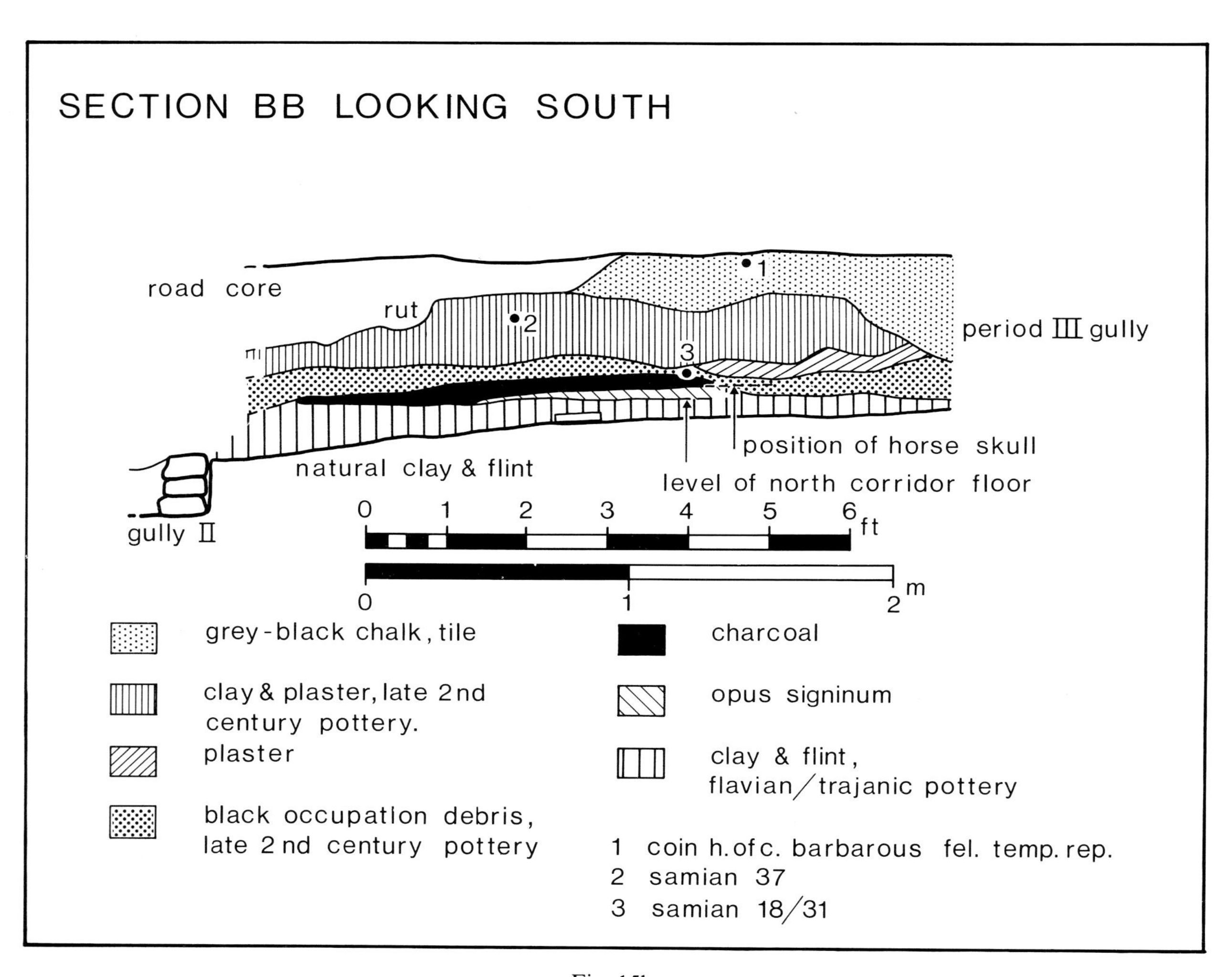
SECTION BB LOOKING SOUTH
road core
rut
1
2
3
period III gully
position of horse skull
level of north corridor floor
natural clay & flint
gully II
0 1 2 3 4 5 6 ft
0 1 2 m
grey-black chalk, tile
clay & plaster, late 2nd century pottery.
plaster
black occupation debris, late 2nd century pottery
charcoal
opus signinum
clay & flint, flavian/trajanic pottery
1 coin h. of c. barbarous fel. temp. rep.
2 samian 37
3 samian 18/31

Fig. 15b.

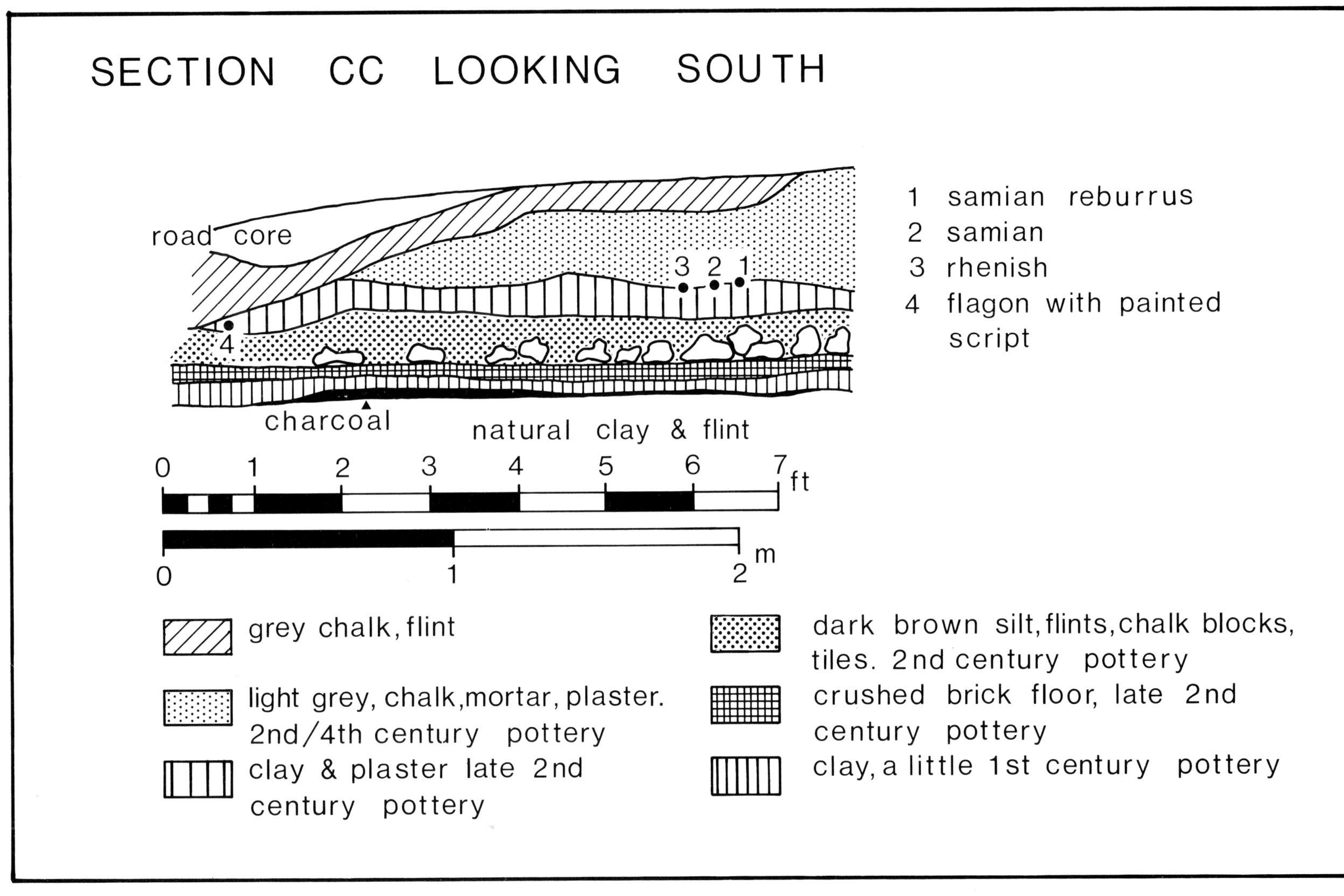
SECTION CC LOOKING SOUTH
road core
3 2 1
4
charcoal
natural clay & flint
0 1 2 3 4 5 6 7 ft
0 1 2 m
1 samian reburrus
2 samian
3 rhenish
4 flagon with painted script
grey chalk, flint
light grey, chalk, mortar, plaster. 2nd/4th century pottery
clay & plaster late 2nd century pottery
dark brown silt, flints, chalk blocks, tiles. 2nd century pottery
crushed brick floor, late 2nd century pottery
clay, a little 1st century pottery

Fig. 15c.

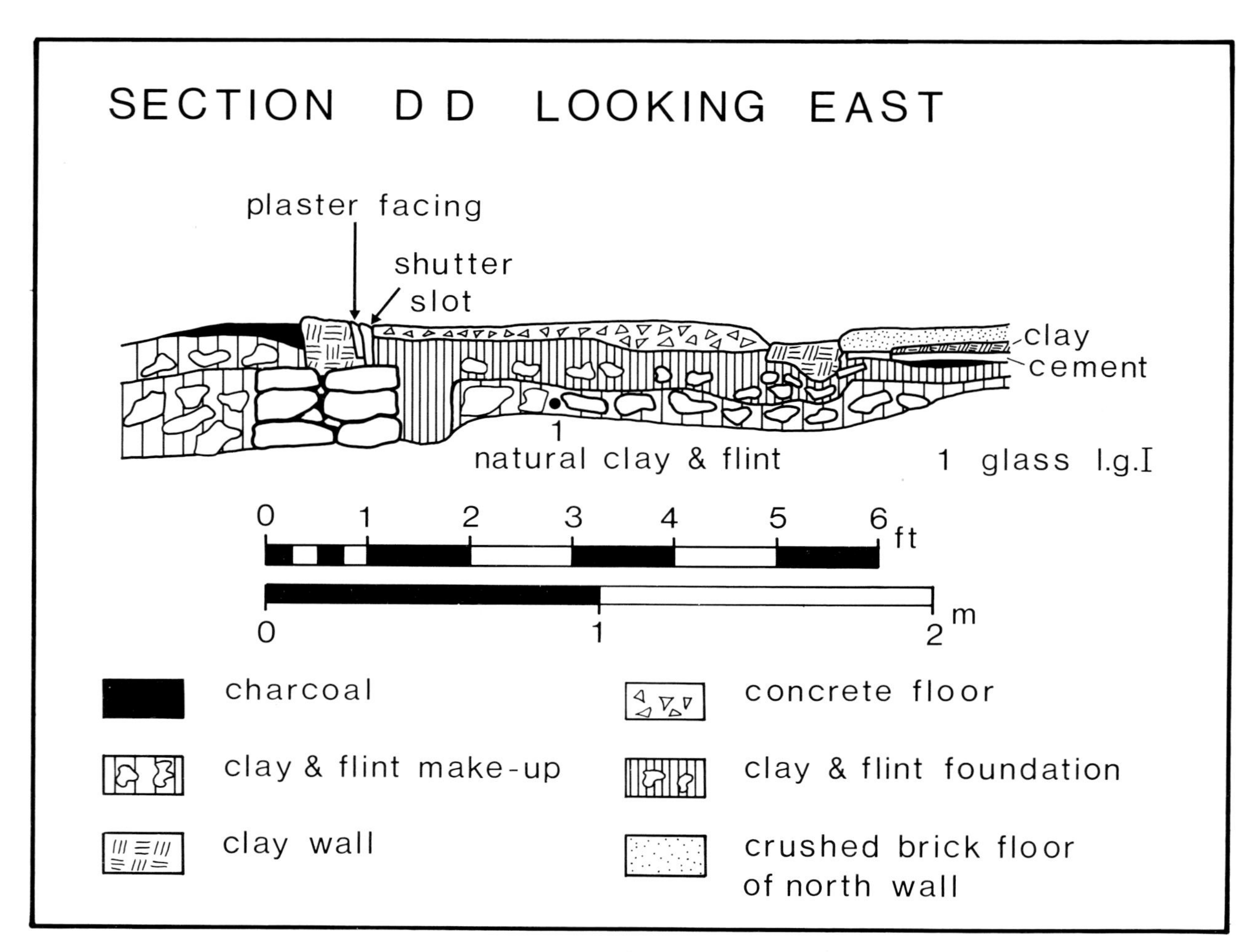
SECTION DD LOOKING EAST
plaster facing
shutter slot
clay
cement
1
natural clay & flint
1 glass I.g.I
0 1 2 3 4 5 6 ft
0 1 2 m
charcoal
concrete floor
clay & flint make-up
clay & flint foundation
clay wall
crushed brick floor of north wall

Fig. 15d.

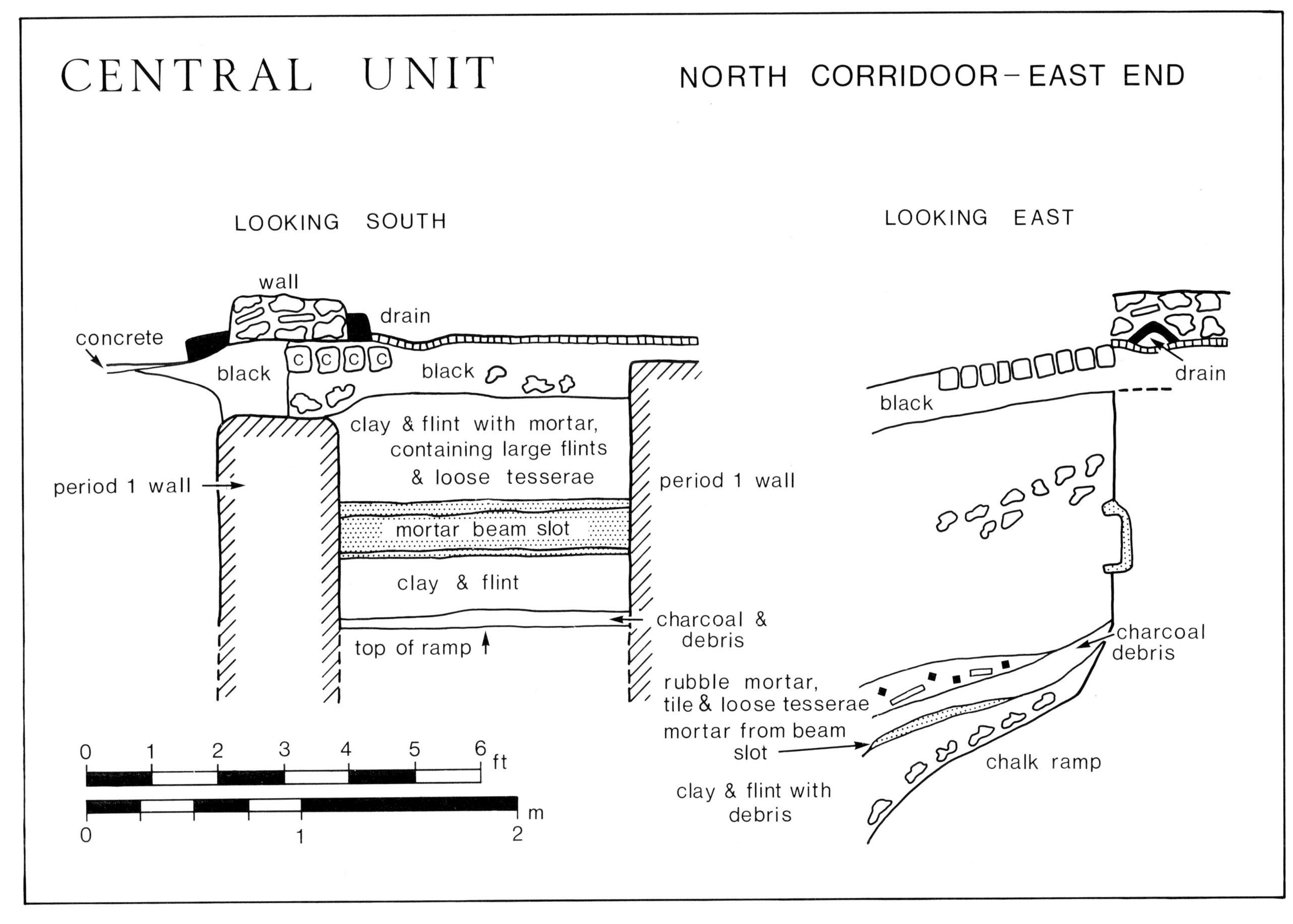
CENTRAL UNIT
NORTH CORRIDOOR – EAST END
LOOKING SOUTH
wall
drain
concrete
black
c c c c
black
clay & flint with mortar, containing large flints & loose tesserae
period 1 wall
period 1 wall
mortar beam slot
clay & flint
charcoal & debris
top of ramp
0 1 2 3 4 5 6 ft
0 1 2 m
LOOKING EAST
drain
black
charcoal debris
rubble mortar, tile & loose tesserae
mortar from beam slot
chalk ramp
clay & flint with debris

Fig. 16.

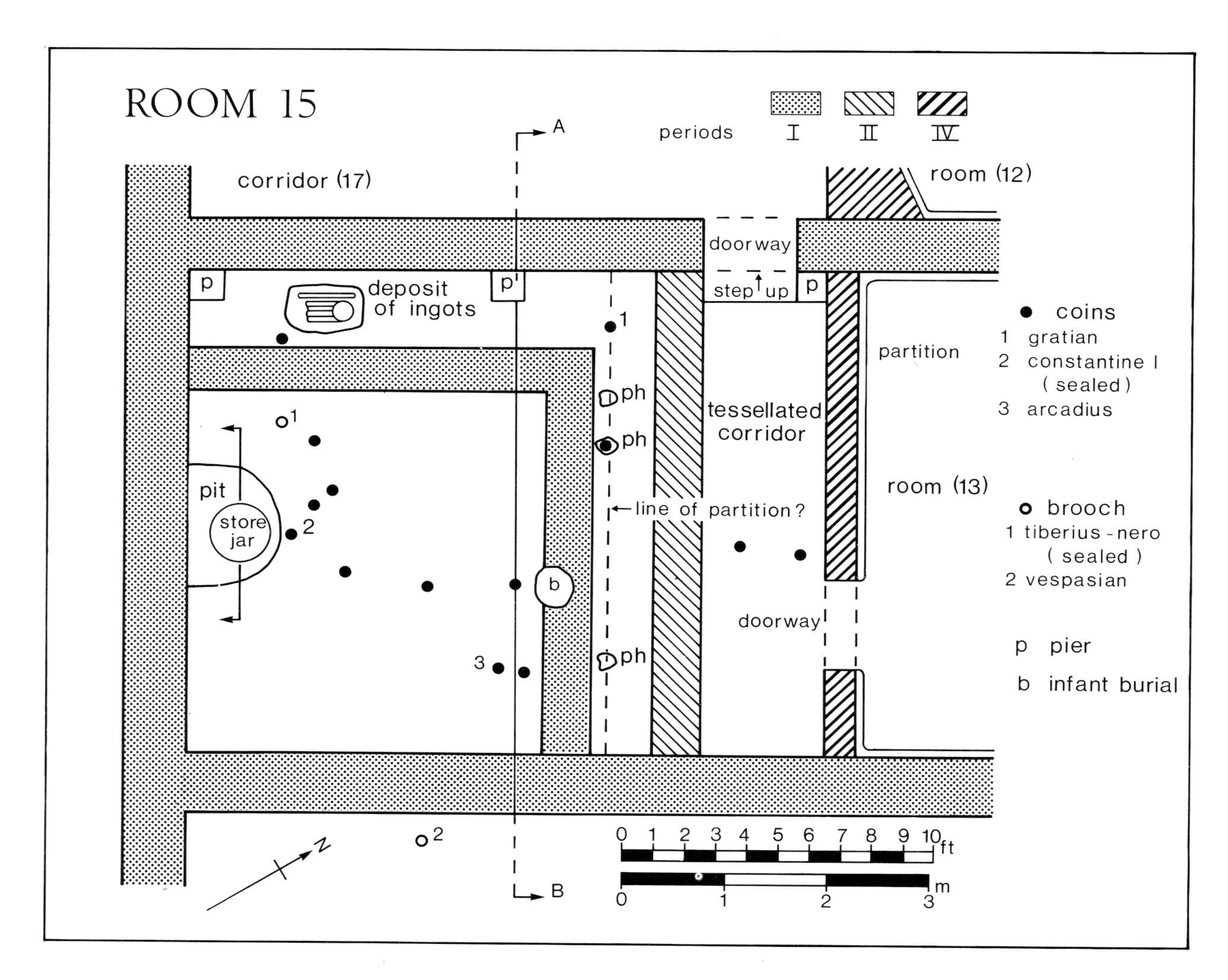
ROOM 15
periods
I
II
IV
A
B
corridor (17)
room (12)
doorway
p
p
deposit
of ingots
step up
p
1
ph
ph
tessellated
corridor
partition
room (13)
line of partition?
pit
store
jar
2
1
b
3
doorway
ph
2
coins
1 gratian
2 constantine I
(sealed)
3 arcadius
brooch
1 tiberius - nero
(sealed)
2 vespasian
p pier
b infant burial
N
0 1 2 3 4 5 6 7 8 9 10 ft
0 1 2 3 m

Fig. 17a.

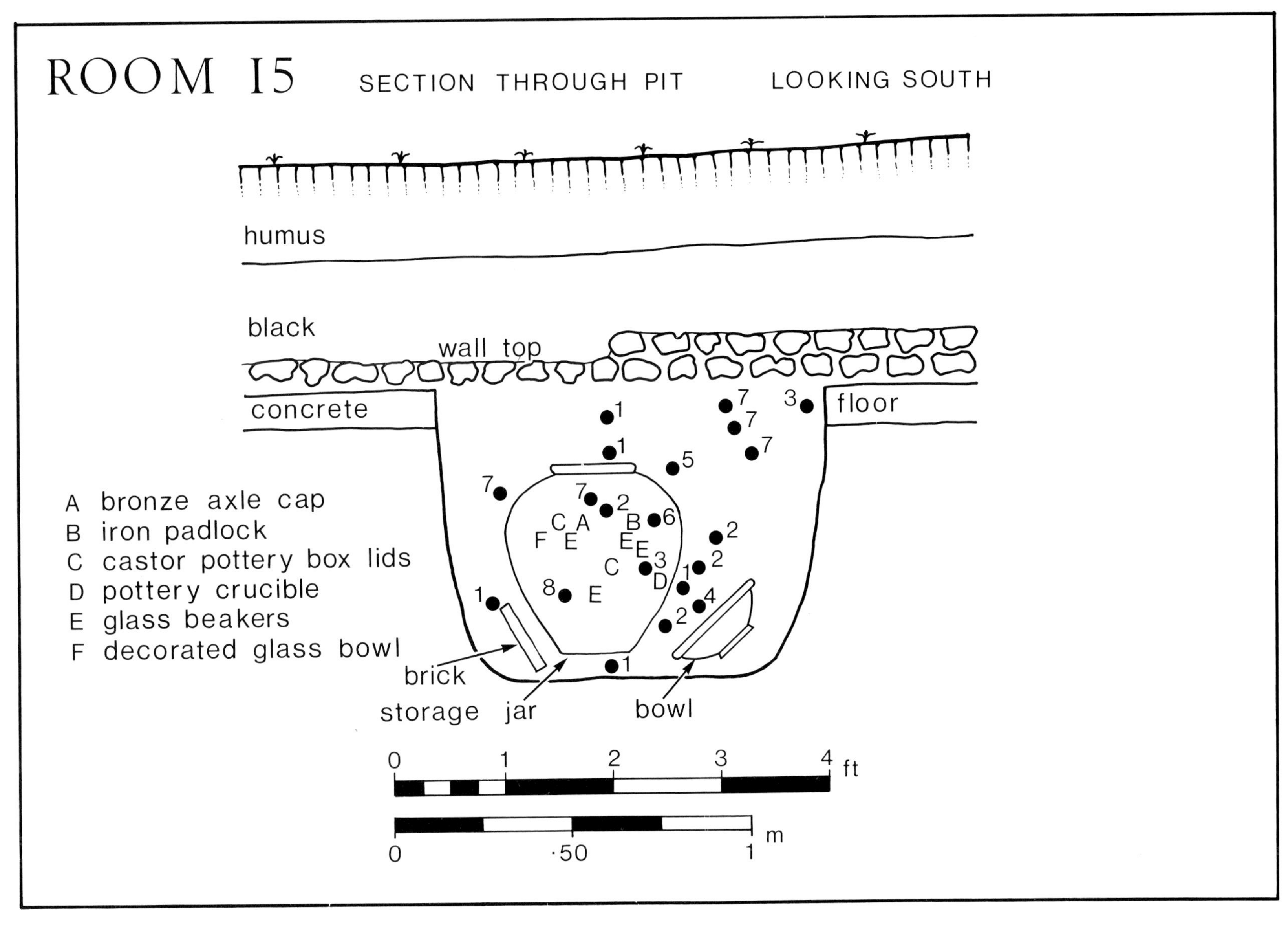
ROOM I5
SECTION THROUGH PIT
LOOKING SOUTH
humus
black
wall top
concrete
floor
brick
storage jar
bowl
A bronze axle cap
B iron padlock
C castor pottery box lids
D pottery crucible
E glass beakers
F decorated glass bowl
0 1 2 3 4 ft
0 ·50 1 m

Fig. 17b.

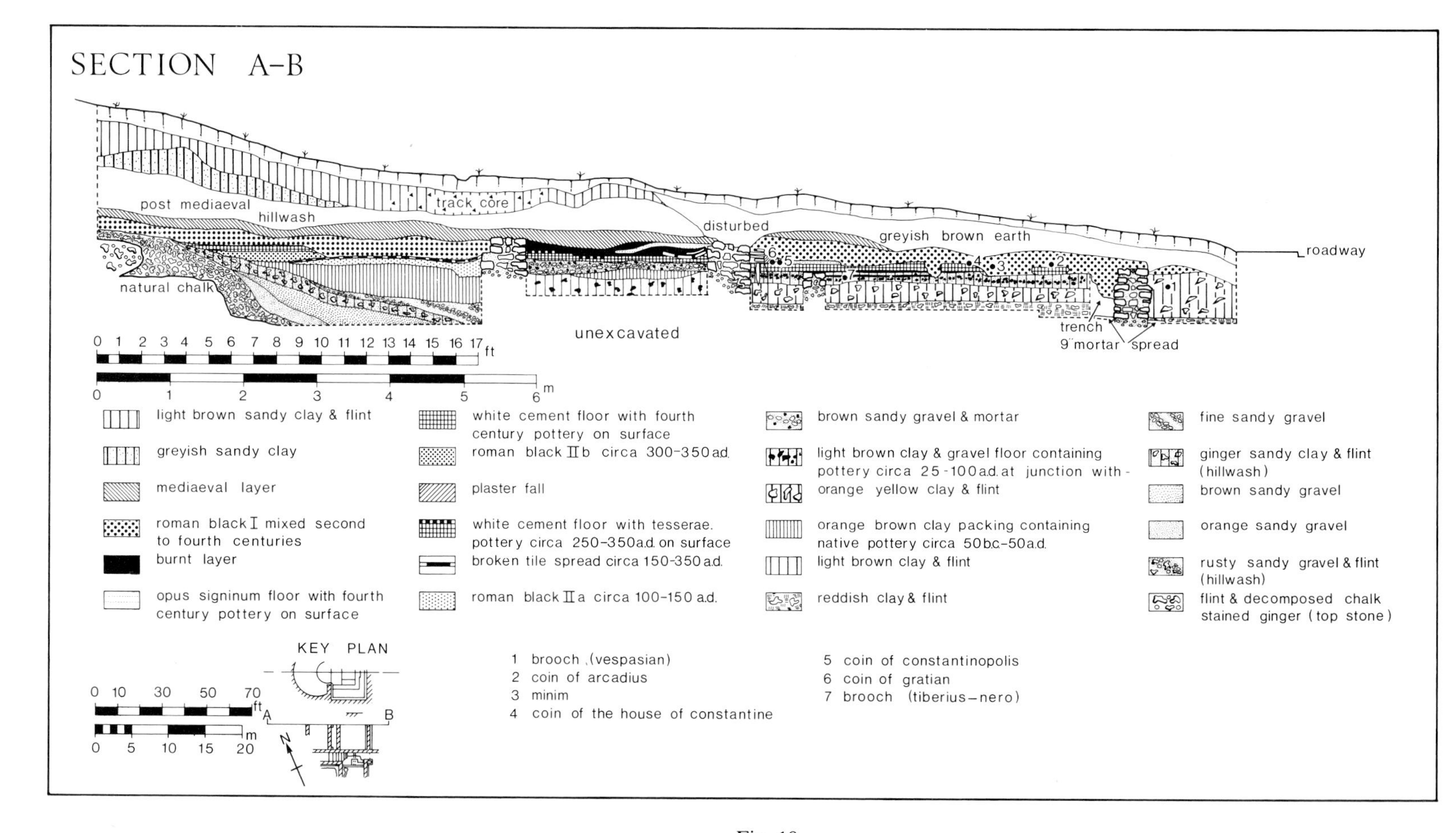
SECTION A–B
post mediaeval
hillwash
track core
disturbed
greyish brown earth
roadway
natural chalk
unexcavated
trench
9" mortar spread
0 1 2 3 4 5 6 7 8 9 10 11 12 13 14 15 16 17 ft
0 1 2 3 4 5 6 m
light brown sandy clay & flint
greyish sandy clay
mediaeval layer
roman black I mixed second to fourth centuries
burnt layer
opus signinum floor with fourth century pottery on surface
white cement floor with fourth century pottery on surface
roman black IIb circa 300–350 a.d.
plaster fall
white cement floor with tesserae. pottery circa 250–350 a.d. on surface
broken tile spread circa 150–350 a.d.
roman black IIa circa 100–150 a.d.
brown sandy gravel & mortar
light brown clay & gravel floor containing pottery circa 25-100 a.d. at junction with -
orange yellow clay & flint
orange brown clay packing containing native pottery circa 50 b.c.–50 a.d.
light brown clay & flint
reddish clay & flint
fine sandy gravel
ginger sandy clay & flint (hillwash)
brown sandy gravel
orange sandy gravel
rusty sandy gravel & flint (hillwash)
flint & decomposed chalk stained ginger (top stone)
KEY PLAN
0 10 30 50 70 ft
0 5 10 15 20 m
A
B
N
1 brooch (vespasian)
2 coin of arcadius
3 minim
4 coin of the house of constantine
5 coin of constantinopolis
6 coin of gratian
7 brooch (tiberius–nero)

Fig. 18.

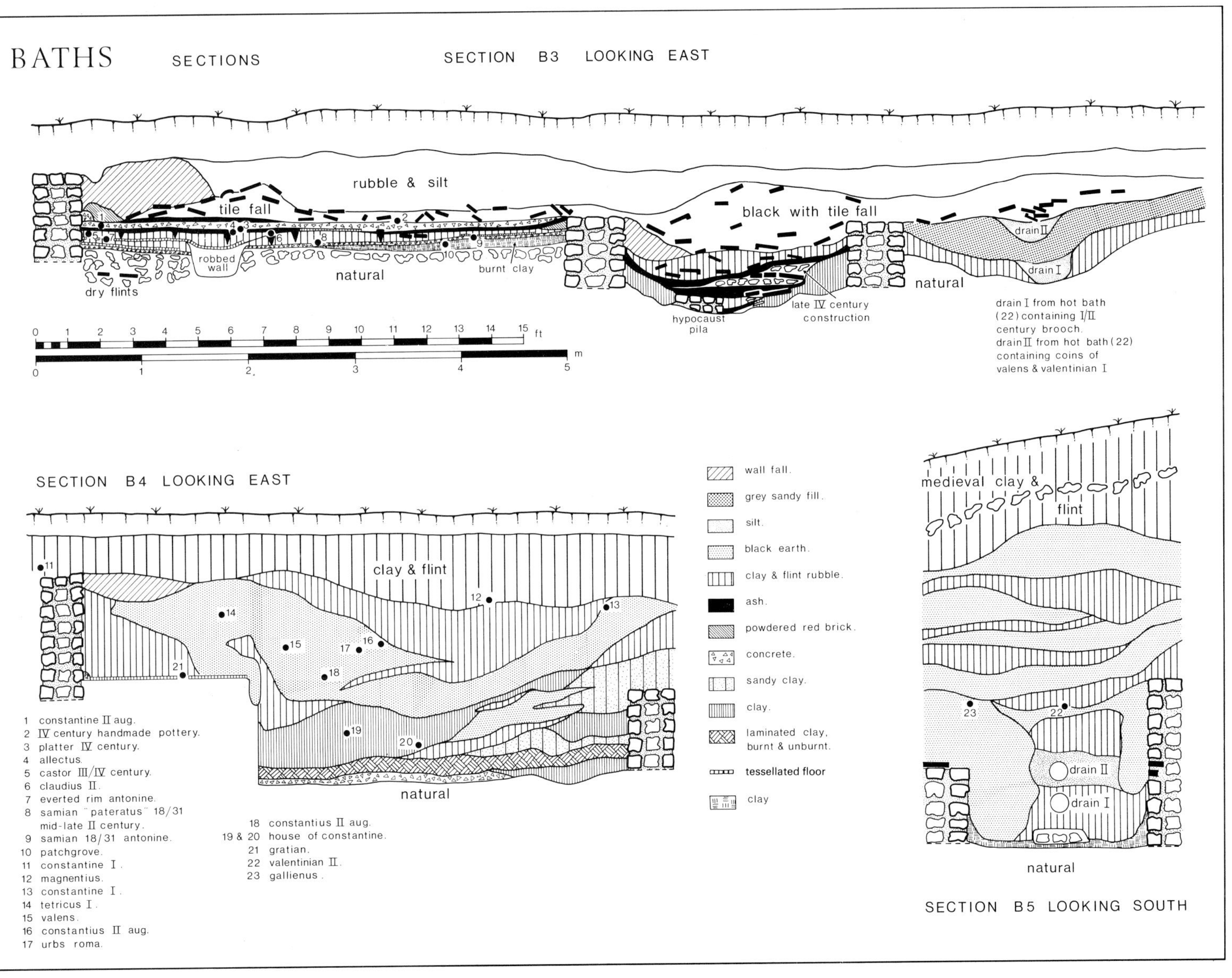
BATHS
SECTIONS
SECTION B3 LOOKING EAST
rubble & silt
tile fall
robbed wall
dry flints
natural
burnt clay
black with tile fall
hypocaust pila
late IV century construction
natural
drain II
drain I
drain I from hot bath (22) containing I/II century brooch.
drain II from hot bath (22) containing coins of valens & valentinian I
0 1 2 3 4 5 6 7 8 9 10 11 12 13 14 15 ft
0 1 2 3 4 5 m
SECTION B4 LOOKING EAST
clay & flint
natural
1 constantine II aug.
2 IV century handmade pottery.
3 platter IV century.
4 allectus.
5 castor III/IV century.
6 claudius II.
7 everted rim antonine.
8 samian "pateratus" 18/31 mid-late II century.
9 samian 18/31 antonine.
10 patchgrove.
11 constantine I.
12 magnentius.
13 constantine I.
14 tetricus I.
15 valens.
16 constantius II aug.
17 urbs roma.
18 constantius II aug.
19 & 20 house of constantine.
21 gratian.
22 valentinian II.
23 gallienus.
wall fall.
grey sandy fill.
silt.
black earth.
clay & flint rubble.
ash.
powdered red brick.
concrete.
sandy clay.
clay.
laminated clay, burnt & unburnt.
tessellated floor
clay
medieval clay & flint
drain II
drain I
natural
SECTION B5 LOOKING SOUTH

Figs. 21a, b, c.

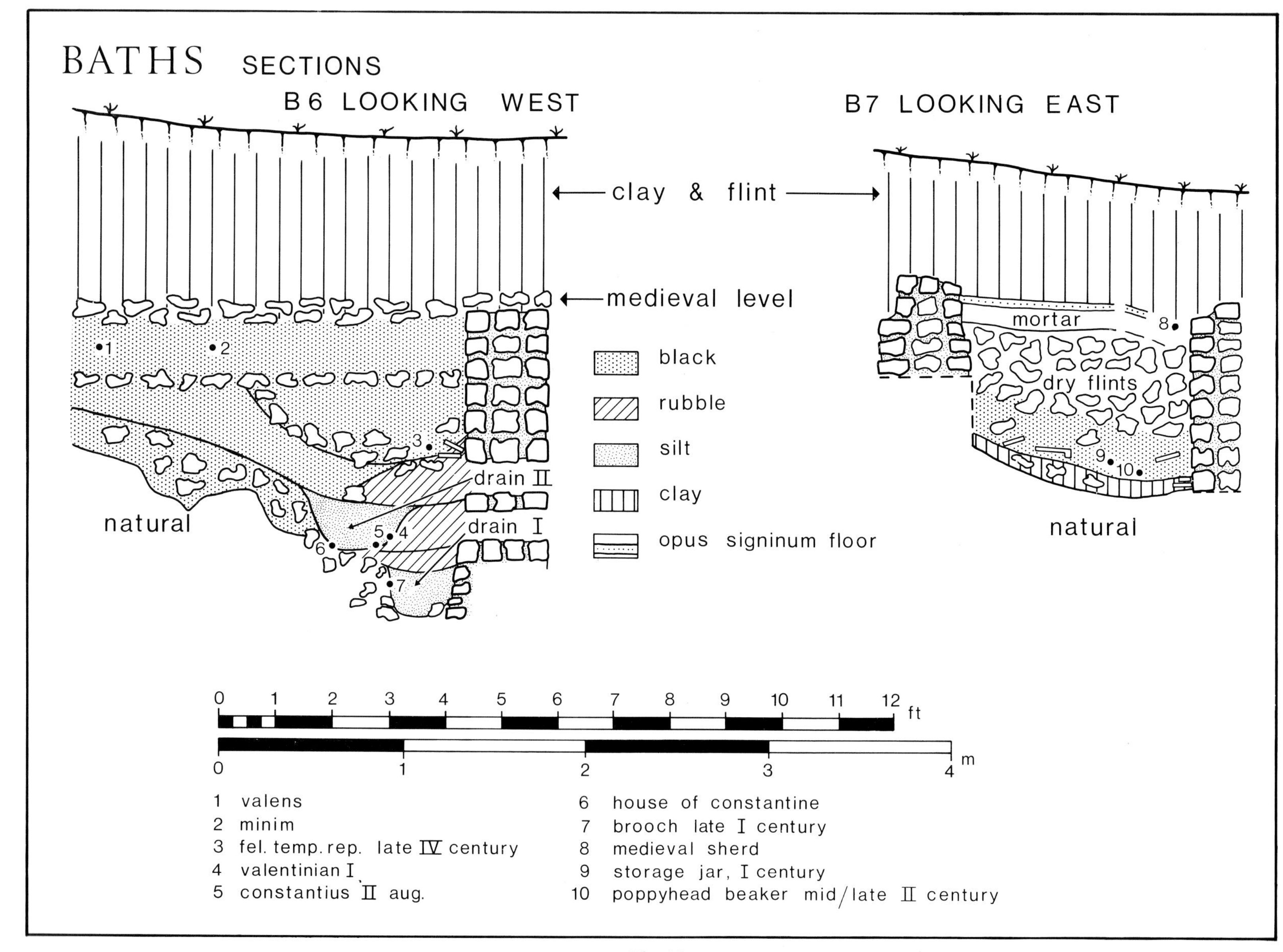
BATHS SECTIONS
B6 LOOKING WEST
B7 LOOKING EAST
clay & flint
medieval level
mortar
dry flints
drain II
drain I
natural
natural
black
rubble
silt
clay
opus signinum floor
0 1 2 3 4 5 6 7 8 9 10 11 12 ft
0 1 2 3 4 m
1 valens
2 minim
3 fel. temp. rep. late IV century
4 valentinian I
5 constantius II aug.
6 house of constantine
7 brooch late I century
8 medieval sherd
9 storage jar, I century
10 poppyhead beaker mid/late II century

Fig. 22a.

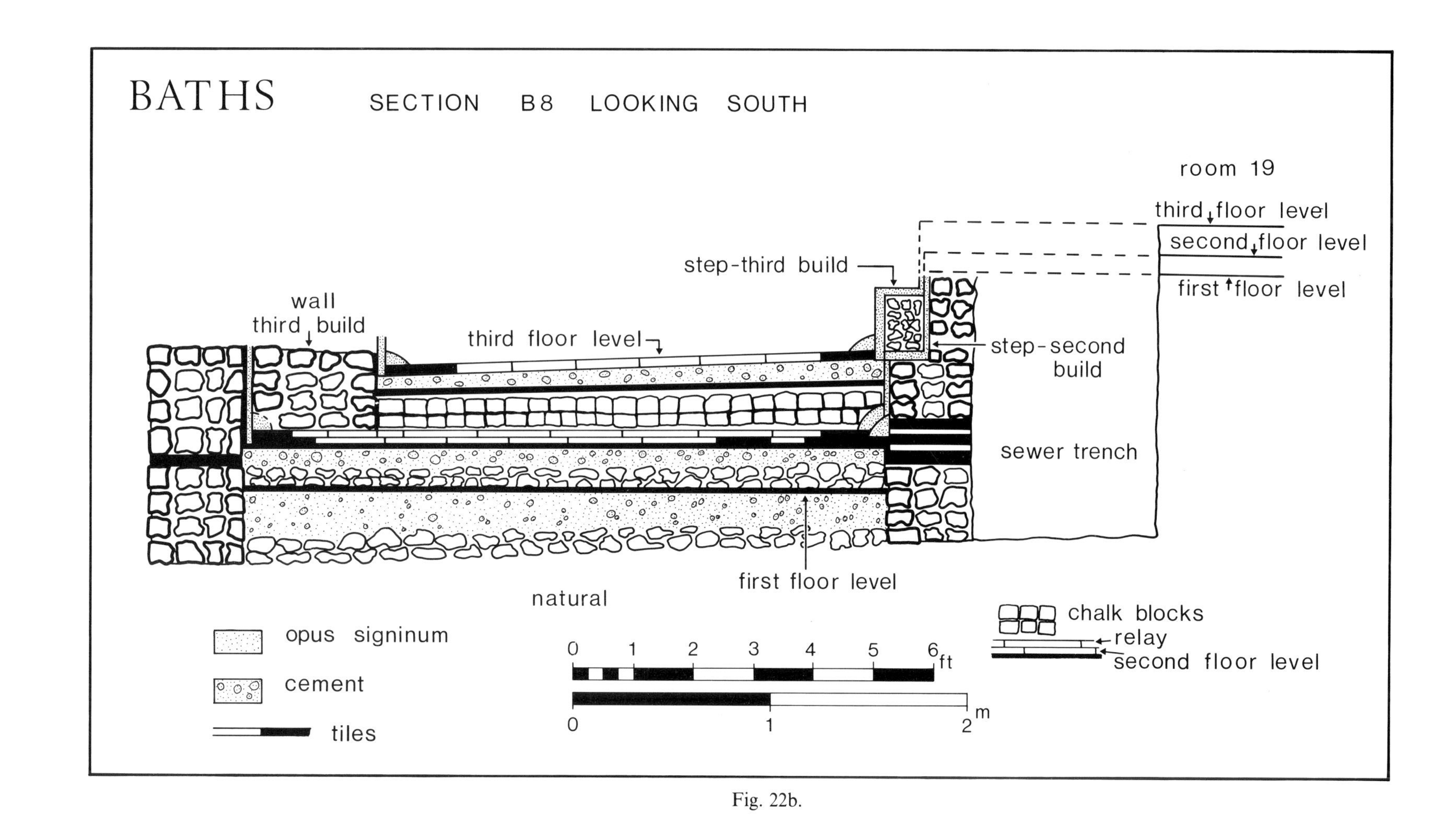

BATHS
SECTION B8 LOOKING SOUTH
room 19
third floor level
second floor level
first floor level
step-third build
wall
third build
third floor level
step-second build
sewer trench
first floor level
natural
opus signinum
cement
tiles
0 1 2 3 4 5 6 ft
0 1 2 m
chalk blocks
relay
second floor level

Fig. 22b.

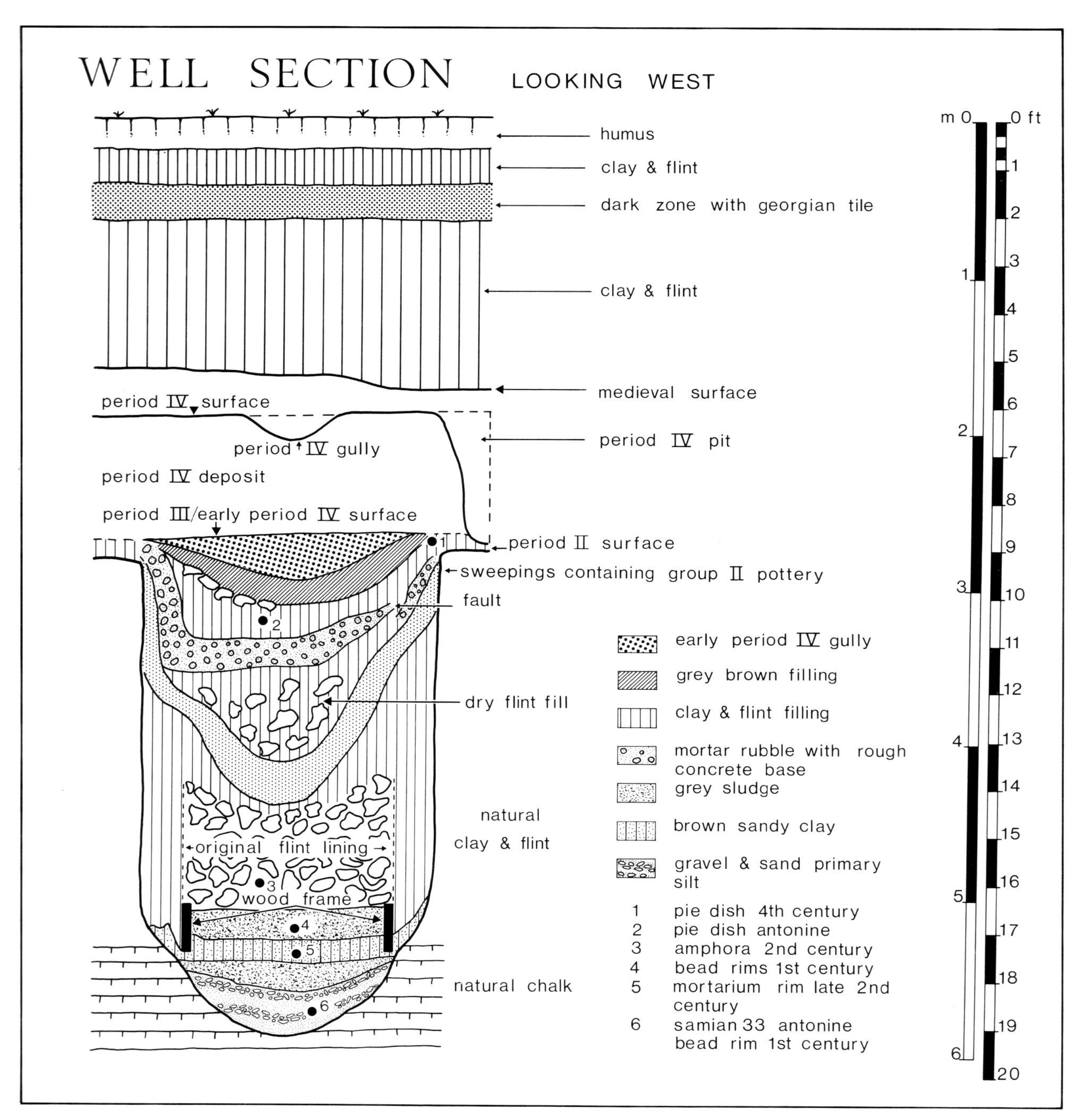
WELL SECTION LOOKING WEST
humus
clay & flint
dark zone with georgian tile
clay & flint
medieval surface
period IV surface
period IV pit
period IV gully
period IV deposit
period III/early period IV surface
period II surface
sweepings containing group II pottery
fault
dry flint fill
natural
clay & flint
original flint lining
wood frame
natural chalk
early period IV gully
grey brown filling
clay & flint filling
mortar rubble with rough concrete base
grey sludge
brown sandy clay
gravel & sand primary silt
1 pie dish 4th century
2 pie dish antonine
3 amphora 2nd century
4 bead rims 1st century
5 mortarium rim late 2nd century
6 samian 33 antonine bead rim 1st century
m 0
1
2
3
4
5
6
0 ft
1
2
3
4
5
6
7
8
9
10
11
12
13
14
15
16
17
18
19
20

Fig. 23.

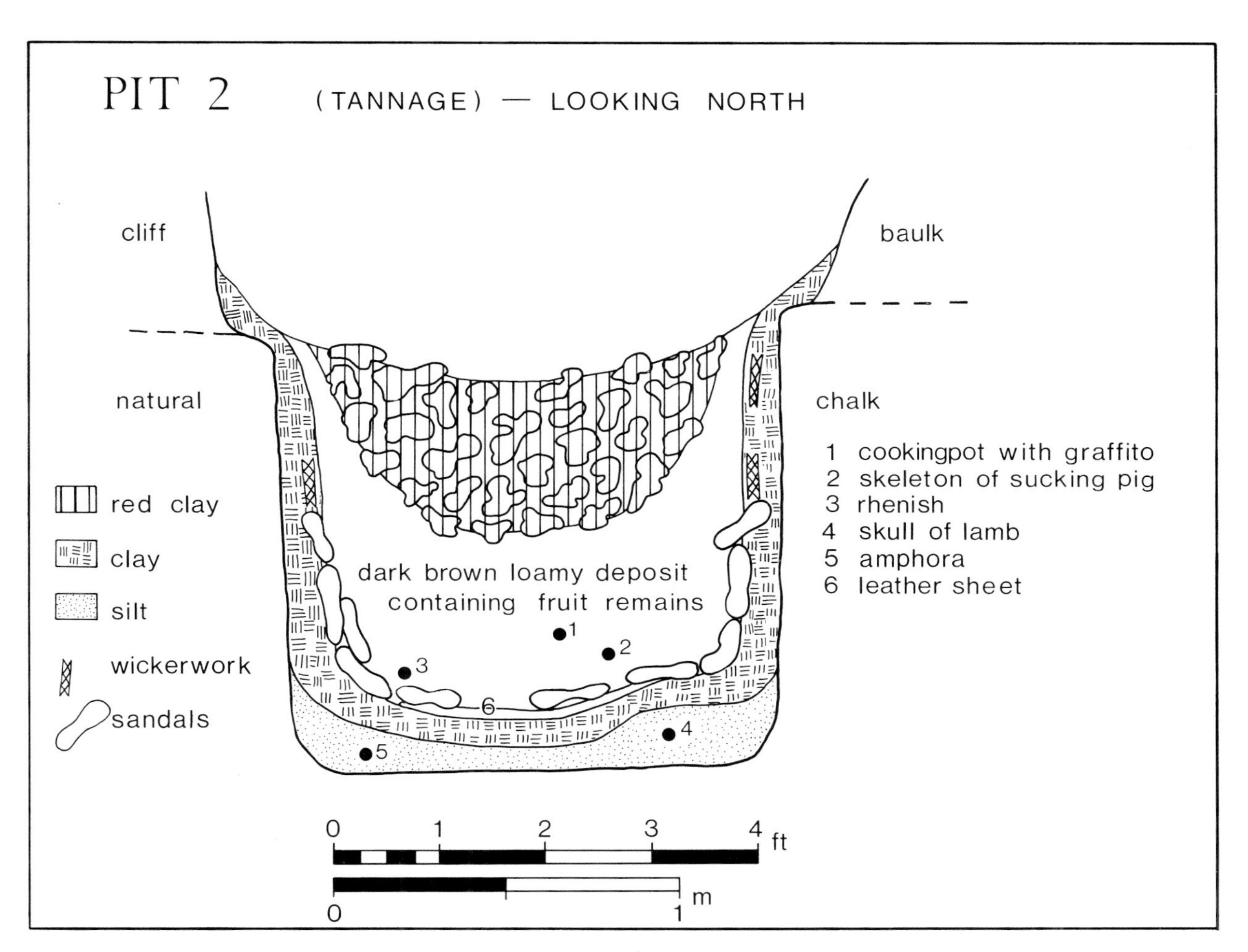
PIT 2 (TANNAGE) — LOOKING NORTH
cliff
baulk
natural
chalk
1 cookingpot with graffito
2 skeleton of sucking pig
3 rhenish
4 skull of lamb
5 amphora
6 leather sheet
red clay
clay
silt
wickerwork
sandals
dark brown loamy deposit containing fruit remains
1
2
3
4
5
6
0 1 2 3 4 ft
0 1 m

Fig. 26a.

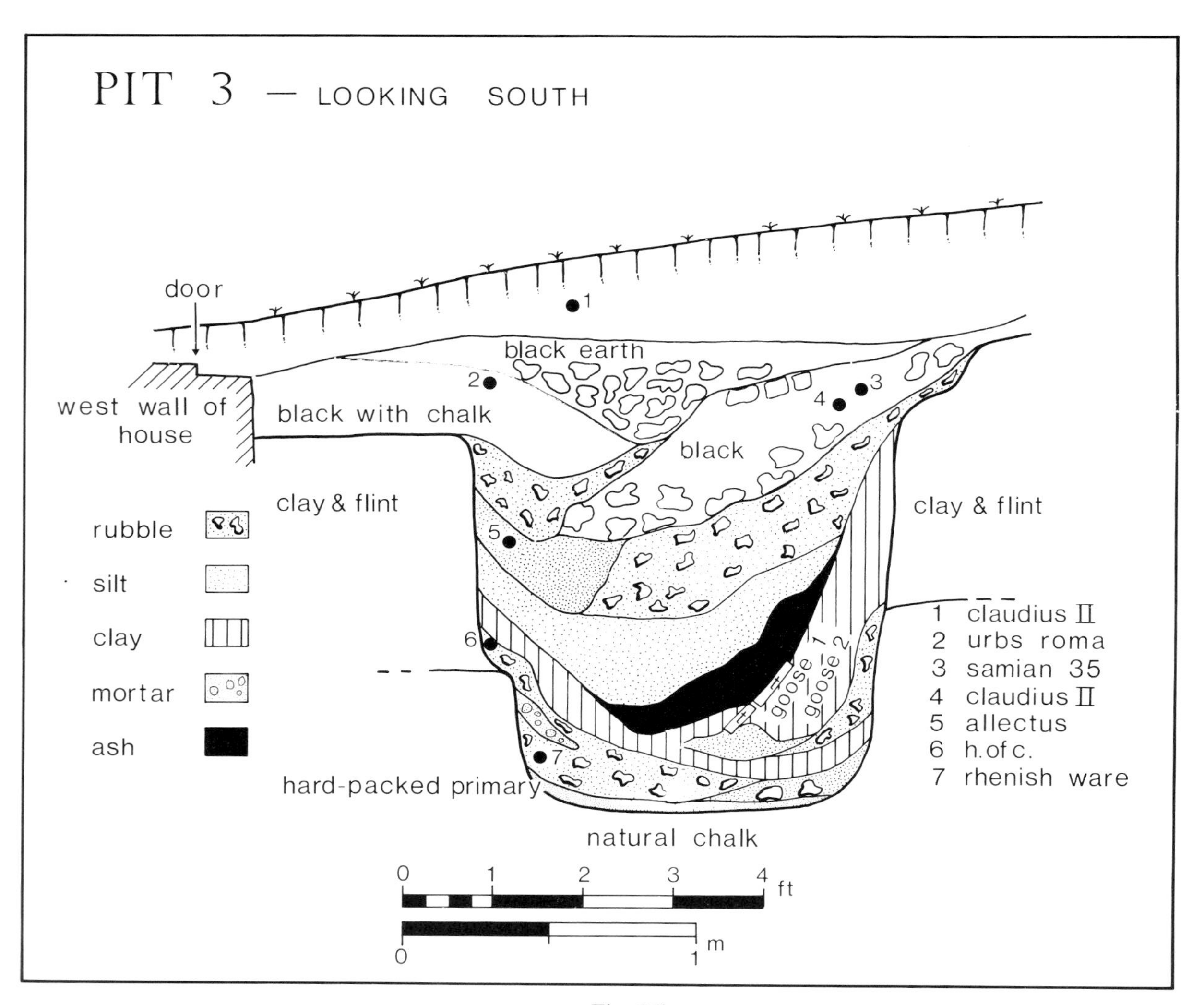
PIT 3 — LOOKING SOUTH
door
west wall of house
black earth
black with chalk
black
clay & flint
clay & flint
rubble
silt
clay
mortar
ash
goose 1
goose 2
hard-packed primary
natural chalk
1 claudius II
2 urbs roma
3 samian 35
4 claudius II
5 allectus
6 h.of c.
7 rhenish ware
0 1 2 3 4 ft
0 1 m

Fig. 26b.

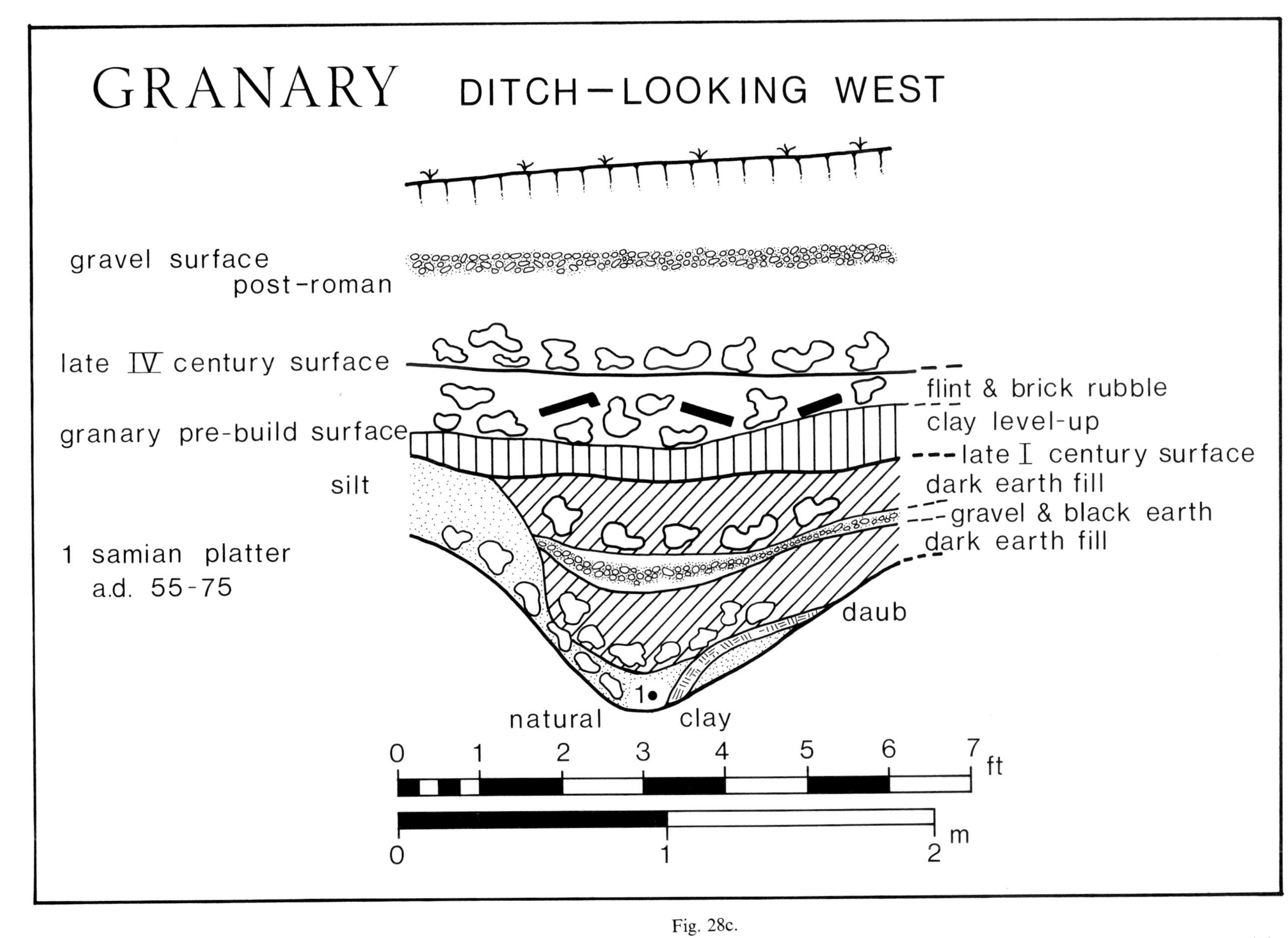
GRANARY DITCH–LOOKING WEST
gravel surface
post-roman
late IV century surface
granary pre-build surface
silt
1 samian platter
a.d. 55-75
flint & brick rubble
clay level-up
late I century surface
dark earth fill
gravel & black earth
dark earth fill
daub
1
natural clay
0 1 2 3 4 5 6 7 ft
0 1 2 m

Fig. 28c.

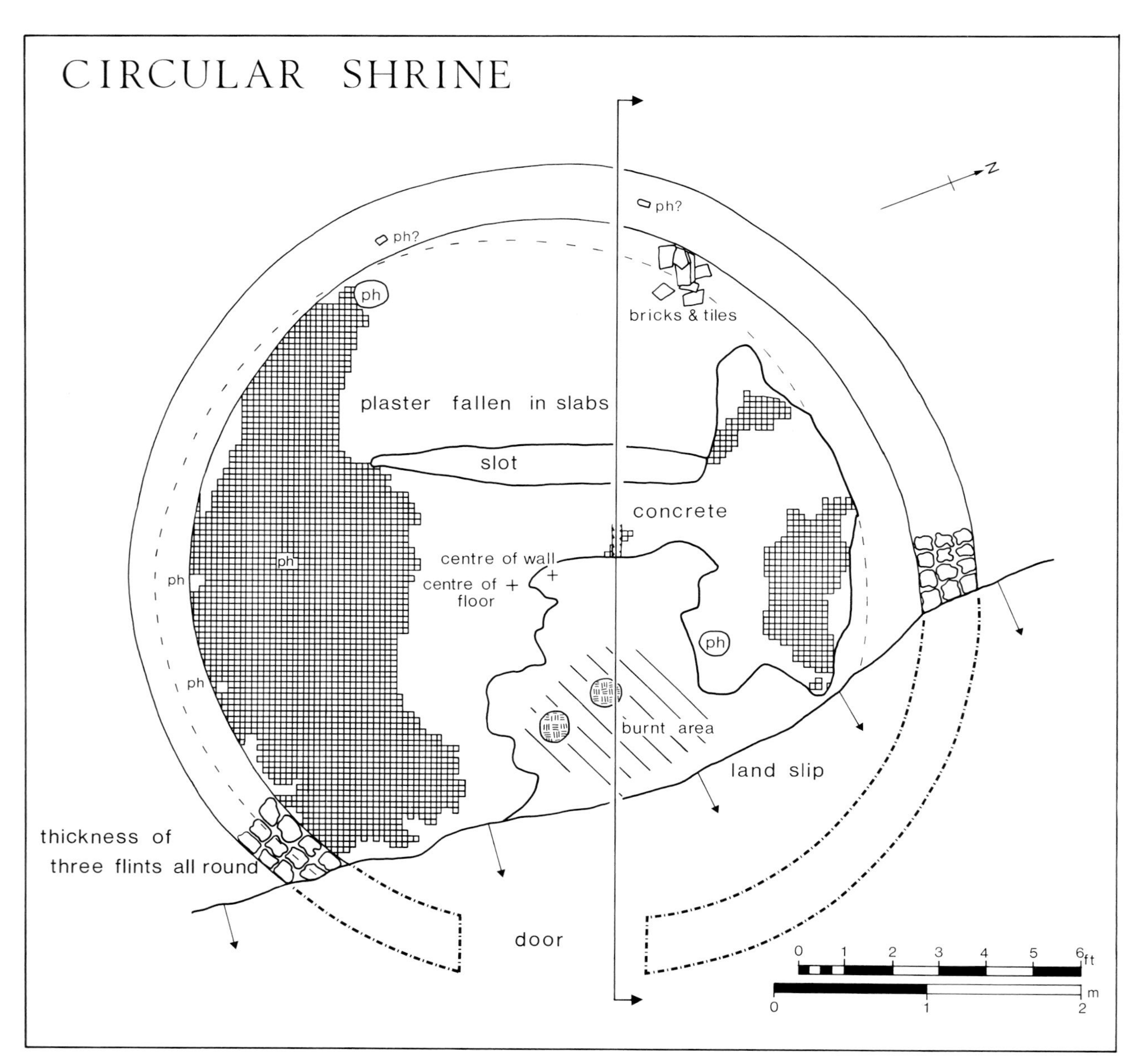
CIRCULAR SHRINE
N
ph?
ph?
ph
bricks & tiles
plaster fallen in slabs
slot
concrete
ph
centre of wall
ph
centre of + floor
ph
ph
burnt area
land slip
thickness of
three flints all round
door
0 1 2 3 4 5 6 ft
0 1 2 m

Fig. 29.

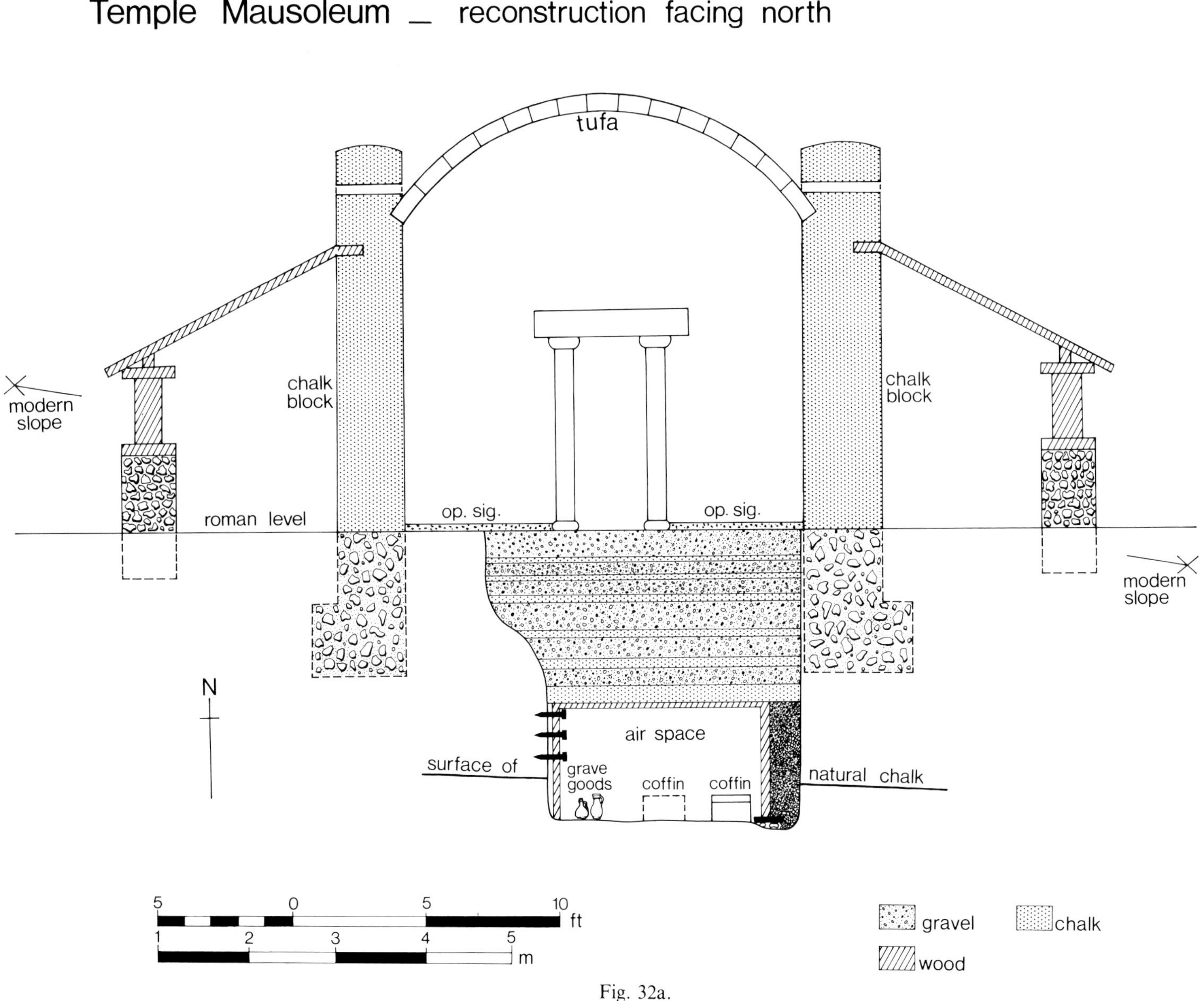

Temple Mausoleum — reconstruction facing north
tufa
chalk block
chalk block
modern slope
modern slope
roman level
op. sig.
op. sig.
N
air space
surface of
grave goods
coffin
coffin
natural chalk
5
0
5
10
ft
1
2
3
4
5
m
gravel
chalk
wood

Fig. 32a.

Temple Mausoleum – plan of tomb chamber

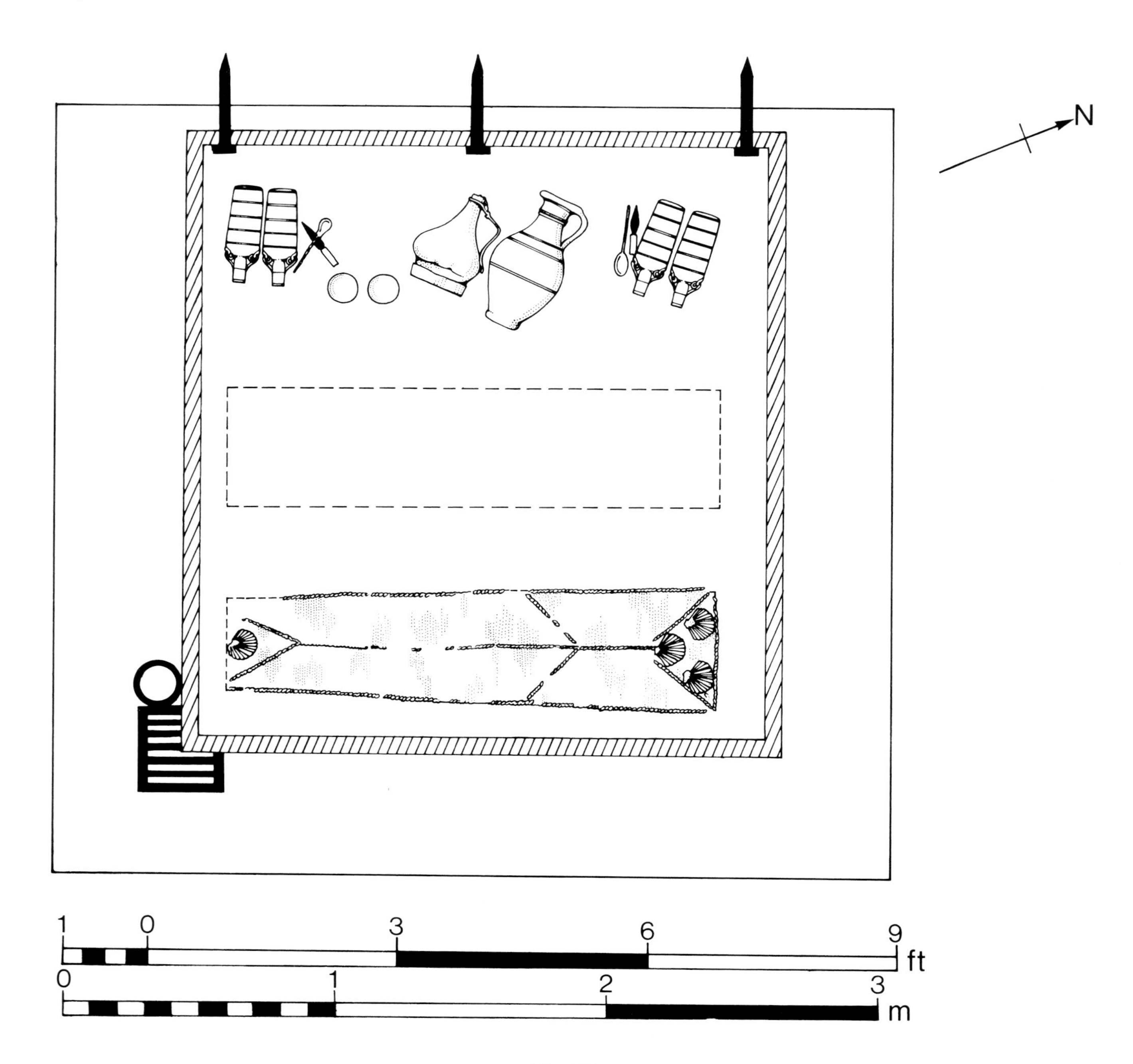

Fig. 32b.

Plates

a. Deep Room: First-Century Staircase-Well, looking South. Room (13) in Background.

b. Deep Room: Site of First-Century Loading Platform, looking North-East. Late Second-Century Wall-Block in Background.

a. Deep Room: Bust I and Plinth of Bust II as found, looking North.

b. Deep Room: Bust I and Plinth of Bust II as found, showing Steps. Site of Bust II (removed) on right.

c. Deep Room: Bust II as found.

a. Deep Room: Busts as found, Shoulder of Plinth of Bust II snapped off at Edge of Step, and SVAVIS Pot in Concrete Floor. Third-Century Wall-Block behind.

b. Deep Room: Busts replaced in original Positions.

a. Deep Room: SVAVIS Pot as found.

b. Deep Room: SVAVIS Pot cleaned.

c. Deep Room: Companion Pot (2) with SVAVIS Pot (1) as found, looking South.

d. Deep Room: Niche in south Wall, showing Painting of Water-Nymphs as found.

a. Deep Room: Section looking East, with central Sump and Fourth-Century Plinths right and left.

b. Deep Room: Carbonized Plank and Cover of Pot (4) beneath lowest Step, looking South.

c. Deep Room: The four Votive Pots.

a. Deep Room: Fourth-Century Plinths against north Wall.

b. Deep Room: The *Opus signinum* Podium as found, looking South. Fourth-Century Plinth on right, and Site of Pot (3) beneath fallen Podium.

c. Deep Room: The Limestone Block.

d. Deep Room: Limestone Column as found, looking East.

a. Room (10): Tiled Stairs, looking South-West, with Landing and blocked Turn into Deep Room on left. Second-Century 'Trellis' Plaster on Wall.

b. Room (10): Section across Steps, looking West.

a. Room (10A): Third-Century Wall-Block with Arch, looking South-West. Steps from Ambulatory (2) on left, with Deep Room in Background.

b. Room (10): North-East corner, showing Arch partially excavated, Box-Flue in Third-Century Wall and Steps to Ambulatory.

a. Room (10): Third-Century North Wall with Box-Flue, and Stub of First-Century Wall in middle Ground. Tiled Steps, Foreground and right. Sections right and left.

b. Room (10): Fourth-Century Post-Hole Complex, looking South. Section on right.

c. Room (10): Ox Skull beside north Wall, looking West.

a. Room (11): Looking North-East, showing exterior Entrance in north Wall and Entrance to Ante-room of House-Church in east Wall, with Room (10) beyond.

b. Room (10A): Fourth/Fifth-Century Oven in South-East Corner, looking South-West.

a. Northern Complex: North Ambulatory of Temple, looking South-East, showing Clay Walls, with Horse Skull in Foreground.

b. Northern Complex: Miniature Pot mortared into interior Face of east Wall of Temple.

c. Northern Complex: Close-up of north Clay Wall, showing Plaster and Flint Foundation. Exterior Drainage Gully in Background.

d. Northern Complex: Close-up of Section of Clay Wall, showing Plaster and Flint Foundation.

a. Northern Complex: Slab of fallen Plaster on east exterior Wall of Temple.

c. Northern Complex: Exterior Drainage Guillies with Sump on right, looking West.

PLATE XIIIb

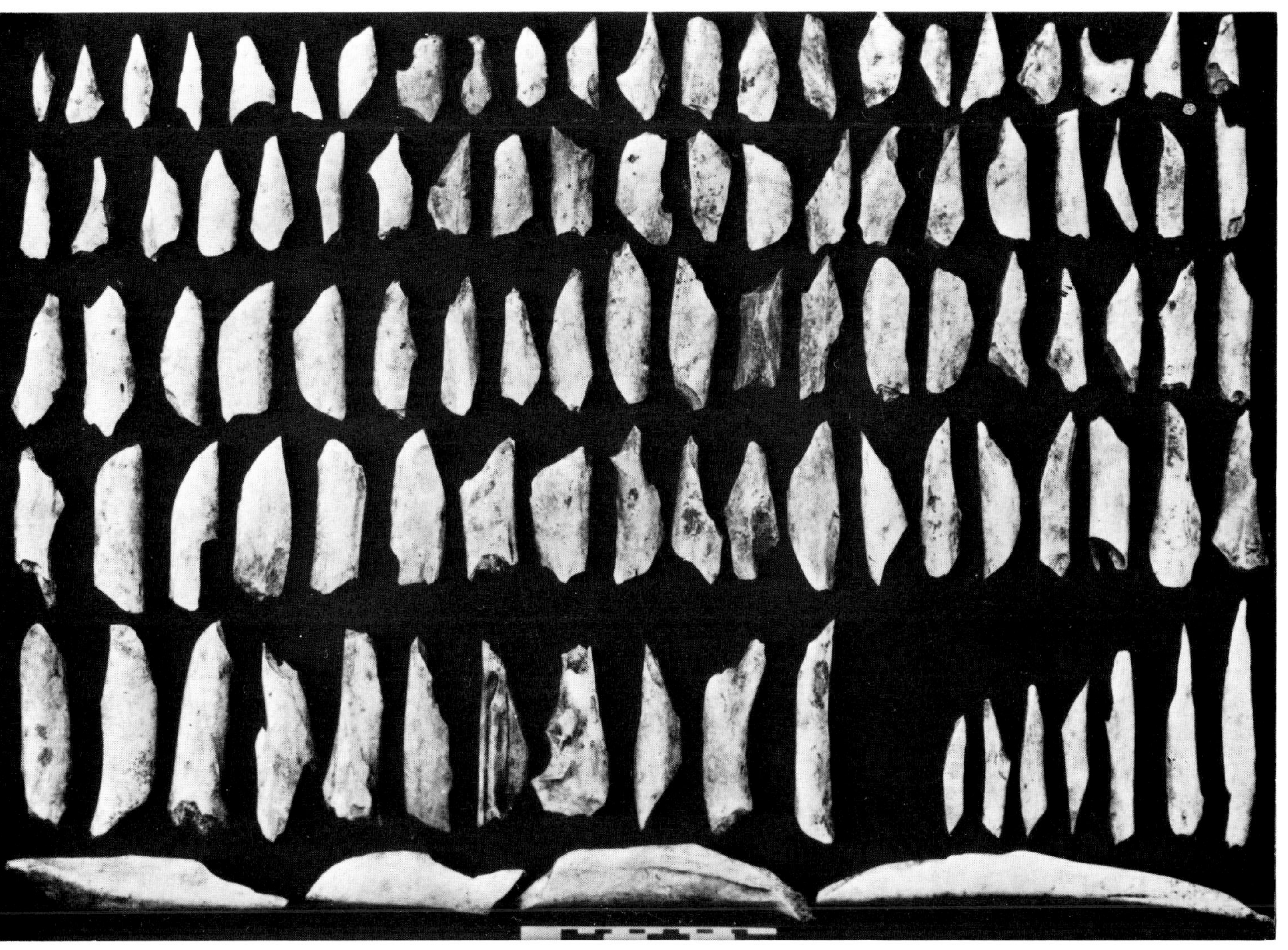

Northern Complex: Group of pointed Bone Fragments from north Exterior of Temple.

a. Room (13): East End of north Corridor, looking South-East. Chalk Wall overlying First-Century Staircase-Well, Room Drain in right Background.

b. Room (13): Hearth beneath north tessellated Surround of Mosaic Floor.

c. Room (13): East End of north Corridor, looking South-East. Section down to Ramp in First-Century Staircase-Well.

d. Room (13): South Corridor. Plaster on Base of south Wall of Room (13), looking West.

a. Rooms (12) and (13): General View looking East, showing Holes for eighteenth-century Park Fence.

b. Room (12): The Europa Panel.

Room (13): The Bellerophon and Seasons Panel.

Room (13): Close-up View of the Bellerophon Panel.

Room (13): Close-up View of 'Spring' Season.

b. Room (13): The 'Swastika' Panel, looking South.

c. Rooms (12) and (13): Looking North-West, showing Mosaic Step and 'Swastika' Panel.

a. Room (13): Drain in north-east Corner, looking East.

b. Entrance Corridor: Drain from Room (13), looking North-West.

c. Room (15): Casting and Patch Grove Vessel as found. (Ingots beneath, unexcavated).

d. Room (15): Ingots and Casting as found, looking South-West.

a. Baths: View looking North-West. Steps in Background.

b. Baths: Close-up View of Steps, looking West.

a. Baths: Cold Room (19), looking East, showing successive Floors.

b. Baths: Furnace Flue, looking East into Hot Room (21).

c. Baths: Holes for Grid in Furnace Flue, looking West (at top).

d. Baths: Hot Room (21), looking East, showing *Pilae*.

a. Baths: Semi-circular Trough with Sand Filling, looking West.

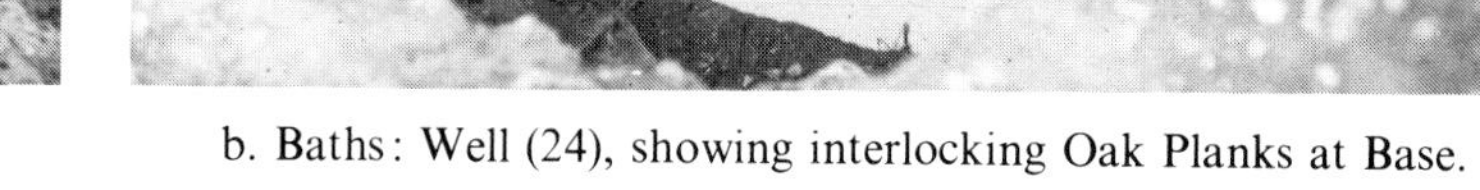

b. Baths: Well (24), showing interlocking Oak Planks at Base.

c. Baths: Concrete Floor with Post-Holes, north Exterior of Furnace (16), looking North. Semi-circular Trough right foreground.

a. Kitchen Area: Western Part of Concrete Platform, looking South, with Post-Holes and Ovens, the further Oven underlying the Tannage Complex. Site of Infant Foundation Burial extreme right Foreground.

b. Tannery: Steeping-Tank in Background, Oven on right with Post-Hole Complex. Second-Century Oven beneath on right. Looking South-West.

c. Kitchen Area: Infant Foundation Burial, looking South.

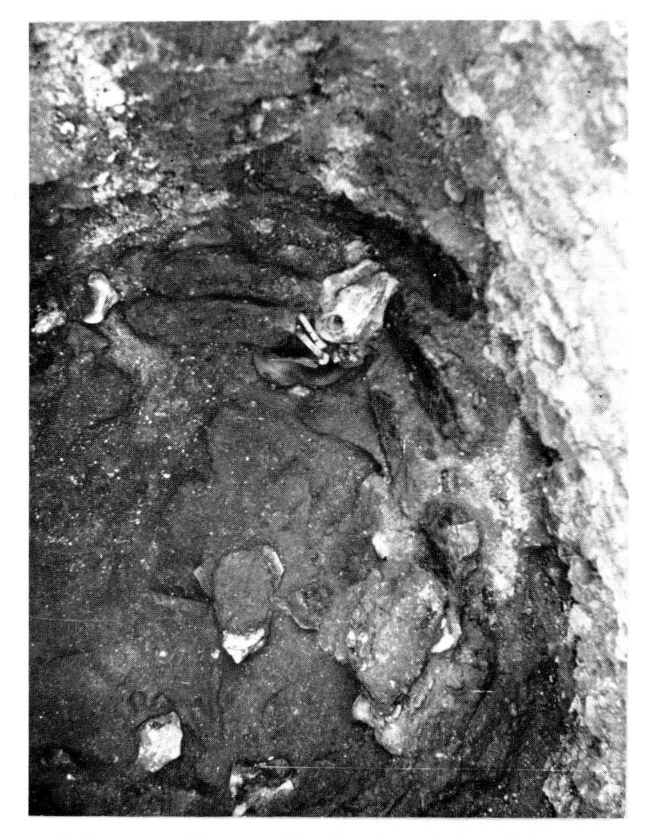

d. Tannery: Tannage Pit, showing Lining of Sandals.

a. Granary: View looking North-East, with two North–South Sections.

b. Granary: Close-up View of blocked Arch into South Sub-Compartment, looking South-East.

a. Granary: Central 'Boxes', looking North-East.

b. Granary: West End, looking North, showing Floor-Plinths and Seatings for wooden Uprights in Foreground.

a. Granary: First-Century Ditch at north-west Corner, looking East, showing overlying west Wall of Granary.

b. Granary: First-Century Ditch at north-west Corner, looking West.

a. Circular Shrine: Looking North-West, Reserved Area in Background.

b. Circular Shrine: Section to Site of Entrance, looking West, showing Post-Holes (pegged) and Fall of *Tesserae* (labelled).

a. Temple Mausoleum: North Ambulatory, looking West. North Wall of *Cella* on left, north Wall of Church left background.

b. Temple Mausoleum: South Ambulatory, looking North-East. Exterior Entrance right background. Entrance to *Cella* left Background, Tomb Chamber far left background.

c. Temple Mausoleum: Laminated Levels *in situ* in north-east Corner of *Cella*, looking North-East.

d. Temple Mausoleum: Laminated Levels fallen upon Lead Coffin, looking South-East.

a. Temple Mausoleum: Lead Coffin as found, looking South-East and showing 'Scallop-Shell' Decoration left.

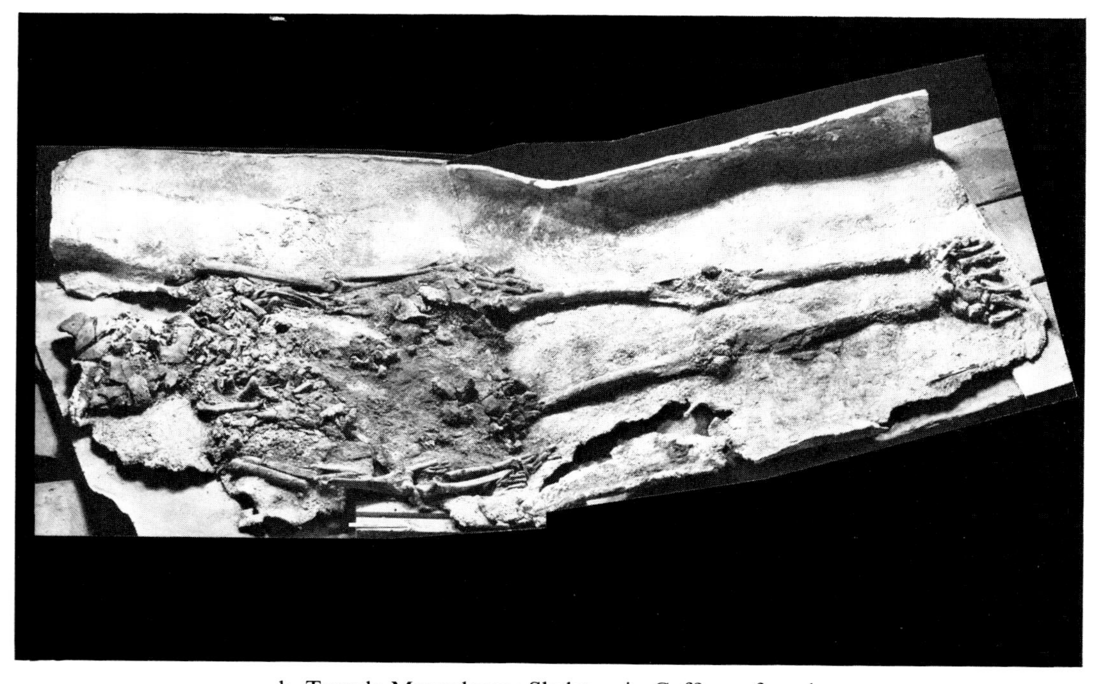

b. Temple Mausoleum: Skeleton in Coffin as found.

a. Temple Mausoleum: Grave Goods from Tomb Chamber. Background: Bronze Flagon, Glass Bottle, Pottery Flagon. Foreground: Bone Objects, Set of Glass Gaming Pieces, Spoons.

b. Temple Mausoleum: The Bone 'Medusa' Roundel.

Reconstruction of Villa *c.* A.D. 360, by Alan Sorrell.

INDEX

INDEX